The Lives Of The Presidents: James Madison, James Monroe And John Quincy Adams

William Osborn Stoddard

THE LIVES OF THE PRESIDENTS

JAMES MADISON

JAMES MONROE

AND

JOHN QUINCY ADAMS

BY

WILLIAM O. STODDARD

Author of "The Life of George Washington," "The Lives of John Adams and Thomas Jefferson," "The Life of Ulysses S. Grant," etc., etc.

NEW YORK
FREDERICK A. STOKES
SUCCESSOR TO WHITE, STOKES, & ALLEN
1887

PORTRAIT OF JAMES MADISON.

CONTENTS.

JAMES MADISON.

CHAPTER XV.

CHAPTER XVI.

JAMES MONROE.

CHAPTER I.

CHAPTER II.

CHAPTER III.

CHAPTER IV.

CHAPTER V.

CHAPTER VI.

CHAPTER VII.

CHAPTER VIII.

CHAPTER IX.

CHAPTER X.

CHAPTER XI.

CHAPTER VIII.

CHAPTER IX.

CHAPTER X.

CHAPTER XI.

CHAPTER XII.

CHAPTER XIII.

CHAPTER XIV.

CHAPTER XV.

JAMES MADISON.

FOURTH PRESIDENT.

By WILLIAM O. STODDARD.

CHAPTER I.

*The Madison Family—Birth of James Madison—
School-days—The Friendship of Thomas Jefferson
—A Hard Student—Going to College.*

In the days of Pocahontas and Captain John
Smith and Powhatan, the romance days of the Virginia Colony, in the year 1623, a list was written of
the names of all its men and women and children.
In that list is the name of Captain Isaac Madison,
and there are fragmentary records which indicate
that he was an Indian fighter.

Thirty years later, in 1653, a patent for lands on
the shore of Chesapeake Bay, between the York
and James rivers, was taken out by John Madison.

This is very nearly all that is known of the earlier
history of the Madison family in Virginia.

According to an imperfectly attested genealogy,
a son of that John Madison was named John also,
and at this point the uncertainty seems to cease.

The next Madison in succession was named Ambrose, and became a planter, as his father had been before him. His son was named James, and married a very estimable young lady named Nelly Conway. He was the owner of an estate called Montpellier, in Orange County, Virginia. His son James was one of the strong men who planned and founded the United States of America.

When ex-President Madison was an old man, in 1834, he wrote to Dr. Lyman C. Draper about himself :

"His grandfathers were also planters. It appears that his ancestors on both sides were not among the most wealthy of the country, but in independent and comfortable circumstances."

Mrs. Nelly Conway Madison's father owned a plantation at Port Conway, in King George County, on the northern bank of the Rappahannock River, and she made a long visit home in the spring of the year 1751. During this visit at Port Conway, on the 16th of March, her first child was born, a boy, and he was named James Madison, after his father.

Other children were born to James and Nelly Madison as the years went by, until the family circle at Montpellier contained four sons and three daughters.

There was ample provision for them all, and the style of living may be described as plentiful, but primitive. There seems to be every reason for believing that the affairs of the household were conducted upon the best models provided by the social conditions of the old colony times. When, however, the Montpellier plantation is called "an estate," and its owner is spoken of as "a large landed proprietor," both terms may be correctly applied without implying riches. Virginia forests were unprofitable property, and the returns from even the best improved lands were moderate.

All the ordinary domestic service, as well as all the farm drudgery of such an establishment, was performed by colored slaves, with results which are much better understood now than they were then. The children of the family were sure to receive the idea, from infancy, that they belonged to the privileged and ruling class. It was especially true of the elder son that he would probably grow up with a strong conviction that he had a career before him. Something like an expectation of leadership was sure to take form in the mind of any boy so situated, if his natural gifts were at all above mediocrity. How strong an effect this may have had upon the aspirations and lives of the bright boys of that generation may be at least guessed at by anybody who will examine the roll of the noted men of the early days of the Republic. It is very remarkable how many of them were sons of Virginia planters.

When James Madison was born, in 1751, two boys who, more than all other human beings, were to influence his character and life were already at school. Thomas Jefferson, aged eight, was busy with his first books over in Albemarle County. George Washington, aged nineteen, having finished his career as a surveyor, had received his commission as major in the Virginia militia, and was study-

ing military works and receiving lessons in the
manual of arms and in swordsmanship.

James Madison, Sr., was a man of intelligence
and worth, and took an active part in the public
affairs of his county. There had been no schools at
all in Virginia when he was a boy, and he deeply
felt the disadvantages he labored under from a lack
of early education. He determined that his children
should have all they could obtain from the schools
now available, and he made an early beginning with
his oldest son. He was a prosperous planter, with
the work of many careless Africans to oversee, and
it is likely that his hands were full ; but Mrs. Nelly
Madison was every way competent to direct the
first steps of her boy's mental training. The deep
devotion with which he cared for her in after years
bears witness to the strength of the tie created
between them in his childhood.

Not all his early educational influences came from
books, however. There were tendencies born in
him which required the rough freedom of rural life
in a rude time to oppose them and make a man of
him. He was to be through all his life a studious
and thoughtful man, associated with men of progress and of action, and it was early impressed upon
him that he had been born into a world of very
positive and terrible realities.

When he was only four years of age the news of
Braddock's defeat by the French and Indians came.
It was a message of terror to the country homes of
all that part of Virginia, and the rising tide of savage war threatened to reach the very threshold of

Montpellier. During two years following, the horrors which were transacting all along the near frontier formed the staple of all fireside and neighborhood talk, and the children listened. The name they heard most frequently mentioned and learned to love the sound of was that of Colonel George Washington, the young hero in command of the Virginia riflemen, who was keeping back the red marauders. To the end of his life James Madison retained memories of that time with a vividness which attested the strength of the impressions then made.

An Ohio school-boy, like Ulysses S. Grant, might drive a wood wagon at eight years and a plough at eleven. A Yankee school-boy, like John Adams, had chores to do as soon as he was old enough to do them. All that was left out of the first training of the son of a Virginia planter, with colored servants around him. There is no record of how far advanced was little James in years or learning when he was deemed fitted to be sent from home to his first regular school. This was in King and Queen County, and was kept by a Mr. Donald Robertson.

Whatever English branches were included in the course of instruction laid down for the young beginner, careful mention is made of the fact that Greek, Latin, French, and Spanish were on the list. Mr. Robertson was a competent teacher, as President Madison himself testified many years later. After remaining with him for a length of time which is not clearly indicated, a piece of uncommon good fortune fell to the share cf the youthful student.

The Rev. Thomas Martin, clergyman of the parish containing the Montpellier estate, came to make his home with the Madison family and to take charge of its eldest son as private tutor. James not only had now a teacher all to himself, but from that time forward his reading and his preparation for college could go hand in hand with home comforts. These should have included the riding, fishing, hunting, and general sociability which belonged to planter life in the Old Dominion. To a certain extent they did so, but his liking for them was not sufficiently strong. James Madison had been born to an undefined ambition, and it was now overmastering him. The father's idea of the vast importance of scholarship to human success was taking possession of the son in an exaggerated form. He was in danger of becoming a book-worm, and all the more so because of half-wise counsel he received from a young man whom the bookish boys of that part of Virginia were beginning to look up to as a model. Thomas Jefferson, of Shadwell, Albemarle County, was only twenty-three years of age, but had already won a reputation for learning and for rare industry as a student. He had entered upon the practice of the law with remarkably rapid success, and young Madison went to hear him argue a case before a court. He afterward placed upon record the fact that, while Jefferson spoke fluently and forcibly, he was no orator, and attempted no flights of eloquence. This did not seem, however, to interfere with the other fact that he had a habit of winning his cases. Madison, when seventeen years of age, went to him

for advice as to a course of study to be pursued by
such a youth as himself, determined upon attaining
eminence. The reply was not to be commended,
for Jefferson laid out a process of merciless and
health-sacrificing book-eating such as his own iron
constitution was with difficulty sustaining. His enthusiastic young friend undertook the task piled up
for him, and the consequences were detrimental.

Shadwell was only a fair day's ride from Montpellier, and the influence of the older ambition upon
the younger could not have been otherwise than
powerful. Political and moral and even theological
tendencies were sure to be communicated along with
literary advice. Three years earlier Jefferson himself had listened to Patrick Henry's burning eloquence in the Virginia House of Burgesses in behalf
of his famous resolutions. He was by no means the
man to have omitted from his talk with the bright
boys who visited him a full declaration of his own
opinions concerning the current disputes between
the colonies and the mother country. He was
therefore a very important factor in the agencies
employed for the education of the man who was to
succeed him as President of the United States.

In religion the Madison family were stanch supporters of the Established Church. So strong was
their adherence to its authority that among the
reasons assigned for not sending the eldest son of
the house to the College of William and Mary, in
Virginia, is that the doctrinal tendencies of the
faculty were unorthodox. A better reason was
found, perhaps, in the notoriously defective per-

sonal character of some of the same men and of the
educational facilities offered by them. These were
all sure to be given due weight by the Rev. Mr.
Martin, himself a New Jersey man, disposed to
favor the college at Princeton. The Established
Church in Virginia, however, was at that time doing
all in its power to repel such of its young men as
were beginning to feel the new impulses toward
human freedom. The persecution of dissenters,
against which Jefferson and Patrick Henry were
protesting, was vigorously pressed during Madison's school-days. In the year 1768 three Baptist
preachers were arrested near Montpellier, one Sunday morning, for daring to preach. They were
brought first to the parish church-yard, where three
magistrates who waited for them put them under
bonds of a thousand pounds each to answer the
crime alleged. They afterward spent forty-three
days in the Spottsylvania jail, doing good service
for the cause of religious freedom in America. This
and many another similar occurrence made their due
impression upon the mind of the studious, ambitious
boy, and the result was afterward very plainly declared.

All preliminary studies were finished in the year
1769, and James Madison went to college, at Princeton, uncommonly well prepared to avail himself of
whatever facilities might be there afforded him.

It was a memorable year in the history of America.

Already, in May, the Virginia House of Burgesses
had assembled at Williamsburg to pass the four

resolutions declaring colonial rights and providing for an appeal concerning them to His Majesty King George III., and then to be promptly dissolved for their patriotic presumption by Governor Lord Botetourt. They had then reassembled in the ballroom of the old Raleigh Tavern to take action which fixed and declared the position of the Virginia colony in the struggle for liberty.

Already British regiments were concentrating at Boston to overawe the rebellious province of Massachusetts.

At all the colonial centers of political thought and action the new life of freedom was stirring to fever-heat, and the several clusters of patriots were drawing nearer to each other in mutual hope and purpose. The colonies were rapidly preparing to become States and to solidify in due time as the United States, requiring a Constitution and a President, at the very hour when James Madison went away from home.

When Thomas Jefferson, some years earlier, went to the college of William and Mary, he also went to become a member of the daily dinner-table coterie of Governor Fauquier and to listen to Patrick Henry.

When John Adams went to Harvard he might as well have gone to Boston itself, so far as his political education was concerned.

When James Madison went to Princeton he sought the most retired corner of the most quiet colony owned in America by the British king. New Jersey was yet to have more battles fought upon

her soil than were fought upon that of any other
State except New York, and was to be more rich in
revolutionary war memories ; but at this time her
suppressed political heat had no distinct crater.
Nevertheless, a young man from the seclusion of a
Southern plantation was sure to find himself in a
new world at Princeton, and to form the acquaintance of other men, young and old, from the middle
and northern colonies whose ancestry, traditions,
training, and habits of thought were altogether
different from his own. The crust of provincial
narrowness was sure to be broken.

CHAPTER II.

*College Life—A Patriotic Bonfire—Results of Over-
work—Graduation—At Home at Montpellier—An
Interval of Quiet.*

JAMES MADISON went to college with well-settled
habits and purposes as a student. He also carried
with him a stainless moral character, which he succeeded in keeping clean in spite of all the tempta-
tions of a coarse and profligate time. The vices
and the frivolities from which he turned away were
the deadly enemies of the high ambition which had
been so long growing within him. Like Jefferson
at Williamsburg, he reacted from the evils around
him with a repulsion too strong to be clear-sighted,
and he discarded even healthful amusements and
needful bodily exercises.

His religious tendencies were very strong, and
theology had a large place in his course of reading.
Concerning this also he had consulted with his friend
Jefferson, and among the list of books commended
to his thoughtful perusal by that learned young
lawyer are mentioned : '' Bible ; New Testament ;
commentaries on them by Middleton in his works,
and by Priestley in his ' Corruptions of Christianity '
and ' Early Opinions of Christ ; ' the sermons of
Sterne, Massillon, and Bourdaloue.''

Precisely that selection would not have been made

by Madison's very orthodox tutor, the Rev. Thomas Martin, minister of the parish, but it may have had something to do with the fact that the pupil's religious tendencies did not lead him into the clerical profession. It is stated that he gave a year to the study of Hebrew after completing his college course. That is a tongue of small use except to theologians, but his investigation of it probably indicates a condition of mind rather than any definite purpose.

The regular college tasks could not have been burdensome to a brain so capable as his and so well prepared by previous training. Not much more should have been attempted, but Madison heaped toil upon toil in a feverish, ill-advised struggle for the attainment of learning, until his health broke down. All that is known of his student life at Princeton testifies to the unswerving zeal with which he sought for scholarship for its own sake. The head of the institution, Dr. Witherspoon, himself an able and accomplished scholar, had succeeded in giving a tone of serious, philosophical inquiry to the thoughtful young men under his direction. Among them were many who afterward attained eminence and exceptional usefulness.

Madison's college friends and associates were naturally such as would be drawn to him by kindred tastes and aspirations, but it would be a mistake to suppose that any American boys of that time could so bury themselves under school-books as not to know what was going on outside of college. Least of all could this be so with a neighbor and correspondent of Thomas Jefferson. The boys kept track of the events of the day, and were enthusiastic patriots. Dr. Witherspoon himself held opinions concerning American liberty which were sure to be received in full strength by the ardent young spirits around him.

On July 23d, 1770, James wrote to his father at Montpellier :

" We have no public news but the base conduct of the merchants in New York, in breaking through their spirited resolutions not to import, a distinct account of which, I suppose, will be in the Virginia *Gazette* before this arrives. Their letter to the merchants in Philadelphia, requesting their concurrence, was lately burned by the students of this place in the college yard, all of them in their black gowns and the bell tolling."

The picture of the black-gowned boys around the bonfire on the green, punishing with wrath a copy of the hated letter, while one of their number tugged at the college bell, is grotesquely funny, but it was full of important meaning. Not a great while afterward some of the black gowns were replaced by Continental uniforms. Other boys just like them, who had expressed their feelings during the previous winter by snowballing redcoats on Boston Common, were yet to wait behind the breastwork on Breed's Hill while the lines of red came up the slope to be met by balls not made of snow.

Madison remained at Princeton three years, being graduated, in 1771, with the degree of Bachelor of Arts. He appears to have remained to pursue a post-graduate course of study for a while, but, whether that record is accurate or not, he was at his Montpellier home in 1772. Here he assisted his father in the management of the estate, undertook the post of tutor for his younger brothers and his sisters, and continued to be a laborious and thoughtful student. The condition of mind and body to which his college over-work had brought him may be gathered from a passage in a letter to an ex-classmate, William Bradford, Jr., of Philadelphia, dated November 9th, 1772. He said of himself :

"I am too dull and infirm now to look out for extraordinary things in this world, for I think my sensations for many months have intimated to me not to expect a long or a healthy life, though it may be better for me after some time ; but I hardly dare expect it, and therefore have little spirit or elasticity to set about anything that is difficult in acquiring and useless in possessing after one has exchanged time for eternity."

He was in a sad state of despondency and disability for a youthful patriot for whom such stirring times and important duties were preparing. The sensations he referred to really intimated the folly of so much mere book-work and the necessity of vigorous exercise in the open air.

The year 1773 was comparatively quiet, so far as politics were concerned. There was temporarily a better feeling between the colonies and the mother country, but the leaders of colonial thought seem to have understood that it was only a lull before a storm, and their committees of correspondence were continually busy. In Boston, at least, there was no lull worth mentioning, and the events of previous years were under ceaseless discussion among the villages, farm-houses, and neighborhoods in the interior of every colony. The country was under-going a sort of ripening process, and young men like James Madison were getting ready for the times to come without being well aware of it.

CHAPTER III.

*Religious Freedom—The Port Bill and the Fast Day
—The Indian War—Madison and the Committee
of Safety—Following Jefferson—Outbreak of the
War of Independence.*

THE ripening processes of the year 1773 included
in their operation the British king and his ministers.
Before the year was over the latter had devised a
thinly cunning plan for retaining the right to tax
the colonies. They had sent over many shiploads
of tea to be employed by the people of several
American ports as practical tests and illustrations
of colonial determination not to be taxed. The
methods varied at the several ports, and their particulars, such as the Boston Harbor tea-party, December 18th, 1773, are matters of general history.
The action taken by the Philadelphians, however, in
refusing to receive the tea, enabled young James
Madison to put upon record the precise point to
which his patriotism had risen at the beginning of
the new year which was to be so full of great
events. He wrote to his friend William Bradford,
in Philadelphia, January 24th, 1774 :

" I congratulate you on your heroic proceedings with reference
to the tea. I wish Boston may conduct matters with as much discretion as they seem to do with boldness. . . . I verily believe
the frequent assaults that have been made on America (Boston especially) will in the end prove of real advantage."

It is not always easy to determine what is or is not discretion, and the Mohawks who emptied the tea-chests into salt water may, after all, have been the wisest men in Boston. Madison could not have been aware of that act when writing to his friend.

Another passage in the Bradford letter shows that the young planter-student had reached solid ground upon the question of religious freedom. Here, at least, he was almost ready to lay aside discretion, for he wrote : " But away with politics ! . . . That diabolical, hell-conceived principle of persecution rages among some ; and, to their eternal infamy, the clergy can furnish their quota of imps for such purposes. There are at this time in the adjacent country not less than five or six well-meaning men in close jail for publishing their religious sentiments, which in the main are very orthodox. I have neither patience to hear, talk, nor think of anything relative to this matter ; for I have squabbled and scolded, abused and ridiculed so long about it to little purpose that I am without common patience."

Jefferson and Patrick Henry and others were as angry as he, but they all were compelled to work patiently for many years before they obtained the blessing of religious freedom for Virginia.

The storm of the coming war gathered fast during the next ninety days. The King and Parliament of Great Britain decided that the presumptuous colonies required a warning. Boston had so behaved as to select itself a fitting example by whose fate all other American communities might be instructed. As a harbor it was to be shut up, in

order that as a town it might perish. The Boston
Port Bill and its associated legislative measures were
passed by Parliament and approved by the king in
precisely the same blundering arrogance which led
them to send over more regiments and stronger
fleets, instead of treating American Englishmen as
the fellow-citizens of the other Englishmen yet residing on the British islands.

The Virginia House of Burgesses was in session
at Williamsburg when, late in May, the news arrived
that the port of Boston was to be tyrannically shut
up on the first day of June. The members had
come together in an uncommonly loyal state of
mind, and had prepared a grand ball in honor of
Lady Dunmore. Instantly all was changed, although the ball was duly given and attended. On
the 24th a resolution was unanimously adopted
appointing the first of June " a day of fasting,
humiliation, and prayer, to implore Heaven to avert
from us the evils of civil war, to inspire us with firmness in support of our rights, and to turn the hearts
of the king and Parliament to moderation and
justice."

There were to be public religious services in all
the parish churches. When the news of this important resolution came to the homes of planters
like the Madisons, it plainly notified them, as it did
the British Government, that to the minds of the
men who voted for it a civil war threatened to come.
With the announcement of the Fast Day came the
news that Governor Lord Dunmore had promptly
dissolved the Assembly for appointing it ; that the

members had at once reassembled in the Raleigh Tavern ; that they had invited an ANNUAL CONGRESS of delegates from all the colonies ; that they had adjourned to meet again on the first of August, and had gone home to stir up their constituents.

The fast was kept with great solemnity, and as a rule the clergy did their duty with patriotic energy. The Boston Port Bill was made to have its full effect upon the people of the rural districts.

Other subjects than British tyranny were vexing the hearts and minds of the people of the border counties of Virginia. At about this time young Madison made a visiting tour among old friends in New Jersey and at Philadelphia. On his return he wrote a letter to William Bradford which gives a sad picture of the harassed frontier :

" I am once more got into my native land, and into the possession of my customary employments, solitude and contemplation ; though I must confess, not a little disturbed by the sound of war, bloodshed, and plunder, on the one hand, and the threats of slavery and oppression on the other. From the best accounts I can obtain from our frontiers, the savages are determined on the extirpation of the inhabitants, and no longer leave them the alternative of death or captivity. The consternation and timidity of the white people, who abandon their possessions without making the least resistance, are as difficult to be accounted for as they are encouraging to the enemy. Whether it be owing to the unusual cruelty of the Indians, the want of the necessary implements and ammunition for war, or to the ignorance and inexperience of many who, since the establishment of peace, have ventured into these new settlements, I can neither learn nor with any certainty conjecture. However, it is confidently asserted that there is not an inhabitant for some hundreds of miles back (which have been settled for many years), except those who have been forted in or embodied by their military commanders. The state of things has induced

Lord Dunmore, contrary to his intention at the dissolution of the Assembly, to issue writs for a new election of members, whom he is to call together on August 11th.

"As to the sentiments of the people of this colony with respect to the Bostonians, I can assure you I find them generally very warm in their favor."

He added exceptional notes concerning some of the conservative and mercantile classes which somewhat increase the light thrown by this letter upon his own position with reference to current events. Youth, ill-health, and habit of mind combined to curb the zeal of his patriotism and incline him to take, as yet, the part of an observer rather than of an actor. He could speak of " solitude and contemplation" in the very letter which depicted the desolation of the Virginia border, and disclosed the fact that he had been sounding the political views of his neighbors.

The Virginia voters selected the same men to represent them in the House of Burgesses summoned by Lord Dunmore and in the Williamsburg Convention which was to meet, eleven days earlier, to name delegates to the first Continental Congress. When they came together for the latter purpose they also provided for committees of safety, to take charge of the military preparations going forward in each county, and thereby invited young James Madison to perform his first public duties.

Congress met in Philadelphia on September 5th, and remained in session, with closed doors, for fifty-one days. Only the printed results of its proceedings reached the public eye or ear, but there was a general impression, at home and abroad, that it had proved itself a rarely capable and dignified body of men, well fitted to be intrusted with the cause of American liberty.

The county committees of safety were selected from time to time after neighborhood consultations. That of Albemarle County was not chosen until January 1st, 1775, with Thomas Jefferson for chairman. George Washington and Patrick Henry were already chairmen of their respective county committees. James Madison, Sr., was at the head of the eleven men elected by the freeholders of Orange County, and his son's name was also on a list of them recorded December 22d, 1774. The other names are those of men of the highest rank and wealth in the community, and the presence of both the Madisons, father and son, sufficiently indicates the estimation in which they were held and the pronounced position which they had already taken with reference to public affairs. A month later, January 20th, 1775, James Madison wrote to his friend Bradford :

" We are very busy at present in raising men and procuring the necessaries for defending ourselves and our friends in case of a sudden invasion. The extensiveness of the demands of the Congress and the pride of the British nation, together with the wickedness of the present ministry, seem, in the judgment of our politicians, to require a preparation for extreme events. There will by the spring, I expect, be some thousands of well-trained, high-spirited men ready to meet danger whenever it appears, who are influenced by no mercenary principles, but bearing their expenses, and having the prospect of no recompense but the honor and safety of their country."

The military preparations of Virginia were well made, and she contributed men and material, as well as a general, to the Continental Army before Boston. Nevertheless, from the beginning to the end of the war the condition of her frontier described by Madison, and the necessity of keeping the savage tribes in check, was a serious drain upon her resources.

The first visible approach of an appeal to arms decided one problem of the life of James Madison. His bodily strength, uninured to exertion or exposure, and wasted by study and confinement, was insufficient to meet the demands of camp and field service. He had not one trace of the born military instinct essential to success as a soldier or a leader of soldiers. All his training, all his habits of thought, prepared him for the council and the legislative chamber. He was but twenty-three years of age, and, however ambitious, had peculiarities of temperament which prevented him from pushing himself into undue prominence. It does not follow that he lacked clear convictions and fixed principles because he was in need of leaders, men of rougher mould, stronger and more aggressive than himself. It is better to say that he selected his captains with unerring judgment, and followed them unswervingly until his own turn came to lead, because they expressed his own perceptions of truth and right and sound public policy. The index of his career may be found in the fact that his first and last captain in political matters was Thomas Jefferson.

The news of the day came slowly and imperfectly

to plantation neighborhoods like that of Montpellier, but it was all of a nature to keep the zeal of patriotism at fever-heat. The Things were getting worse and worse in Massachusetts, and now, in the last week of April, startling tidings arrived from nearer home. The Virginia Colony owned some powder, stored for safe keeping in the public magazine at Williamsburg. On the night of April 20th Governor Lord Dunmore ordered a squad of marines ashore from a British man-of-war in the harbor. He sent them as an escort of one of his own wagons to steal fifteen half barrels of the powder and convey it on shipboard. The next morning the town of Williamsburg was in an uproar, and then swift messengers aroused the patriots of the interior. Mounted riflemen rallied fast, but all were restrained from decisive measures except one band gathered in Hanover County by Patrick Henry. These men rode right on, joined by others as they went, until they were within sixteen miles of Williamsburg. They were but one hundred and fifty strong, but for all Lord Dunmore knew they were an army. At all events, he sent his family on board the Fowey man-of-war for safety, and sent a messenger to settle for the powder. He received a written acknowledgment which was as good as a proclamation to the people of Virginia. It read as follows :

" DONCASTLE'S ORDINARY, NEW KENT, *May* 4, 1775.

" Received from the Honorable Richard Corbin, Esq., His Majesty's Receiver-General, 330 pounds, as a compensation for the gunpowder lately taken out of the public magazine by the governor's order ; which money I promise to convey to the Virginia delegates at the General Congress, to be, under their direction, laid out in gunpowder for the colony's use, and to be stored as they shall direct, until the next Colony Convention or General Assembly, unless it shall be necessary, in the mean time, to use the same in defence of the colony. It is agreed, that in case the next Convention shall determine that any part of the said money ought to be returned to the said Receiver-General, that the same shall be done accordingly.

"Patrick Henry, Jr."

Some of the money was so returned as being in excess of the value of the powder, but the Committee of Safety of Orange County at once wrote a letter to the Hanover men. It is in the handwriting of James Madison, Jr., and bears date May 9th, 1775. Among its other expressions of aggressive patriotism is the following :

" We take this opportunity also to give it as our opinion that the blow struck in the Massachusetts government is a hostile attack on this and every other colony, and a sufficient warrant to use violence and reprisal in all cases in which it may be expedient for our security and welfare."

The blow referred to had been struck at Lexington and Concord, and with the tidings of the events around Boston came word that Governor Dunmore was a fugitive on board the Fowey.

The Orange County committee further expressed its zeal by a public burning of ministerial pamphlets and other anti-American publications, and it was shortly to become evident that the part taken by young Madison was such as to make him a man of mark in spite of his youth and his moderation.

CHAPTER IV.

The Burning of Norfolk—Madison Elected to the Legislature—Congress and the Declaration of Independence—Reconstruction of Virginia.

THE year 1776 opened darkly for the colonial cause. Everywhere arose discontented murmurs against the as yet untried commander-in-chief. He was accused of inactivity, for he had not intrusted all men with the secret of how defective were the forces with which he was besieging the British Army in Boston. Something of temporary vacillation and unreadiness palsied the action of Congress. The people of Virginia in particular received, on New Year's Day, a dark warning of what might yet be included in the vengeance of the British ministry. Already they had been threatened with the horrors of a servile insurrection ; the savages of their harassed border were being stirred to fiercer activities by British emissaries ; and now, January 1st, 1776, a British fleet wantonly bombarded and destroyed Norfolk, the largest and richest town in the colony. Five thousand people were rendered houseless in midwinter, and it was plainly declared that similar devastation would soon be visited upon the entire seaboard and the tide-water settlements.

The aspect of affairs brightened shortly with the

evacuation of Boston by the British troops and the transfer of Washington's headquarters to New York, but the general feeling of the Virginia people was one of bitter exasperation mingled with dark forebodings.

It was in such a state of mind that the April elections were held for members of the Convention which was to assemble in May at Williamsburg. The precise impression already made by young Madison upon his neighbors is well defined by the fact that at such an hour they selected him to represent them. He was chosen to membership in a body of men whom the Norfolk fire had prepared for independence as completely as Bunker Hill and the winter camps had prepared the constituents of John Adams. It was nevertheless a time when that sturdy but imprudent radical was himself shunned in the streets of Philadelphia and on the floor of Congress as a disloyal fanatic, a dangerous man, going too fast and too far in his hot-headed dreams of separation from the mother country. Concerning himself and the state of public opinion at this date, Mr. Madison wrote to Jared Sparks, the historian, January 5th, 1828 :

"My first entrance into public life was in May, 1776, when I became a member of the convention in Virginia which instructed her delegates in Congress to propose the Declaration of Independence. Previous to that date I was not in sufficient communication with any under the denomination of leaders to learn their sentiments or views òn that cardinal subject.

"I can only say, therefore, that so far as ever came to my knowledge, no one of them ever avowed or was understood to entertain a pursuit of independence at the assembling of the first

Congress or for a considerable period thereafter. It has always been my impression that a re-establishment of the colonial relations to the parent country, as they were previous to the controversy, was the real object of every class of the people, till despair of obtaining it, and the exasperating effects of the war and the manner of conducting it, prepared the minds of all for the event declared on July 4th, 1776, as preferable, with all its difficulties and perils, to the alternative of submission to a claim of power at once external, unlimited, irresponsible, and under every temptation to abuse from interest, ambition, and revenge. If there were individuals who aimed at independence, their views must have been confined to their own bosoms or to a very confidential circle."

Before the end of May the Virginia delegates in Congress received copies of the resolutions adopted by the Williamsburg Convention on the 15th, instructing them to urge an immediate Declaration of Independence. From that hour forward the result was sure, and deliberation and debate in Congress related mainly to the manner of announcing the new nationality and the forms and methods by which it should be defined and maintained.

In the same breath with which the Virginia Convention had advised the associated colonies to become a nation, it had assumed for the Old Dominion the character of an independent State. The next duty upon its hands, therefore, was to devise ways and means for its local self-government. The first legislative work and experience of James Madison was consequently with reference to the Virginia Bill of Rights and Constitution. He was a member of the committee to whom was assigned the duty of drafting the Constitution. It became speedily manifest in the committee-room that more

than ordinary powers of mind had been under preparation for usefulness during his long years of excessive study and deep thinking.   The slight-framed,
quiet-mannered, youthful member from Orange was
no debater, no orator, he had never before been
heard of in public affairs ; but he had that in him
which made men listen to him and give weight to
whatever he might say upon the vitally important
questions before the Assembly.   He was a man
whose courtesy and kindliness of address gave
offence to none, and whose cheerful gayety made
him a pleasant companion over the dullest and
weariest of prosaic work.

The writings of Washington, Jefferson, and many
other competent witnesses entirely sustain Madison's
record of the state of public opinion, up to this time,
with reference to separation from the mother country.   He himself, like his associates in that convention, was but barely ready, goaded by the scalpings
on the frontier and the piracies on the seaboard, to
the indignant adoption of the resolutions which
nerved the Continental Congress to its work.   Upon
another subject than that of national independence,
however, he was advanced beyond his older colleagues.   The arrests and fines and imprisonments
of Baptist ministers, under the Virginia code, had
given him object lessons upon freedom of conscience.
Voices came to him through the bars of jails, and
he now echoed them upon the floor of the Convention.

Fourteen articles of the Bill of Rights were mainly
the work of George Mason, three more being drafted

by other hands. The fourteenth article proposed by Mr. Mason contained the following :

" All men should, therefore, enjoy the fullest toleration in the exercise of religion, according to the dictates of conscience, independent and unrestrained by the magistrate, unless, under color of religion, any man disturb the peace, the happiness, or the safety of society."

The idea of restraint by a magistrate implied that of the general supervision and censorship of religious doctrine by some established church, empowered by law to exercise toleration. Madison proposed to amend so that the article should declare, concerning religious freedom, that " all men are entitled to the full and free exercise of it according to the dictates of conscience. . . . No man or class of men ought, on account of religion, to be invested with peculiar emoluments or privileges, or subjected to any penalties or disabilities, unless, under color of religion, the preservation of equal liberty and the existence of the State are manifestly endangered."

The convention was not ripe for untrammelled religious freedom, but Madison succeeded in having a declaration of equal right substituted for the word and idea of toleration. The clause concerning restraint was simply omitted and the great question of practical liberty was left to the long discussions of other years. Mr. Madison himself recorded, in his ripe age, that his part of the work upon the Constitution was of a minor sort. " Being young and inexperienced," he writes, " I of course had little agency in those proceedings."

How was it, then, that so young a member, never heard of before, made so deep an impression upon the able and discerning men who composed that memorable convention?

The answer is like a key-note to his entire career, and may in part be found in the tribute paid to him by his friend Thomas Jefferson in that statesman's memoir of his own life:

" Mr. Madison came into the House [Virginia] in 1776, a new member and young ; which circumstances, concurring with his extreme modesty, prevented his venturing himself in debate before his removal to the Council of State in November, 1777. From thence he went to Congress, then consisting of few members. Trained in these successive schools, he acquired a habit of self-possession which placed at ready command the rich resources of his luminous and discriminating mind and of his extensive information, and rendered him the first of every Assembly afterward of which he became a member. Never wandering from his subject into vain declamation, but pursuing it closely, in language pure, classical, and copious, soothing always the feelings of his adversaries by civilities and softness of expression, he rose to the eminent station which he held in the great national convention of 1787 ; and in that of Virginia which followed, he sustained the new Constitution in all its parts, bearing off the palm against the logic of George Mason and the fervid declamation of Mr. Henry. With these consummate powers was united a pure and spotless virtue which no calumny has ever ventured to sully."

The man who could and did receive such a training and attain such results had already in his boyhood developed the high character and strong personality which made the Virginia delegates careless of his youth and his attenuated body. His father was county lieutenant of Orange, chairman of the Committee of Safety, and a man of wide social influence ; but that could not have secured the election of his son to the Convention if the high-spirited planters and sturdy yeomen had not already discovered the intrinsic worth of their scholarly neighbor.   It was the more remarkable at a time when the minds of all men were turning toward military affairs, and when soldierly qualities, on the one hand, and oratorical power, on the other, were sure passports to the foremost places.   The silent force of Madison's character must have been precisely such as is indicated in the eulogy pronounced by Jefferson.

Immediately after the adoption of the Constitution, Patrick Henry was chosen first governor of the new State.   War measures of various kinds were adopted.   An election of State Senators was provided for.   The Convention adjourned, July 5th, to meet again on the first Monday in October, to act as the House of Delegates until the next April election.   Senate and House together were to constitute the General Assembly of the Commonwealth of Virginia.

When the adjournment took place the news had not yet reached Virginia that the Liberty Bell in Philadelphia had pealed so loudly the previous afternoon in proclaiming the Declaration of Independence.

CHAPTER V.

A STORM of military events followed the formal
assumption of nationality by the young republic.
There were minor successes here and there, but all
these were lost sight of in the gloom caused by the
defeat on Long Island and the subsequent reverses
to the central army under Washington. It was
under that cloud that the Virginia Assembly met,
October 7th, 1776, and took up the noble work of
reconstructing the social system of the State, its
laws, its customs, its entire administration and rela- .
tion to the rest of the world, at the same time that
redoubled efforts were made to sustain the common
cause.

The independent companies, one in each county,
organized in the beginning by the Committees of
Safety, had aggregated about six thousand men.
From these had been largely recruited the first
forces sent to the Continental Army. James Madison's brother Ambrose, four years younger than himself, had gone with the volunteers from Orange
County. The good men and true of the Old
Dominion were pouring into the ranks, and upon the

Assembly fell the duty of equipping and maintaining them. No other State did better, from first to last.

The work of civil reconstruction began at once, but Madison was not to have any considerable immediate share in it. At a later day he fell heir to the legislative outlines then marked out by others. Most of the proposed reforms lingered unfinished through long years. They did so, writes Jefferson, " until after the general peace, in 1785, when by the unwearied exertions of Mr. Madison, in opposition to the endless quibbles, chicaneries, perversions, and delays of lawyers and demi-lawyers, most of the bills were passed by the Legislature with little alteration."

There was nothing brilliant in the young legislator's first term of service, but he would almost undoubtedly have received a re-election if it had not been for a bold effort that he made for the reform of a pernicious abuse. It was the Virginia custom, borrowed from the mother country, that candidates for elective offices should not only make a personal canvass and stoop to ask for votes, but should provide unlimited liquor on election day. Madison was willing to canvass, with due regard to self-respect, but he rebelled especially against the practice of treating, and refused to furnish any liquor. He did so, as he declared, because " the reputation and success of representative government depends on the purity of popular elections."

There can be no doubt but what the better men around him approved of his course, but they were

not the majority. The innovation was too sudden
and too great, and the old bad custom beat him.
An attempt afterward made to contest the election
on the ground of corrupt influence failed entirely,
but the young reformer was not to remain at home.
On November 13th of the same year, 1777, the Virginia Assembly, in a joint session of both Houses,
elected a Council of State. The vote was by ballot,
and James Madison did not know that he was to be
a candidate until his friends had elected him by a
handsome majority.

The Council of State consisted of eight members,
and shared the executive functions of the governor,
who could perform no official act without their advice. There were special reasons, apart from his
character for probity and general ability, why Madison was selected for a post of such honorable distinction. His well-known scholarship had much to
do with it. When the Council came together it
was found that no other member of it was versed in
foreign languages. There were letters from abroad
to be read and answered ; there were occasional
emissaries from the continent of Europe to be received and conferred with ; more than all, there
were many European military men continually
arriving, seeking commissions in the forces of the
new republic. With reference to all the varied
business thus indicated, the youngest member of the
Council became of great assistance to his colleagues
and to Governor Patrick Henry. With the latter
he soon formed a close and confidential friendship.
So much of the entire mass of executive correspond-

ence fell to the share of Madison, before long, that many people inexperienced in the new official titles described him as Secretary of State rather than Councillor of State.

The struggle for American freedom swayed to and fro during two long and dark and trying years. The campaign which included the battles of the Brandywine and Germantown had ended with Washington's army in the terrible winter camp at Valley Forge. Then had followed a campaign in which partial successes like the battle of Monmouth were counterbalanced by disasters like the fall of Savannah and blood-chilling horrors like the Wyoming Valley massacres. The winter of 1779–80 found the Continental Army as badly off as it had been at Valley Forge. Continental paper money had so fallen that forty dollars of it could be purchased by one dollar in silver, and there was reason to believe that its utter repudiation must quickly follow. Congress itself had seemed to lose much of its unity of purpose and vigor of action.

Just as the year 1779 was closing, on December 14th, James Madison was chosen a delegate to Congress from Virginia, and on March 20th, 1780, he took his seat. There was something noteworthy in the action of the Assembly in taking from the governor's Council of State its busiest member to represent the Commonwealth in its relations to the general Government. He was not yet thirty, but he had evidently worn well before the eyes of the anxious-hearted men who so expressed their confidence.

Only one week after his arrival in Philadelphia
Mr. Madison addressed a letter to Governor Thomas
Jefferson which affords a complete picture of the
situation.   It suggests also the extent and character
of the legislative duties upon which the writer was
entering and the difficulties he was to contend with
and to largely assist in surmounting.   Governor
Henry's term of office had expired some months
before, so that the old friendship between the boy-
student of Montpellier and the young Albemarle
County genius, then of Shadwell and now of Monticello, had grown stronger in the close association
of confidential official intercourse.   Madison wrote
to Jefferson :

"Among the various conjectures of alarm and distress which
have arisen in the course of the Revolution, it is with pain I affirm
to you that no one can be singled out more truly critical than the
present.   Our army threatened with an immediate alternative of
disbanding or living on free quarter ; the public treasury empty ;
public credit exhausted—nay, the private credit of purchasing
agents employed, I am told, as far as it will bear ; Congress com-
plaining of the extortion of the people, the people of the improvi-
dence of Congress, and the army of both ; our affairs requiring the
most mature and systematic measures, and the urgency of occasions admitting only of temporizing expedients, and these expedients generating new difficulties ; Congress recommending plans
to the several States for execution, and the States separately re-
judging the expediency of such plans, whereby the same distrust of
concurrent exertions that has damped the ardor of private individuals must produce the same effect among the States themselves ;
an old system of finance discarded as incompetent to our necessi-
ties, an untried and precarious one substituted, and a total stagna-
tion in prospect between the end of the former and the operation
of the latter.

"These are the outlines of the picture of our public situation.

I leave it to your own imagination to fill them up. Believe me, sir, as things now stand, if the States do not vigorously proceed in collecting the old money and establishing funds for the credit of the new, we are undone ; and let them be ever so expeditious in doing this, still the intermediate distress to our army and hindrance to public affairs are a subject of melancholy reflection. General Washington writes that a failure of bread has already commenced in the army, and that, for anything he sees, it must unavoidably increase. Meat they have only for a short season ; and as the whole dependence is on provisions now to be procured, without a shilling for the purpose and without credit for a shilling, I look forward with the most pungent apprehensions."

The republic was then in the chaotic state preceding its first stages of definite formation. It had no executive, no national judiciary, no departments of administration: No State had understood relations to other States or to the Confederation, the central Government which included them all. Nobody knew what were or what were not the powers of Congress, or how soon it might lose all that it seemed or professed to have. The evil consequences were plainly set forth in Mr. Madison's letter. It was an official report, in which the writer did somewhat more than appeared in even his vivid and striking delineation of the crisis. He left it plain to our eyes that he was at that time studying these evils, their causes and their remedies. So were other able and patriotic men, with whom he was to be associated. Every failure, every disorder, every civil or military disaster seeming to threaten the existence of the new experiment in human government, warned him and them that behind it, causing it, was something or other which

must be discovered and avoided or rooted out. So
he went to work, and so did they all ; but none
better than he ; and the result was that a stable
" government of the people, by the people, and for
the people shall not perish from the earth.''

CHAPTER VI.

Inventing a New Government—No Taxes, no Treasury—Practical Lessons for Congressmen—Getting Acquainted with Washington—Borrowing Money to Live on.

THE first idea entertained by the colonies concerning American liberty was that it was a blessing which might be fought for and won and enjoyed as a part of the general liberty of the British Empire.

When that delusion perished, the men who had escaped from it were as ready as ever to fight or to make pecuniary sacrifices for American liberty standing alone. They knew that no man could be really free except under a free government, and they were now blindly groping around in the general confusion of the war time for something of that sort. The first clear idea they had of it was that it must be a power which could pay its debts, especially to its army contractors and soldiers. The best of men had only crude notions of financial science in that day. The entire Continental currency had to melt away to nothing and disappear before it was thoroughly understood that the power to issue paper promises must be backed by the power to levy taxes and collect cash enough to fulfil the promises. That power to tax was slowly and jealously surrendered by the several States to the general Government.

A great deal of instruction was obtained by public men from European financiers among whom they undertook to borrow money. All the shrewd money-lenders began at once to ask questions about the national sources of revenue. The French Government lent some money from time to time, but it was only because it was a cheap way of maintaining an important part of the force with which she assailed her old enemy, England. French statesmen regarded America as a sort of left wing of their army, and paid money to keep it in fighting condition—not one franc more.

The general drift of military events during that first year of Madison's service in Congress, 1780, was not unfavorable to the American arms.

General Gates had been defeated at the battle of Sanders Creek, but there had been good fighting at the South.

Arnold's treason had been felt as a disaster and dishonor by the entire nation, but he had been alone in it.

Spain and Holland had joined the foes of England, and were as a re-enforcement to America and France.

Under all the difficulties pictured by Madison in his letter to Jefferson, Washington had managed to keep his suffering army together, and every month during which he could do so was as a lost battle to England, for her power to maintain the costly struggle was ebbing away.

With the close of the year the long-tried patience of the Continentals wavered a little. There was a

serious mutiny of the Pennsylvania line on New
Year's Day, 1781, at Morristown, New Jersey. Even
General Wayne was unable to control the starving
men, and thirteen hundred of them, with six field
pieces, marched toward Philadelphia with an avowed
intention of bringing Congress to terms. The men
behaved admirably on their march and afterward.
Their demands were in part met, they were pacified,
and returned to duty without actually marching into
Philadelphia. They had, however, set the facts of
the case before Congress and the entire country in
such a forcible manner as to render debate unnecessary. A few weeks earlier, in November, 1780,
Madison had written that the want of money "is
the source of all our public difficulties and misfortunes. One or two millions of guineas properly
applied would diffuse vigor and satisfaction throughout the whole military department, and would expel
the enemy from every part of the United States."

Continental currency was at that date circulating
slowly at about a hundred for one, and two millions
of golden guineas, ten millions of actual dollars,
must have seemed a large sum. It was a slightly
exaggerated statement, such as Madison did not
often make ; but a mere fraction of the sum named
would have prevented the January mutinies and
many mournful scenes in all the camps that winter.

Congress had received important lessons in finance
from Wayne's mutineers, and Madison himself was
soon to obtain a practical acquaintance with pov-
erty. His unostentatious, well-regulated life had
been passed in comfortable independence, and he

had never known the need of money until the year 1781. Even then it came to him peculiarly as a member of Congress depending on his pay. Each State made such provision as it saw fit for its own delegates, and Virginia had intended to deal liberally with her own. She had provided that each man sent to represent her at Philadelphia might charge his housekeeping expenses to her account, including three servants and four horses, fuel, and house rent. He must keep due accounts, and was to be reimbursed quarterly. Added to this, he was to have two dollars a mile for distances travelled, and twenty dollars a day for time spent in attending to Congressional duties.

When the law making this provision was passed the State of Virginia was paying cash. When James Madison, in 1781, tried to make both ends meet with the paper money Virginia was paying then, he found himself a sort of legislative pauper. Thirteen thousand dollars paid to Jefferson in reimbursement of a loan of gold to the State did but buy him an overcoat. James Madison's pay was insufficient to feed him. There is no wonder that he devoted himself day and night to thought and study upon the national finances, for matters grew worse as time went on.

The next great lesson, perhaps, was in the discovery that no military success, however brilliant, could increase the value of a national promise-to-pay until the victory could be transmuted into some method for collecting a national revenue. The year 1781 was crowned by the surrender of Corn-

wallis at Yorktown, and all the world agreed with
Lord North, Prime-Minister of England, that "it
is all over" with British rule in America. Nevertheless, the financial and other difficulties continued
undiminished, and members of Congress were often
almost as badly off as if they had been officers in
one of Washington's unpaid, half-fed, half-clad,
and now indignant regiments. The general himself
spent that entire winter of 1781–82 in Philadelphia
urging the adoption of vigorous measures and the
maintenance of a bold military front until the final
removal of the last British soldier from the soil of
the United States. This was Madison's first opportunity for cultivating a close acquaintance with the
nation's hero. Each was utterly absorbed in the
performance of his duty to his country, and could
understand and sympathize with the other. The
records of committee work and legislative business
at this time prove the unflagging diligence with
which Madison was toiling, while his letters frequently remove the veil from the very disagreeable
circumstances under which his work was done.

To his friend Edmund Randolph he wrote : "I
cannot in any way make you more sensible of the
importance of your kind attention to pecuniary re-
mittances for me than by informing you that I have
for some time past been a pensioner on the favor of
Haym Solomon, a Jew broker."

Nobody cared to buy drafts drawn upon Virginia.
From week to week the pressure upon penniless
Congressmen grew more and more distressing. The
very wolf was at the door in some cases. In fact,

a sort of death by famine seemed to threaten the life of the young republic. It was not entirely driven away until at last Washington summoned the genius of Hamilton to solve the problem of taxation and revenue. Before that could be done, however, there was a vast amount of work for the hands of Madison and his brother legislators who could not meet their board bills. He wrote again to Randolph :

"The kindness of our little friend in Front Street [the broker], near the coffee-house, is a fund which will preserve me from extremities ; but I never resort to it without great mortification, as he obstinately rejects all recompense. The price of money is so usurious that he thinks it ought to be extorted from none but those who aim at profitable speculation. To a necessitous delegate he gratuitously spares a supply out of his private stock."

CHAPTER VII.

*The Old Confederation—Surrender of Cornwallis—
An Industrious Legislator—Monarchical Notions
Presenting Themselves—Madison's Disappointment
—Once more in the Virginia Legislature.*

JAMES MADISON was very young, speaking by the
record of dates, when he went to Congress, but
there were reasons why he was a somewhat old
young man. One was that he had never been thoroughly a boy. His earliest letters and pursuits
evince uncommon maturity all over one side of his
character. Amiable, cheerful, sociable, he nevertheless did not present to his older colleagues any unpleasant suggestion that his years were in the way
of their meeting him on equal ground. He never
bubbled over with a hundredth part of the hot-
headed enthusiasm which at times made John
Adams seem absurd and ill-balanced, which made
Jefferson's rhetoric swell into inflation, which so
easily heated Patrick Henry to the boiling-point, or
which made Washington lose his temper altogether.
He had deep convictions and an abundance of
warmth concerning them, but no tide of feeling ever
swept him away or prevented him from dealing with
either victory or disaster with a calm and scholar-
like analysis of its real importance.

When the allied French and American armies

paraded through Philadelphia, on successive days, marching to the capture of Cornwallis, Madison watched the passing regiments with an interest so intense that he at once sat down and wrote about them to his friend Judge Pendleton. His letter begins : " This letter will be the most agreeable of any I have long had the pleasure of writing ;" and so beyond all doubt it was ; but it is a picture sadly lacking in color. He praised the sturdy ranks of the old Continentals, in all sorts of uniforms and without uniforms other than the rags to which they were reduced by the failure of Congress to provide for them. He praised the admirable equipment and soldierly bearing of the French troops. Still, he did not burst out into any kind of exuberance then, nor did he afterward when Washington's masterpiece of military strategy was crowned with success.

It is entirely possible that the portentous difficulties with which he was contending as a statesman and legislator, and which he perceived more clearly than did most other men, weighed habitually upon his mind and kept him down. So, too, did his intense, persistent, self-sacrificing toil.

The inherent defects of the temporary form of government first adopted by the revolted colonies offer too wide a field for analysis in a mere biography. A sufficient summing up may be made in saying that thirteen State governments were too loosely harnessed together to pull together. The result was that when the country had piled up a debt of forty millions of dollars and was abundantly able to pay it off in two years, the central Government was unable to even meet the interest, and was compelled to borrow money for that purpose from France in a most humiliating way.

That this was so was no fault of James Madison. The record shows that his efforts as a member of the Congressional Committee on Finance were directed by a far-sighted and intelligent statesmanship. As to financial measures proposed, he seems in nearly all cases to have been in accord with Alexander Hamilton. The records of debates and of committee work were then imperfectly kept, but they testify abundantly to the estimation in which Madison was held by his colleagues. They also prove that he had entirely .put away any lack of self-confidence, and was able to uphold his views with fluency and force against the foremost debaters of the day. Questions of vast importance to the future of the country as well as to the present were rapidly looming up ; questions involving historical precedents, international law, existing treaties between other powers, the manifest interests and ambitions of European nations, such as England, France, Spain. In dealing with all and each in turn the speeches of Mr. Madison and the papers prepared by him show that now, as in earlier life, he was an industrious and capable student. That he was so and that he found his search after needed information unduly hampered is strikingly testified to by a vigorous attempt that he made to induce Congress to lay the foundation of a Congressional Library. He had a committee appointed, with himself as chairman, and reported a catalogue of works which he declared ought at once to be purchased for the use of Congress. The intelligent performance of their duties by other members required that they should have at hand for reference and should consult the authorities he himself had found indispensable, and many more ; but there were too many men in the House who were willing to go on, as before, without burdening themselves with book learning, and no library was provided.

The germs and beginnings of future political differences and discussions came to the surface from time to time in various forms, but none of the questions upon which parties were one day to divide were ripe for consideration or for settlement. It was an era of expedients and makeshifts, and the ablest men in the land frankly, sorrowfully declared themselves unable to forecast by what precise form of permanent government all this chaotic uncertainty was to be overcome and replaced.

It should by no means be forgotten that republicanism in America during the latter years of the war of independence was quite another thing from the democratic-republicanism which includes all parties and permeates all political education at the present day. There was a vast amount of inherited or acquired caste and aristocracy. The entire population had been born and brought up under a monarchy, and monarchical ideas had only in part passed away. The existing republicanism was English rather than American, and afterward expressed itself in the Federal Party until the new political idea had time to take possession of the minds of men.

The Continental Army itself placed upon record a sufficiently clear definition of the political situation during Mr. Madison's last year in Congress. Peace with England had not yet been attained, but was evidently near at hand, and it almost seemed as if the country had cast off the burden of feeding soldiers whose bayonets it was soon to need no more. At the same time it was undeniable that not even Congress itself had so strong a hold upon the popular heart and confidence as had the commander-in-chief, who had for so long been very nearly a dictator as well as wholly a patriot.

The men who had endured so much and so un-flinchingly for liberty were surely not behind other men in what was then understood as republicanism, and yet, in 1782, while peace negotiations were pending, they offered the crown of a constitutional monarchy to General Washington. He received a letter from Colonel Lewis Nicola, a veteran and in-fluential officer, who spoke for others as well as for himself. He discussed possible forms of government, favoring that of England, and added :

" In that case it will, I believe, be uncontroverted that the same abilities which have led us through difficulties apparently insur-mountable by human power to victory and glory, those qualities that have merited and obtained the universal veneration and esteem of an army, would be most likely to conduct and direct us in the smoother paths of peace. Some people have so connected the idea of tyranny and monarchy as to find it very difficult to separate them. It may therefore be necessary to give the head of such a constitution as I propose some title apparently more moderate ;

but if all other things were once adjusted, I believe strong arguments might be produced for admitting the title of king, which, I
conceive, would be attended with some material advantages."

Washington's severely indignant refusal destroyed
in its infancy the dream of constitutional monarchy
in America, but the end was not yet. To him Congress and the country were again indebted, during
the following spring, for the unequalled firmness,
tact, and courageous devotion with which he restrained his justly indignant veterans during the
trials of patience which preceded their disbandment.
But for him the army would have disbanded Congress.

A general treaty of peace was signed at Paris on
January 20th, 1783, and preparations began at once
for the removal of the British forces ; but the hands
of Congress did not seem to be immediately strengthened. It was rather as if the several States held off
for a moment, each desiring to consider the new
situation and to determine what might yet be most
for its own interest when the outside pressure of the
war with England should be removed. It was
through such a condition of affairs that Mr. Madison's term in Congress drew toward its close month
after month. Under the Virginia law, as it then
stood, he was not eligible for a second successive
term, and it seemed as if an era of his public life
were finishing very early.

A very different era, belonging to his personal
history, had come to the young-old statesman somewhat late, and was also about to be finished for him
by a law beyond his control. Among his warm

friends in Congress was General William Floyd, of
Long Island, and he had brought his daughter with
him, in 1783, to brighten the gloom which had
settled over the business of legislating for the republic. She is represented as very bright and attractive. She must also have been mature beyond
her years, for she reached her sixteenth birthday in
April, 1783, and yet was more than merely permitted by her father to receive the attentions of the
distinguished young Virginian. He paid them as-
siduously, for he was deeply in love. He proposed,
was accepted, and all things seemed to be going forward smoothly toward a wedding day, when the
young lady discovered that she had made a mistake.
It was not so much that Mr. Madison was fully
twice her age or that he was at all lacking in the
qualities which she had seemed to find in him ; her
eyes were opened by the arrival of a young clergyman, whose accomplishments were of a different sort
from those of the man who was to be " first of every
assembly afterward of which he became a member."
The law of love prevailed against all obstacles ; the
temporary fetter which bound her to Mr. Madison
was in due progression sundered, and Miss Floyd
afterward married the young clergyman. Her
father is said to have been much disappointed at the
dismissal of his friend, of whom as a son-in-law he
had fully approved. Woman had her way, but the
rejected lover felt his dismissal keenly. He had
not bestowed his affections wisely, but his devotion
to a girl incompetent to appreciate him had been
genuine. He deserved and received the sympathy

of those who knew him. The intimacy of his personal relations with Jefferson can be better understood, as it should be, with reference to their political association, when we find the latter writing to him at this time :

" I sincerely lament the misadventure which has happened, from whatever cause it may have happened. Should it be final, however, the world presents the same and many other resources of happiness, and you possess many within yourself. Firmness of mind and unintermitting occupation will not long leave you in pain. No event has been more contrary to my expectations, and these were founded on what I thought a good knowledge of the ground. But of all machines ours is the most complicated and inexplicable."

Jefferson's first romance had come to him when he was yet a mere law student under age, and subsequent events had taught him something. Once more he had loved, more deeply, tenderly, absorbingly than at first, and once more he had lost, for he had not yet recovered from the prostration caused by the death of his wife in 1782. He soon wrote again to Madison, suggesting a sort of dream of the future. Another of his young friends, James Monroe, had talked of buying a small farm near Monticello, and retiring there for studious years of philosophic contemplation. Another named William Short was probably equally available. Why, he urged, should not Madison also turn away from the disturbances and cares of the world and buy a farm close by ? With Monticello and its library and its hospitalities for a centre, could not four such friends attain all that was left to them of human felicity in mutual consolation, companionship, and congenial scholarly pursuits?

It was not altogether so absurd as it seems, looked at from a distance, but these men were not to live for themselves alone, and their mutual friendship was to be of vast service to the country, for which they were to toil during so many years of close companionship.

Madison's first reply, although not favorable to the dream of his friend, gave as a reason the necessity he was under of superintending the Montpellier estate, for his father was growing old. He had returned home at once upon the close of his Congressional term, and had added law studies to his duties as a planter. In the spring of that very year, however, 1784, the call of duty came to both of them. The Orange County electors decided that they wished James Madison to represent them in the Virginia Assembly, and did not compel him to solicit votes or to supply election-day liquor. They had no other man among them whom they were willing to send instead of him on any account. On May 17th Congress selected Jefferson as a plenipotentiary commissioner to France, in association with Benjamin Franklin and John Adams, and he accepted the appointment, taking along William Short as Secretary of the Legation. His last token of confidence in James Madison was to commit to him the supervision of his nephews, sons of his friend Dabney Carr. He wrote to him:

" I have a tender legacy to leave you on my departure. I will not say it is the son of my sister, though her worth would justify it

on that ground ; but it is the son of my friend, the dearest friend
I knew, who, had fate reversed our lots, would have been a father
to my children.   He is a boy of fine dispositions, and of sound,
masculine talents.   I was his preceptor myself as long as I stayed
at home ; and when I came away I placed him with Mr. Maury.
There is a younger one, just now in his Latin rudiments.   If I did
not fear to overcharge you I would request you to recommend a
school for him."

CHAPTER VIII.

*The States and the Union of States—How the Move-
ment for a Better Union Began—Call for a National Constitutional Convention—The Legislature
Visited by Washington and Lafayette.*

THE Virginia Legislature of 1784 contained many
patriotic men whom it was easy to lead in measures
relating to the reform and advancement of their
own State, provided that they were not led too fast
or asked to surrender more than one old error at a
time.

There were not so many members who had any
clear idea that Virginia was, and for her good must
continue to be, an integral part of a great, new
nation called the United States of America.

Mr. Madison had been thoroughly trained, during
his three years in the severe school of the war Congress, to be a national statesman, with wide and
widening views of America's political future. He
had studied the finances, commerce, and foreign
affairs of the nation as a whole and its relations to
the several States. He at once became the ruling
mind of the Legislature. Patient and courteous
with all, while as persistent as he was far-sighted,
all the reforms accomplished and all the good work
done bear the impress of his hand, and testify to the
firmness, tact, and skill with which he overcame the

obstacles thrown in his way by ignorance, narrowness, sectarianism, State pride, class prejudices, and
mistaken greed. No catalogue of what he accomplished for the welfare of Virginia can be given
here. Thomas Jefferson's testimony as to its extent and value has been already quoted. In serving
his own State well, however, and especially in labor-
ing for a better adjustment of its relations with the
general Government, he rendered lasting service to
the nation as a whole.

While in Congress Mr. Madison had acquired the
friendship and confidence of leading men from other
States. With many of these, especially with such
as were at this time members of the national legislature, he was in correspondence and intelligent co-
operation. The great work of unifying the customs
system, and with it the commerce of the country,
took form very slowly, for the several States were
averse to surrendering control of their ports and
rivers. It is easy to see that in the minds of many
stubborn ex-colonists the Confederation, which had
not yet become a Union, stood in the attitude of a
friendly foreign power with which the State of which
they formed a part was chaffering over a long series
of sharp bargains. Each other State was also more
or less a foreigner with whom a close treaty of alliance for common defence existed, but whose conduct was to be closely watched. It is needful to
keep the State rights jealousy in mind in order to
appreciate the work of men who, like Madison, were
giving lives of thoughtful toil to the construction of
a great nation out of these colonial fragments. Not

one of the fragments, the States so to be fitted together, was yet in good shape either to stand alone or to become a working member of the general body, the Union. Madison labored manfully to get Virginia ready. One of his most important achievements grew out of an attempt to adjust conflicting claims of Virginia and Maryland to the control of Potomac River navigation. The matter was peculiarly within his province as chairman of the Committee on Commerce. Even before the meeting of the Legislature he had taken counsel with Mr. Jefferson, and he afterward reported a resolution, adopted June 28th, 1784, providing for the appointment of commissioners by the two States to negotiate a final settlement. He was himself named one of the four Virginia commissioners. Maryland was slow in appointing her representatives, and the Commission did not meet until the spring of 1785. When they came together they discovered that other States, particularly Pennsylvania and Delaware, were interested in the navigation of the Potomac and of Delaware Bay, and should be represented in such a conference. The subject seemed to widen as it was looked at, and the Maryland Legislature proposed that the general subject of American commerce should be brought before a convention of delegates from all the thirteen States. Mr. Madison himself, through his friend Mr. Tyler, introduced into the Virginia Legislature a resolution providing for a convention of five commissioners from each State " to take into consideration the trade of the United States ; to examine the relative

situations and trade of said States ; to consider how
far a uniform system in their commercial regulations
may be necessary to their common interest and their
permanent harmony ; and to report to the several
States such an act, relative to this great subject, as,
when unanimously ratified by them, will enable the
United States, in Congress, effectually to provide
for the same."

The phrases of this resolution present a condensed
statement of the absence of a national government
with adequate powers.   The fact that it was permitted to lie asleep on the table for two months
illustrates the absorption of the several State legislatures in their own affairs and their comparative
indifference to the idea of a unification of the thirteen Commonwealths.   It was passed on the last
day of the session, .1786, largely on account of action
taken in the mean time by Maryland.   Mr. Madison
was, of course, named as one of the commissioners.
These shortly came together, appointed the second
Monday of September, 1786, as the day in which
the convention should be held, named Annapolis,
Maryland, as the place of meeting, and sent proper
invitations to the other States.

On September 11th the convention met at Annapolis, and seemed to find itself a complete failure. ·
Georgia, South Carolina, Maryland, and Connecticut
had not sent any commissioners.   North Carolina,
Rhode Island, Massachusetts, and New Hampshire
had appointed commissioners, who, for various
reasons, had not come.   New York, Virginia, Delaware, New Jersey, and Pennsylvania were duly rep-

resented, but five States were not enough to proceed
to the business assigned to the convention, and so
something vastly better was done. An address prepared by Alexander Hamilton was adopted and sent
out to all the States, asking them to appoint commissioners to a convention, to be held in Philadelphia,
on the second Monday of May, 1787, "to devise such
further provisions as shall appear to them necessary
to render the Constitution of the Federal Government adequate to the exigencies of the Union."

When the Virginia Legislature selected its delegates to that important convention, it was inevitable
that the name of George Washington should stand
first. James Madison's name was equally sure to be
among those which followed, for he had been a leading spirit in every step that had led to the result,
and few other men were so well prepared for the
vast work now to be undertaken.

During all this time Mr. Madison's general duties
as a legislator and reformer had gone steadily forward. He had been the special champion of religious freedom, and in every phase of law revision
he had been the advocate of enlightened and pro-
gressive ideas.

Thomas Jefferson's original committee of law revision finished its labors in the year 1779, and reported to the Legislature one hundred and twenty-
six distinct bills. Nearly all of these, owing to the
impossibility of properly attending to them in the
dark days of the war, descended to Mr. Madison as
a species of legislative inheritance, and owed to him
their final shape and adoption.

Neither the thoughts nor the efforts of the future President were limited to the concerns of his own State, much business as these gave him, nor even to the domestic relations of the family of States. While in Congress he had had much to do with the various questions in which the interests of America were complicated with those of European powers. He had made the present and future of the Mississippi Valley an especial study, all the more because of Virginia's claim to the Ohio River country. The mouth of the Mississippi was then under Spanish control, as it afterward became under French. On August 20th, 1784, Mr. Madison addressed a long letter to Mr. Jefferson, in Paris, advocating the perpetual free navigation of the river, and exhibiting a statesmanlike fund of information as to the international control of European rivers passing through or bordered by two or more States. The letter is noteworthy, moreover, as an illustration of Mr. Madison's lifelong devotion to the commercial interests of the United States, and to this he had been first led while studying the ways and means of levying taxes and obtaining revenue wherefrom to pay and feed the half-starved Continental Army.

At the close of the legislative session of 1784 two months were faithfully spent among books in the quiet and seclusion of Montpellier. Then followed a study of a different kind, for Mr. Madison had never yet visited the Northern and Eastern States, and felt the need of a better knowledge of them. He laid out more travel than he was able to accomplish, but he succeeded in making a memorable excursion. At Baltimore he met with the Marquis Lafayette, fresh from his visit with Washington at Mount Vernon, and on his way to attend a grand gathering of the Six Nations at Fort Schuyler, New York.

The Iroquois retained their old liking for the French, and Lafayette, whose Indian name was Kayewla, was heir to all of it. He possessed, moreover, a personal popularity and influence among the red men which enabled him to aid the United States Commissioners in completing the Fort Schuyler treaty and to promote general cordiality at the council.

Mr. Madison availed himself of so good an opportunity to impress upon Lafayette his own views of the free navigation of the Mississippi.

New York had been seen, and the chiefs of the Iroquois, but methods of travel were slow, and but little more sight-seeing could be done. As it was, the Legislature had been two weeks in session when its most influential member returned from his very first long excursion. A few weeks later, in November, they received a ceremonious visit from Washington and Lafayette in company. The latter had come strictly as a guest, but the former to stir up Mr. Madison and others upon the great subject of internal navigation and improvement. The result was that Mr. Madison prepared and introduced and advocated measure after measure in accordance with views which he could so thoroughly adopt and make his own. The last was offered and passed at the close of the session, in the first week of January,

1785, and by it the Legislature gave to Washington, with glowing expressions of their appreciation of his services, fifty shares in the Potomac Company, worth $444 each, and a hundred shares in the James River Company, worth $200 each. Washington transferred the gifts to charitable uses, but Mr. Madison and his friends had been enabled to express themselves.

The autumnal session of the Legislature of 1785 was signalized by the passage of the declaratory act for " the establishment of religious freedom." Jefferson was its author, but its final triumph was mainly due to the unflagging zeal of James Madison.

CHAPTER IX.

*Books and Walks—Natural History—Doctor of Laws
—Once More in Congress—Meeting of the Constitutional Convention—The Rising Sun.*

THE correspondence between friends like Jefferson
and Madison necessarily included other than public matters. The former's two nephews, sons of
Dabney Carr, were under Madison's guardianship,
and faithful reports of their educational and other
progress were frequently made. Europe was at that
time the book-shop of America, and Jefferson was a
haunter of the Paris book-stalls. The orders he received for purchases on account of Madison were
many. While they included such historical, legal,
and other works as might be required in the library
of a statesman who was all the while preparing himself for the duties which came to him, step by step
and year by year, it was pleasant to find that he was
indulging other tastes. In a letter dated April
27th, 1785, he wrote :

" Of Buffon, I have his original work of thirty-one volumes, ten
volumes of his supplement, and sixteen volumes on birds. I shall
be glad of the continuation as it may from time to time be published. I am so pleased with the newly invented lamp that I
shall not begrudge two guineas for one of them."

He also mentions among his wants a pocket-com-
pass and a portable magnifying-glass. With the

latter he proposed to make more minute inspections
of the objects of interest encountered by him in his
walks around the Montpellier neighborhood.   The
study of natural history was eminently adapted to
the preservation of mental and bodily health.   The
latter, indeed, he had long since sufficiently regained
to enable him to endure the unremitting strain of
his many duties.

Friendship with Jefferson had something to do,
and public service somewhat more, with another
friendship, which began in 1784, during Mr. Madison's leadership of the Virginia Legislature.   He
and James Monroe did not meet during their boyhood, and they had been sent to different colleges.
The latter had left William and Mary College to
enter the Continental Army, and had served with
distinction.   He was now a member of Congress,
serving his second term, having been first elected in
1783 as Mr. Madison's successor.   The precise date
of their first meeting is not recorded, but they were
nearly of one mind upon the great questions of the
day, and a confidential correspondence soon sprang
up between them.   Their friendly exchanges of
views with reference to national commerce, an increase in the powers of the general Government, and
other public matters bore important fruit as the
years went by.

In February, 1785, Mr. Madison received the degree of Doctor of Laws from the college of William
and Mary.   At about the same time a cordial invitation came from Jefferson to pay him a visit in
Paris.   The trip was to consume five months, and

would cost but a thousand dollars or so. "You will," he said, "for that have purchased the knowledge of another world." The reply expressed a full appreciation of the offer, but set forth imperative duties and studies which compelled him to decline it. His place of work must be, for the present, in his own country, and for that reason he declined also to consider favorably an effort made to induce him to go abroad in connection with the diplomatic service.

During the vacation of the Legislature, in the fall of 1785, another trip North was made, after a visit to Washington at Mount Vernon, but extended travel was once more prevented. Congress was in session in New York, and there was much consultation to be had with its membership with reference to the relations of the Federal Government and the States and other important matters. Not even the study of natural history had taught Madison how to enjoy a holiday or how to make the best use of a vacation.

A letter to Jefferson, written a little before this trip, speaks of an act passed by the Legislature of Virginia giving to a man named Rumsey a ten years' monopoly of a mechanism he had invented, "by which a boat might be worked with little labor, at the rate of from twenty-five to forty miles a day, against a stream running ten miles an hour."

The inventor had been ridiculed until "he exemplified his machine to General Washington and a few other gentlemen, who gave a certificate of the reality and importance of the invention which opened the ears of this Assembly." He was to obtain similar rights from other States severally, for there was no national Patent Office. The steamboat and the law protecting inventors were alike in their infancy.

Mr. Madison's term of service in the Virginia Legislature closed with the year 1786. Having once more become eligible, he was chosen one of Virginia's delegates in Congress, and took his seat in February, 1787. Shortly after his arrival he once more wrote a letter, this time to Edmund Randolph, as he had written in 1780 to Governor Jefferson, picturing the political situation and striking the key-note of his own subsequent speech and action. He wrote :

"Our situation is becoming every day more and more critical. No money comes into the national treasury, no respect is paid to the federal authority, and people of reflection unanimously agree that the existing Confederacy is tottering to its foundation. Many individuals of weight, particularly in the eastern district, are suspected of leaning toward monarchy. Other individuals predict a partition of the States into two or more confederacies. It is pretty certain that if some radical amendment of the single one cannot be devised and introduced, one or the other of these revolutions—the latter no doubt—will take place."

So perceiving and so believing, he and other clear-headed, strong-hearted patriots took counsel of one another and gave themselves to the great work of devising and introducing the needed radical amendments. What these ought to be were but vaguely indicated by the existing evils which all men saw, for the whole structure to be builded was a new experiment in the science of government. These men were as much entitled to the name of inventors as

was the inventor Rumsey, who brought his steamboat mechanism to General Washington and ex-
plained it to him and his friends in secret.

The prevalent discontent, the seditious, turbulent
fermentation of the popular mind, took form during
the year 1786 in New England, in what is known as
Shays's Rebellion. It was easily suppressed, but it
offered a salutary warning that the time had come
for a thorough adjustment of the machinery of government so that it should work without so much
dangerous friction.

The second Monday, the 14th of May, 1787, had
been fixed as the date for the assembling of the
Constitutional Convention at Philadelphia. Some
States had acted promptly and had chosen their
delegates willingly. Others had acted slowly, with
reluctance, making it very plain beforehand that in
the end they would rigidly examine before accepting any piece of work which the Convention might
succeed in producing. Nowhere did there appear
any drift toward monarchy, but in many places the
idea of a division into two or more confederacies
was presented with threatening clearness. There
were important measures before Congress, but all
the possible work of that body seemed small compared with that proposed for the Convention to do,
and men who, like Mr. Madison, were members of
both bodies turned their thoughts and studies from
the lesser to the greater. When he left New York
for Philadelphia, on May 2d, he carried with him
written outlines of the work which he believed
should be performed. He had corresponded with

Jefferson, and had counselled with Washington, Hamilton, and many other leading men ; but he was afterward able to say that the digest he had written was " the earliest sketch on paper of a constitutional government for the Union (organized into the regular departments, with physical means operating on individuals), to be sanctioned by the people of the States acting in their original and sovereign character."

That is, he believed himself to be the first American statesman to sail right past State governments and boundary lines and discover beyond them all the people, who were really one people and should act as one. As to whether or not a sufficient number and weight of other men could be induced to make the same discovery, he was much in doubt. Three weeks earlier he had written : " The nearer the crisis approaches the more I tremble for the issue. The necessity of gaining the concurrence of the convention to some system that will answer the purpose, the subsequent approbation of Congress, and the final sanction of the States present a series of chances which would inspire despair in any case where the alternative was less formidable."

The alternative so formidable was the idea of no government, with consequent ruin, anarchy, and probable foreign domination. The half-hostile attitude of England and Spain, and even the powerful savage tribes on the frontier, made parts of that alternative, and it was presented at every critical juncture throughout the proceedings of the Convention.

So tardily did the delegates arrive in those days of slow travelling, that it was May 25th before a quorum of the Convention was obtained. Seven States out of the thirteen were then duly represented, and the great deliberative assembly organized itself for work, with George Washington as its presiding officer.

The delegates of two more States, Massachusetts and Connecticut, arrived on the 28th, those of Georgia and Maryland a few days later, those of New Hampshire much later still, while Rhode Island finally refused to send any.

The paper prepared by Mr. Madison was laid by him before his colleagues from Virginia, and formed the basis of what was known as the Virginia Plan, presented by them to the Convention. In the subsequent debates his own part was pre-eminently conspicuous, for he was advocating or defending propositions which he had hammered out into shape through long, toilsome years of thought and study, and painful experience as a legislator and statesman. There were abundant reasons, therefore, why the able men who worked with him should bestow upon him, as they did, the honorable title of Father of the Constitution.

It is impossible within the limits of a brief biography to follow at all the formative processes through which the Convention worked on to the result which it attained. Very few of the delegates began with any clear conception of what they desired or were willing to do. The two leading ideas which were constantly in collision throughout all the debates were left equally in collision when the Convention adjourned, and remained so for eighty years afterward. The first of these ideas was embodied in the phraseology of the declared purposes for which the delegates had been called together. It was that the existing Confederation should so be amended and tinkered and patched that it should become strong enough to serve as a central State governing thirteen or more smaller but independent States, as States. The opposite idea was that of Mr. Madison, of the formation of an entirely new constitutional machinery for the government of the people by themselves, through State and municipal forms, for some purposes, and through the general Government for other purposes. All history, ancient and modern, was drawn upon by the debaters for illustration, for precedent, or for warning. That of England and its Constitution was made so liberal a use of by the advocates of the Virginia Plan that their opponents were fairly able to accuse them of English leanings. It would have been very wonderful if a set of men who had all been born and brought up as colonial Englishmen had not got something English in them as well as all around them ; but the gibe had a powerful influence in subsequent politics.

One thing was inevitable from the first : the work of such a body of men, so educated, representing such varied and apparently conflicting ideas and interests, had to be a skilfully adjusted series of compromises. What these were, their wisdom or unwisdom, required a great deal of expounding, at the time, before the people could at all understand the matter. To the question of what they were was afterward added the other questions of whether they should be retained, amended, or done away with, and around these questions is grouped the entire history of American politics from that day to this.

The daily sessions of the Convention were opened, at the suggestion of Dr. Franklin, with religious services, and were conducted, from first to last, with a dignity and decorum worthy of the men and the occasion. All summer long the great debates went on, and all the households of the land grew more and more deeply interested in what their representatives were doing. One point of danger after another was passed, and its real or supposed peril provided for, until at last something like unanimity was obtained, each member yielding something of his own to meet the general will. Three members only found themselves unable to conscientiously assent and affix their signatures to the completed work. Their firmness of conviction was entirely honorable, but there was at the time an intense anxiety throughout the Convention that there should be no exceptions. These three, Colonel Mason, Governor Randolph, and Mr. Gerry, remained unmoved, in spite of Alexander Hamilton's declaration that they could not have more to surrender than he himself had given up in assenting.

An enrolled parchment copy of the Constitution was prepared for signature at last, but it was to bear one conspicuous amendment. The ratio of representatives to population had been fixed at one Congressman to each forty thousand, and Mr. Madison and others had earnestly advocated a smaller number. At the very last a motion was made to strike out the word ": forty" and insert "thirty." General Washington arose to put the question, and for the first time took what might be called a part in the debates of the Convention by giving his reasons why he wished the motion to prevail. It was enough, and the change was made by unanimous consent.

State after State, the delegates came forward and affixed their signatures to the parchment record : " Done in convention, by the unanimous consent of the States present, this 17th day of September, in the year of our Lord 1787, and of the Independence of the United States of America the twelfth."

Behind the president's chair there was a painting representing a sun but partly above the horizon. Mr. Madison relates that while the last of the delegates were signing the parchment Dr. Franklin stood gazing at that painting, and remarked to those who stood near :

" I have often and often, in the course of the session and in the vicissitudes of my hopes and fears as to the issue, looked at that behind the president without being able to tell whether it was rising or setting. But now at length I have the happiness to know that it is a rising and not a setting sun."

CHAPTER X.

Ratifying the Constitution — The Federalist — A Strong Opposition — The Virginia Convention — Two Fundamental Doctrines—The New Government in Operation—The Slave Trade—Two New Parties.

PURSUANT to a resolution of the Convention, the Constitution was laid before Congress, then in session at New York, that proper action might be taken for the calling of State conventions to pass verdicts upon its adoption. There were efforts made in Congress to modify the work of the Convention or to prevent its further progress, and here again Mr. Madison manifested great parliamentary ability in defeating every plan of obstruction. The duty as well as the limited power of Congress was made so plain that its agency in forwarding the work of the Convention to the several States was performed by a unanimous vote. The requisite State conventions were duly summoned, but in the mean time such a storm of opposition had arisen against the Constitution that its friends for a moment almost lost hope of its ratification. They at once, however, began its defence through the press and otherwise. Most notable of all the printed arguments put forth was the " Federalist" series of papers, printed in a New York journal, copied throughout the country, and afterward preserved as almost a standard authority of constitutional exposition. There were eighty of these papers, twenty-nine of which were written by James Madison, forty-six by Alexander Hamilton, and five by John Jay.

Hardly in any other State was the opposition to the Constitution more vigorous than in Virginia, and in March, 1788, Mr. Madison went home to defend his work before his own constituents. Washington himself joined in the request made by others that Madison should become a member of the Virginia Convention, and the course of events justified their urgency. Even Orange County elected Mr. Madison only after a personal canvass, and he went to the Convention to find that upon its organization a clear majority of its members were against him. They were led, moreover, by the ablest men and purest patriots in the State, with Patrick Henry at their head. The Convention assembled on June 2d, 1788, and in the very beginning of its debates the great orator clearly declared the dividing line over which the coming battle was to be fought : " Give me leave," he said, with his customary vehemence, " to demand what right they had to say, ' We, the people,' instead of ' We, the States.' "

The hands of the friends of the Constitution had already been strengthened by the action of several States, although everywhere the opposition had been perilously strong. The Massachusetts Convention had passed its vote of ratification on February 6th ; that of Maryland on April 28th ; that of South Carolina on May 23d. Others followed while

the Virginia Convention was ·debating until eight
had acted favorably, and she seemed to hold the
position of being the ninth, the one more State required to declare and secure the adoption of the
Constitution. This apparent fact only made the
opposition more determined, even after, without
their knowledge as yet, it had ceased to be a fact
by the vote of the Convention of New Hampshire.
Mr. Madison's part in the protracted debates may
be indicated by the fact that in the first day of
regular debate upon the text of the Constitution he
was called up and spoke no less than thirteen times.
His activity was continuous, and his success is a
perfect illustration of the great power in debate
which may be attained without the possession of
eloquence—such eloquence as Patrick Henry's. On
June 24th Virginia ratified the Constitution by a
vote of eighty-nine to seventy-nine, a narrow but
sufficient majority. The whole country was assured
that no remaining State would finally prove obsti-
nate enough to remain out in the cold alone when
New York speedily followed Virginia.

Having well completed this great duty, Mr.
Madison returned to his seat in a Congress which
had now little more to do than to provide for the
proper inauguration of the new government, and
whose members took so faint an interest in its existence that it was often without a quorum. He had
accomplished a great success, and was in one sense
" the father of the Constitution." More correctly,
he was author of part, approved of more, and dissented from much, dreading the possible interpreta·

tions afterward to be made. He wrote about it to
Thomas Jefferson in September, 1787 : '' I hazard
an opinion that the plan, should it be adopted, will
neither effectually answer its national object nor
prevent the local mischiefs which excite disgusts
against the State governments.''

His premonitions of trouble to come were entirely
correct, but the new plan of government had now
been adopted, and he was regarded as largely re-
sponsible for it. In due season the parties for and
against the Constitution reappeared as parties acting
under it and holding different views of its interpre-
tation. At the outset the opposition which had
failed in the State conventions continued the fight
in the State legislatures. That of Virginia was
almost entirely under control of Patrick Henry.
His first effort was toward the calling of a second
national constitutional convention. Failing in that,
he turned his attention to the elections of Senators
and Representatives for the new Congress of the
United States. Mr. Madison preferred a seat in the
House, but his friends urged his election to the
Senate, and Patrick Henry's nominee only beat him
by five votes. The next stroke aimed was by means
of the process afterward called '' Gerrymandering.''
In districting the State, Orange County was yoked
together with other counties containing known
majorities against the Constitution. This plan
entirely failed, for Mr. Madison took the stump and
gallantly fought his way to an election by the people.
Perhaps the most significant feature of his canvass
was the fact that his competitor was the same James

Monroe who had so long been his personal friend, and was soon to be his political ally, his associate, and finally his successor.

During the first week of April, 1789, the new Congress succeeded in obtaining a quorum, for which it had vainly waited through the month of March. The electoral votes were formally counted, and George Washington was declared President and John Adams Vice-President of the Republic.

The inauguration of President Washington took place, with simple and solemn dignity, on April 30th, 1789, in the city of New York. Replies to his inaugural address were voted by the Senate and House of Representatives. That of the House was drawn by Mr. Madison, as chairman of the committee to which its preparation was referred. The intimacy of his personal relations with Washington is well illustrated by the fact that the President at once requested Mr. Madison to prepare for him suitable rejoinders to both the Senate and the House. He did so, and this is probably the only case in American history in which any man has acted as both President and Congress by special request of each in turn.

Among the first questions to be settled by Congress was that of the President's title, which was wisely left where it now is. Others of instant importance related to the public revenue, and to the discussion of these Mr. Madison brought the ripe results of long years of intense study and wide legislative experience. The President had called Alexander Hamilton into the Cabinet as Secretary of the

Treasury, and the wisdom of the choice was rapidly and triumphantly attested.   Hamilton and Madison had worked together in the Constitutional Convention ; they had written the Federalist papers in partnership ; they were both intimate and trusted friends of the President ; but, step by step, it soon began to appear that they were not to remain in accord in the work which they had now taken in hand.

Washington belonged to no party, but perfectly represented the whole country and the Constitution itself.   In his own Cabinet were the heads of the two parties which were forming, for he had appointed Thomas Jefferson Secretary of State. Although it was several months before that statesman returned from France to assume the duties of his office, his views upon the questions of the day were clearly understood by his friends, and particularly by the one friend, James Madison, who was already acting as his lieutenant.   The reports of Congress from the beginning testify to the great ability with which Mr. Hamilton also was represented, and to them reference must be made for all the deeply interesting legislative history of the formation period of the Government under which we live.

Mr. Madison placed himself on record with reference to one important question during those first debates.   A proposition was made to levy a duty upon the importation of slaves, and was vigorously contested.   It was finally defeated, and among Mr. Madison's words in the debate were the following :

"It is to be hoped that by expressing a national disapprobation of this trade we may destroy it and save ourselves from reproaches and our posterity the imbecility ever attendant on a country filled with slaves. . . . It is as much the interest of Georgia and South Carolina as of any in the Union. Every addition they receive to their number of slaves tends to weaken and render them less capable of self-defence."

Mr. Madison's opinion of the Constitution was not altogether at variance with those of the men who opposed its adoption. To meet his own objections, as well as theirs, he drafted twelve amendments, ten of which were in due time agreed to in Congress and ratified by the States.

To him also at the outset fell the formal duty of proposing the laws required for creating and defining such Cabinet departments and officers as were immediately required.

Members of Congress from all parts of the country were able to meet at first from day to day, and agree or disagree as to the imposition of duties and as to many other matters, without discovering a dividing line at which they could begin to separate and form political parties. It was not long, however, before two questions, important enough but not at all related, became welded together curiously and answered the purpose of beginning a perceptible division. The first of these arose from the fact that the several States owed Revolutionary War debts of various sizes. For many good reasons Mr. Hamilton, John Adams, and their friends, on one side,

wished the Federal Government to assume and pay
these debts. Mr. Madison, Mr. Jefferson, and their
followers, on the other side, for reasons which to
them seemed good, were opposed to such assumption and payment. One prominent reason advanced
by them was that the creation of a national debt
was a long step toward centralization and the con-
solidation of power in the hands of the Federal
Government. All the old colonial spirit, now
changed into State pride, which had so bitterly
opposed the Constitution, was ready to rally behind
that reason.

The other great question related to the locality
of the permanent Federal capital. At that time a
degree of political importance was assigned to this
matter which was only temporarily real. The day
was to come when the country could see with indifference all its Federal business transacted in a
large village near its eastern border, as the city of
Washington now is. At that time many men
believed that political power would somehow attach
itself to the seat of government, to the disadvantage
of the more distant communities.

Both questions were at last settled by a species of
barter. There were Virginia men opposed to Mr.
Hamilton's plan for paying the State debts, but
willing to permit its passage on condition that the
future seat of government should be finally established upon the bank of the Potomac River, after
ten years of lingering in Philadelphia, by the way.

Mr. Jefferson complained bitterly, though probably not with justice, of the manner in which his

assent to this arrangement was obtained by Mr.
Hamilton ; but the entire nation was afterward
quite willing to be satisfied with it. At the time of
its making it put an end to a series of perilously
sectional and heated debates.

From that day forward Jefferson and Hamilton
were at variance, and the latter found his financial
schemes, when laid before Congress, either subjected to an intensely rigid criticism or strenuously
opposed, as in the case of his plan for a national
bank, by Mr. Jefferson's other self, James Madison.
So around and behind their respective chiefs the
two great parties, Federal and Republican, rapidly
took form, with all the personal animosities and
acrimonies which seem to be inseparable from political party warfare. Through all the successive
struggles the real head of each faction was a member
of Washington's Cabinet, and any measure could be
favored or opposed without unpleasant reference to
the Administration. Mr. Madison led his faction
in the House without impairing in the least his
own personal relations with the President. Nevertheless, the sharp contentions among the men he
trusted, and whose continued presence in the national councils he believed to be essential to the
welfare of the country, were causes of sore disturbance to Washington. They greatly increased his
weariness of public life and his earnest desire to retire to Mount Vernon at the end of his first presidential term.

The desire took the form of a purpose in the
spring of 1792, and he began to consult his more

intimate friends as to the mode and time of making a public announcement. On May 5th he sent for Mr. Madison and laid the matter before him, asking him to consider it well and give him his opinion before going home to Montpellier. The conference was protracted, Mr. Madison arguing against retirement, the President expressing himself strongly concerning the disagreeable and trying features of his position, and declaring his great need and longing for rest. Mr. Madison afterward received from him a written communication to a similar effect, dated May 20th, and replied to it in writing.

There is no doubt but what he had much to do with Washington's decision to put aside all personal considerations and give to his country four years more of anxious toil. Only by his so doing, said the wisest statesmen of that day, was it possible for the new Government to become settled and strong enough to hold together and be handed over to any successor. It is not altogether poetical to say that the first Constitution of the United States was George Washington. Without him, at all events, the work of Mr. Madison and the rest, as they themselves declared, would have been mere wasted paper.

CHAPTER XI.

France and England in American Politics—Madison Acting as Jefferson's Lieutenant — Farming at Montpellier — The Yellow Fever — Courtship and Marriage—Mrs. Dolly Madison.

ONCE more George Washington was unanimously chosen President, while the Federalists could rally only seventy-seven electoral votes for John Adams. They re-elected him Vice-President, but fifty-five votes had been given to other men, and it was evident that a new party was forming strongly.

Many minor questions of a domestic nature had arisen, and had temporarily served to divide strength upon, but their political uses ceased as fast as they were settled. There were purely sectional difficulties which greatly influenced the action and even the composition of the two parties. Outside of all these and beyond any use made of them the new party was greatly aided in getting its forces in order by France and Great Britain.

The opponents of Hamilton and Adams and the Federal Party rightly declared that they discovered something English in it, and in them and in their political ideas and tendencies.

The critics of Jefferson and Madison and the anti-Federal party declared that Jefferson had become a half Frenchman, a radical, an infidel, full of extreme, unsound, and fanatical democracy, and that his followers were no better than their leader.

The great movement for freedom began and rose to its culmination in France, and a great tide of American sympathy arose with it, while every memory of the war of independence aided in making Anglicism, as men called it, unpopular. The natural leaning of American good-will was toward Lafayette and his countrymen in preference to anything associated with King George, his taxes, and his Hessians, until French radicalism sent a chill through the blood of its friends in the United States by the excesses of the Reign of Terror. At the same time there were many and increasing complications in the diplomatic relations between the two countries. There were yet greater causes of ill-feeling continually created by the course of Great Britain toward her former colonies, and it was not easy to say which was the more offensive epithet, " French" or " British," to apply to a politician or a party.

It was in the midst of this condition of ideas and things that the Government of France sent over as its envoy the hot-headed and arrogant " Citizen Genet." She was at war with England, and the special errand of her minister to the United States was to commission American privateers to prey upon British commerce, and to employ every method he could invent for dragging America into the strife. He was foiled by the wise management of Washington and his advisers, but he succeeded in giving them an immense amount of trouble. Mr.

Jefferson, as Secretary of State, conducted his part of the affair with great prudence, while that of Mr. Madison was not officially conspicuous. The line of demarcation between the two parties was deepened in color, notwithstanding, for the position taken by the Federalists was anti-French.

The latter part of the Second Congress was largely devoted to the consideration of foreign affairs, including French and British outrages upon American commerce and the presence of British garrisons in forts within the boundaries of the United States. At the end of the session, early in the spring of 1793, Mr. Madison returned to Montpellier full of a determination to have a genuine vacation for once, and to be as much of a farmer as was possible for a man who was still a statesman, carrying on a large and interesting correspondence with other public men, and publishing political papers through the newspapers. The letters which passed between him and Jefferson, however, related largely to new ploughs, the weather, the appearance of the wheat and other crops, and to other affairs genuinely agricultural.

There is no doubt but what the interest taken by Mr. Madison in rural affairs was hearty and genuine, and included neighborhood interests as well as those of his own plantation. He was the actual head of his aged father's house, and the kindly hospitality extended there was his own, for the guests also were his. It was a time of thorough enjoyment, well earned and every way needful. The return of public duties cut it short, but not until Mr. Madison's constituents had elected him a member of the Third Congress, which was to assemble on the first Monday in December.

About September 1st the yellow fever came to Philadelphia as a virulent and destructive epidemic. The death rate is said to have reached two hundred in one week. One of the first consequences was that the President, writing from Mount Vernon, asked the advice of his Cabinet and of Mr. Madison as to whether he had a right to convene Congress at any other place in case of the continuance of the epidemic. With one exception, Mr. Hamilton, who indicated a modified power, they informed him that he could change the time only for sufficient cause, but not the place. The cause itself passed away before the time came for the assembling of Congress, but not until it had produced another result of life-long importance to Mr. Madison.

In the year 1790 a promising young lawyer of Philadelphia named John Todd married a very pretty and intelligent girl of eighteen named Dorothy Payne. Her family were Quakers of excellent social standing, who had been wealthy, but were then in moderate circumstances. The marriage is said to have been one of ardent love on his part and of filial obedience to her father's wishes, added to affectionate esteem, on her own. Two children were given them within the next three years, and they were living in Philadelphia when the epidemic broke out in September, 1793. Mr. Todd sent his wife and children, one a baby of three weeks, out of town, but imprudently lingered to close business matters. In the very hour when he rejoined them at Gray's Ferry, after losing his own father and mother by the scourge, he was stricken down and died in a few hours. Mrs. Todd was also nearly a victim, and the baby was taken. On her recovery Philadelphia was once more a safe place of residence, and she returned with her remaining child, a son, named after his father. She was only twenty-two, rich, and so very attractive that one of her lady friends is said to have laughingly warned her: " Really, Dolly, thou must hide thy face, there are so many staring at thee."

James Madison took his seat in Congress in December, 1793, one of the foremost men of the nation. He was forty-two years of age, and apparently a confirmed bachelor. The Republican Party to which he belonged was growing fast in power, for the recent elections had given it control of the House of Representatives, and it placed its candidate, Mr. Muhlenberg, in the Speaker's chair by a majority of ten votes. At the same time it was well understood that its leader, Thomas Jefferson, was about to resign from the Cabinet of Washington. He did so on January 1st, 1794, retiring to Monticello, leaving Mr. Madison apparently in sole leadership, but really in such close correspondence and consultation that whatever course was taken by either in any important public matter was as much the act of the other. Mr. Madison's public life during the remainder of Washington's administration is therefore little more than the history of Congressional legislation combined with that of the Republican or anti-Federal Party. His private life, however, grew rapidly more and more interesting.

He may have been one of those to whom Mrs. Dolly Todd's friend, Mrs. Lee, referred when she said that "gentlemen would station themselves where they could see her pass." At all events, Mrs. Lee one day received a note from Dolly, telling her : " Dear friend, thou must come to me. Aaron Burr says that the ' great little Madison ' has asked to be brought to see me this evening."

She is said to have received him in a Quaker dress of rich materials, admirably cut and worn, and the acquaintance which began that evening speedily drifted into a courtship. Among Mrs. Todd's particular friends were the President and Mrs. Washington, and both are recorded as having taken a deep interest in the progress of an affair of such marked social importance. Lucy Payne, a younger sister of Mrs. Todd, had married, in 1792, George Steptoe Washington, a nephew of the general, owning an estate called Harewood, in Jefferson County, Virginia. Mr. Madison's courtship prospered, and a formal engagement was duly announced before the end of the summer. The wedding was to take place at Harewood, September 15th, and early in the month a gay cavalcade set out from Philadelphia. Congress had adjourned, the weather was delightful, all manner of prosperity and hope seemed to accompany the wedding party.

All went merrily at Harewood, and after the wedding ceremony and its accompanying festivities, Mr. and Mrs. Madison drove away together to

Montpellier. Only a few weeks could be spent there, however, for Congress had adjourned to meet again upon November 3d. It did not secure a quorum for business until the 18th, and in the mean time Mrs. Madison had completed her arrangements for re-entering society. She had even yielded to her husband's wish, and had laid aside the Quaker garb.

CHAPTER XII.

A Year at Montpellier—The New House and its Hospitalities—Jefferson and Burr—Madison Appointed Secretary of State—Mrs. Madison and the White House—Peace at Home and Abroad.

MR. MADISON'S career in Congress closed with the end of the Third Congress and the administration of George Washington. John Adams became President, with Thomas Jefferson Vice-President. Under circumstances of great perplexity at home and abroad the country entered upon four years of what was in many respects a political interim between an old order of things and a new. The Federal Party was dying by inches, and the Republican Party was steadily acquiring strength to take its place and to assume absolute and prolonged control of national affairs.

After taking part in the impressive scenes of March 4th, 1797, which may be said to have attended the retirement of George Washington rather than the inauguration of John Adams, Mr. and Mrs. Madison returned to Montpellier to enjoy a year of country life. It was not that he had in any manner lost his interest in public affairs, but that his official connection with them was temporarily severed. He could therefore play farmer and watch his crops and write to Jefferson about improved breeds of sheep,

while his wife superintended the hospitalities of a
house which she rendered more attractive than it
had ever been before. She had brought to him a
large increase of means, also, and it was about this
time that he built upon the old estate a new dwelling, more commodious than the one to which he had
brought his bride. By the end of the year politics
claimed their own. He had not for a day ceased to
be busied with them, and he consented to be once
more elected a member of the Virginia Assembly
for the session of 1799-1800. The duties he so
assumed related largely to the national questions of
the day, but require no record here. They interfered but moderately with the kind of farming which
satisfied his conception of what a farmer might be,
and they gave Mrs. Madison a fine opportunity for
enjoying the good society she was sure to be wel-
comed in during the sessions of the Legislature.

In the autumn of the year 1800 came the fourth
canvass for the election of a President of the United
States. It was the first in which at the outset there
was any general doubt as to the result. It was a
hot contest, and the doubt continued long after the
popular votes were counted, for there was a tie in
the electoral college. Thomas Jefferson and Aaron
Burr had each seventy-seven votes for President,
and the decision was left, under the Constitution,
to the House of Representatives. The affairs of
the nation were in a peculiarly critical condition,
and it was a question of vast moment by what man's
heart and brain they were to be directed. Alexander Hamilton was master of the situation as leader

of the Federal Party. Both of the candidates before the House were his political and personal enemies, and he wisely decided to trust the country with Thomas Jefferson, leaving Aaron Burr Vice-President. In so doing he opened a new career of usefulness to James Madison.

Mr. Madison had at one time been offered a place in Washington's Cabinet, but had preferred, for many good reasons, the position he held in Congress. Now, however, instead of taking a minor place in a discordant council, he was asked to become Secretary of State, head of the Cabinet, under the one man with whom, from boyhood, he had been most perfectly in accord. His own position before the people was such that he added strength to the administration by accepting. A host of men looked upon Jefferson as a radical, an extremist, while, bitterly as Mr. Madison had been assailed by all Federalists, he carried with him into the office of Secretary of State the idea of steadiness and conservatism.

There had been other than political changes during his four years at Montpellier. The seat of government had been removed from Philadelphia to what there was then of the city of Washington. There was a long, wide street, muddy at one time and dusty at another, called Pennsylvania Avenue, and there was a map containing many other streets and avenues. There were already some not at all imposing public buildings, including the Executive Mansion, better known as the White House. There were a few private residences, but not any of these were sufficiently spacious to answer purposes of social entertainment, official or private. The White House itself was the only refuge of Washington society, and President Jefferson seriously embarrassed himself by the open-handed liberality with which he met the emergency and kept open house for friends and foes alike. Fifty dollars a day went often for the mere marketing of the one good table at the capital of the United States. There was good society in the neighboring towns of Alexandria and Georgetown, but much mud had often to be overcome in reaching it.

When March 4th, 1801, arrived, the President-elect had found himself destitute of a carriage, for one that he had ordered had not arrived. He therefore rode on horseback to the Capitol, went in, and took the oath of office. Mr. Madison was not present, having been detained at Montpellier by yet another change, which had for some time been expected. The death of his aged father left him in actual ownership of the estate which he had so long controlled, but did not call for any more than a temporary variation in his plans.

Soon after the arrival of Mr. and Mrs. Madison at Washington they discovered that their relations to the new administration were to be more than strictly official. Thomas Jefferson was a widower, and neither of his two married daughters was able to join him at the Executive Mansion save for brief visits and at long intervals. To Mrs. Madison, therefore, he turned for assistance in the reception of his guests, and she admirably performed the duties of the Lady of the White House, aided by her younger sister, Miss Anna Payne. They were in the habit of receiving such little notes as this :

"*May* 27, 1801.
"Thomas Jefferson begs that either Mrs. Madison or Miss Payne will be so good as to dine with him to-day, to take care of female friends expected."

When George Washington became President a very serious question arose in his mind as to what and how much of formality and ceremonial might be required by the duties and the dignity of his office. He consulted with John Adams, John Jay, Alexander Hamilton, and others, and they managed to surround him with an amount of state and etiquette, against which Mr. Jefferson protested vigorously on his arrival from France. Now that the latter had become President the same question presented itself to him, but under different circumstances. Whatever were his tendencies toward simplicity, he had learned the necessity of law and order in social affairs, especially when these happen to be interwoven with official and diplomatic business. He therefore wrote out with his own hand a series of fourteen " canons of etiquette to be observed by the executive." They contained a great deal of plain, republican common-sense, and Mrs. Madison found her duties simplified by them.

The last work of John Adams as President had been to secure for his country a prospect of peace with France. His successor fell heir to that, and entered upon the duties of his office with a settled purpose of maintaining peace with all Europe. Mr.

Madison, as Secretary of State, was precisely the right man to carry into effect the pacific purposes of the President. If any foreign power should succeed in forcing a quarrel upon a nation whose policy was directed by two such men, it could only be by extraordinary injuries and outrages.

With peace abroad there was also increasing peace at home. The Presidential election canvass had been perilously bitter, but in Mr. Jefferson's inaugural address there had been a distinct and positive effort at conciliation. Only a very few removals of political opponents from office had followed. Except in the New England States, the Federal Party seemed to be losing even local power. The administration controlled both Houses of Congress, and Mr. Jefferson was not only President, but also the unquestioned ruler of his party.

Under such a state of things the machinery of government began for the first time to work smoothly. Not even in the old colonial days had there ever been so near an approach to a general quiet and peace. It was nevertheless true that a man like Madison, discharging ever so well at such a time the duties of second in command under such a captain as Jefferson, was very nearly lost sight of in the shadow of his commander.

CHAPTER XIII.

Mr. Jefferson's Second Term—The Provocation Policy of England—The Embargo—Sarcasm of Napoleon—Mr. Madison Elected President of the United States—Proclamation Repealing the Embargo.

THE people of the United States were entirely satisfied with the first four years of the Jefferson administration. Even socially it was a complete success, for every citizen, male or female, who visited the city of Washington carried home a good report of a hospitable reception. A great many of them had much to say in praise of Mr. and Mrs. Madison. The Presidential canvass of 1804 was therefore hardly a contest. Mr. Jefferson for President and Mr. Clinton, of New York, for Vice-President, received one hundred and sixty-two electoral votes against only fourteen for the Federal Party candidates.

Mr. Madison's labors as Secretary of State continued without a shadow of disturbance, but his wife was deprived of any further assistance from her sister Anna at White House receptions. Miss Payne became Mrs. Cutts, of Maine.

The administration went steadily on to even increased popularity through greater achievements, but the part of Mr. Madison in such matters as the punishment of the Algerine pirates by the young American Navy, the defeat of Aaron Burr's conspiracy, or even the purchase of Louisiana, was altogether official and as a part of Mr. Jefferson's great success. During all this time, nevertheless, there had been a continual strain in America's relations with England, great provocations having been borne with too much patience in the vain hope of better things to come. Very much worse came during the first year of Mr. Jefferson's second term, and in a message to Congress, December 3d, 1805, he described in terms of bitter denunciation the outrages committed by British cruisers and privateers upon the defenceless merchant vessels of the United States. Mr. Madison himself had written of England a little earlier : " She is renewing her depredations upon our commerce in the most ruinous shapes, and has kindled a more general indignation among our merchants than was ever before expressed."

It was sufficiently evident that Great Britain wished for a war with the United States, relying upon her vast naval superiority to enable her to wipe out the commerce of the one nation which threatened to be her rival in the carrying trade of the world. She could not have done more than she did to provoke a war without actually landing troops or destroying towns upon the coast ; but Mr. Jefferson managed to cling to peace of a certain kind to the end of his term of office, and so to hand over the inevitable British war to his successor.

There were protests, negotiations, and further messages to Congress, until in June, 1807, the

British ship-of-war Leopard, just outside of Hampton Roads, fired a broadside into the American frigate Chesapeake, killed or wounded several of her men, forced her to strike her colors, and sent a party on board of her to seize and carry off four American sailors claimed as British subjects.

The country was aroused to a fever of angry excitement by the news, and President Jefferson at once despatched a ship to England with a demand for reparation. He summoned Congress to meet on October 26th, by which time he would probably have heard from England, and the legislators would have had four months of consideration as to the action required by the honor of their flag and the safety of their ships at sea. He issued a proclamation forbidding British ships-of-war to remain in American waters ; but they were there to provoke war, and they contemptuously disregarded his authority. As Mr. Madison wrote to Mr. Monroe : " They continue to defy it, not only by remaining in our waters, but by chasing merchant vessels arriving and departing."

When Congress came together its members were not ready for war, and at the instance of the administration they passed the Embargo Act. They shut up the ports of the United States, so far as their own vessels were concerned, suspended American commerce, and the statesmen of England could not reasonably have asked them to do more. France and Great Britain were issuing decrees, retaliating upon each other, the effect of which was to impose at least a paper blockade upon almost all the ports of Europe, and now the United States blockaded their own ships in their own harbors. Strangely enough, the nation approved for a while, and accepted the delusion that they had somehow struck a blow at Great Britain instead of at their own prosperity. The great distress caused in commercial and financial circles by the operation of the embargo soon extended throughout all classes more or less severely. During the last year of Jefferson's term the eyes of men had opened pretty rapidly. Napoleon Bonaparte helped them somewhat ; among other bitter sarcasms upon the American embargo he issued a decree ordering the seizure of all American vessels found at sea. He did it, he declared, out of friendship for the United States, to aid them in preventing the escape of any of their ships contrary to their own law.

The pressure became unendurable, and it was evident that the days of the embargo were numbered, whatever were to be the consequences of its repeal. Its discussion rendered the Presidential election canvass in the autumn of 1808 more interesting than it otherwise would have been, for the result was known from the beginning. There were three aspirants within the Republican Party : George Clinton, of New York, James Monroe, and James Madison. Mr. Jefferson's autocratic choice gave the nomination to the latter, and Monroe was pacified, for he had only to await his turn, while Mr. Clinton had no appeal from the decision of his party leader. Mr. Madison received one hundred and twenty-two out of one hundred and seventy-five

electoral votes, for the Federal Party had secured
fifty-three with the help of the embargo. Mr.
Jefferson resisted every effort to induce him to
change the existing state of affairs, and the entire
complication, with all its difficulties and responsibilities at home and abroad, was, on March 4th,
1809, transferred to the shoulders of James Madison.

Mr. Jefferson, retiring to Monticello, did not cease
to be the controlling spirit of his party, and the continuous advice he gave to his friend and successor
was that of a statesman who was still able to sway
majorities in either House of Congress. There were
advantages and there were also disadvantages in
having such a powerful counsellor.

During the interval between the election, in
November, and the inauguration on March 4th,
1809, Mr. Madison held conferences with the British
minister to the United States, Mr. Erskine, in the
hope of reaching some basis of settlement with the
British Government. The tone of the American
people and press and of the debates in Congress was
increasingly resentful against England, but Mr.
Madison proposed to do his uttermost in a policy
of conciliation. Mr. Erskine was evidently disposed
to co-operate with him, not being in sympathy with
or perhaps not fully understanding the real policy
of the ministry at home which he represented, and
of which Mr. Canning was the head. He duly reported the result of his conferences with Mr. Madison, and waited for instructions. While he was
waiting the inauguration took place, and the new
administration assumed the direction of affairs.

Mr. Robert Smith, of Maryland, was appointed Secretary of State, but Albert Gallatin, who was retained as Secretary of the Treasury, was probably Mr. Madison's chief adviser in the Cabinet.

Mrs. Dolly Madison was now the Lady of the White House by right and no longer by mere invitation, but the profuse hospitality of Mr. Jefferson's day was not imitated. There was no longer any occasion for it. There had been many improvements in and about the city of Washington. New streets had been opened and improved, and houses had been built. When Anna Payne and Mr. Cutts were married, in 1804, the only church the city contained was at the Navy Yard, and the wedding party and guests drove to it through deep mud. No record states whether any other places of worship had since been built before 1809, but the private residences were now many, and the East Room of the White House was no longer the only parlor large enough to hold an evening party. Mr. Madison was fifty-eight years of age, but his wife was only thirty-seven, and she was every way well fitted for her part of the important business of making his administration popular.

What seemed Mr. Madison's first stroke of statesmanship lifted him at once upon the crest of a great wave of popularity. Mr. Canning's reply to Mr. Erskine arrived in April, and it seemed to give him power to meet Mr. Madison almost half way. The British representative may or may not have exceeded his instructions, but the terms of an agreement between the two countries were settled, and a diplomatic success appeared to be accomplished. Mr. Erskine reported to Mr. Canning what he had done in ignorance of the hidden fact that an agreement, a settlement, a peace giving new life to American commerce, was precisely what Mr. Canning did not wish. Mr. Madison was more than equally ignorant, and he issued a proclamation terminating the acts of embargo and non-intercourse as against Great Britain and her colonies, the repeal to take effect on and after June 10th, 1809.

All through the land the President's proclamation was hailed with enthusiastic approval. In every harbor on the coast the long-deserted wharves and the ships which had rocked in lonely uselessness at their anchors began to swarm with busy men. The hammers rang again in the dock-yards. Work came to the unemployed, food to the half-starving, and the hope of new prosperity to the all but bankrupt mercantile classes in every port and city. Everywhere men blessed James Madison and prepared for a new era, to begin on June 10th. On the morning of that day more than a thousand ships were ready, and crowds were waiting at the wharves in every port to see them spread their wide, white wings once more. Amid cheering and cannon-firing and bell-ringing the good ships went to sea, leaving behind them high hopes which were soon to be blasted, and sailing into a thick mist of disasters caused by the action of a British ministry as coldly cruel as that of George the Third.

CHAPTER XIV.

The Canning Ministry—Embargo Legislation—Providing for but one War at a Time—The War Party Growing—Appointment of James Monroe—War with England Declared—Lessons of Disaster.

MR. CANNING promptly rejected the agreement proposed by his subordinate, Mr. Erskine, but issued a decree in council by which the ships which had gone to sea under cover of it were permitted nominally to pursue their voyages undisturbed. The decree went no farther, and the degree of protection afforded by it was notably defective.

Mr. Madison wrote to Mr. Jefferson at Monticello : " You will see by the instructions to Erskine, as published by Canning, that the latter was as much determined that there should be no adjustment as the former was that there should be one."

It is true, as has been urged by those who have defended Mr. Canning, that the repudiated agreement was defective, wretchedly incomplete as regarded either side of the controversy ; but its worst defect, for which it was destroyed, was that it was a beginning toward the recognition of American rights upon the high seas. Its repudiation can hardly be criticised by itself, as an act standing alone, but rather as a something which fitted into its proper place in the unvarying British policy which required a war to break it up.

Mr. Erskine was soon recalled, and was replaced by a Mr. Jackson, with whom the President was immediately at variance, through the Secretary of State, concerning the conduct of his friend Mr. Erskine.

It was needful now to issue a second proclamation rescinding the first and leaving the embargo in force, and bidding the ships which had been set free to return to their wharves or remain abroad at their own risk. Numbers of captains and owners preferred the risk to their vessels of being scuttled or confiscated to that of rotting in harbor, and did not return. Some of those ships were burned, and some were sunk, and some were confiscated ; but others, swift-sailing craft of Yankee build, left behind them a cheerful tradition of large profits earned during their daring defiance of European blockades and the American embargo.

The people could not say but what Mr. Madison had done all in his power, but the sudden wave of his popularity had spent its course. It was not easy for him or others to solve the problem or see what it was best for America to do next. The winter session of Congress arrived, and was almost entirely consumed in debates upon various propositions ; but in the following May an act was passed which relieved the President of some responsibility, while it still left him master of the situation. It shut out from American ports the war ships of England and France, but suspended the non-importation law for three months following the adjournment of Congress. Should England or France, or both of them, continue their oppressive policy beyond that date, the President was empowered to declare the act in force again against the offending power or powers.

France—that is, Napoleon—at once took advantage of the act of Congress. He was imposing ruinous import duties and restrictions upon American commerce in the ports under his control. Even while doing so, however, he revoked the decrees aimed at by Congress, and left Mr. Madison free to except France from the operation of the non-importation act. Both the acts and the words of Napoleon were manifestly dictated by a thoroughly selfish policy, but they gave the President an opportunity to leave France out of the great quarrel with England, which, he now plainly saw, was only a question of time. The United States had many deep causes of complaint against the government of Napoleon, but they were all put aside, and grievances were submitted to in order that only one too-powerful antagonist might remain.

The people of the United States were steadily becoming more and more deeply exasperated throughout the year 1810. Mr. Madison's letters to Jefferson and others show that he fully understood the situation. During the next session of Congress it became plain that a war party was forming, and that it could not fail to grow in strength so long as its fire should be fanned by successive reports of British outrages upon American merchantmen. Those of France were hardly less in number or extent, but were inflicted for the greater part upon vessels in port. The President himself seems at times to have expected and dreaded war with France sooner than with England, but the general popular instinct was correct. One British claim was aimed, not at property, but at the bodies of men, and her impressment of American sailors from under the American flag, declaring that she had a right to do so, stirred up more angry blood than did all the money losses occasioned by the heartless tyranny of Napoleon. It was for kidnapped sailors rather than for stolen dollars that Henry Clay and John C. Calhoun and other fiery young patriots were able to plead, a little later, with an eloquence which carried the hearts of all men with them for war against England, and her only.

Then and afterward Mr. Madison was accused of too strong a desire for peace at any price, but the charge came mainly from the rising generation rather than from the men who had borne with him the toils and anxieties of the war of independence. Neither have subsequent writers taken into proper account how fully his inclinations toward peace represented the hope and the will of the people. He understood them very thoroughly, and how unready they were for war. He knew not only the condition of the small navy and the insignificant army, but how tardy and insufficient were likely to be the supplies of men and money voted by a nation whose national feeling was yet so very weak. He had, on the other hand, a justly high appreciation of the European naval power, while the capacity of America for improvising a navy had not yet been discovered. He was determined especially that the war which must come should be with but one power at a time. This idea came continually to the surface, as in his letters to the American minister to France concerning French outrages in the Baltic. He assured him that American frigates would at once be sent, "with orders to suppress by force the French and Danish depredations," if it were not that the ships he was able to send were only of the medium size and armament, and would be in "danger of rencounters with British ships of superior force in that quarter." His written and spoken words, public and private, were not those of a weak or timid man so much as of a somewhat too cool and wary statesman upon whose shoulders a great and deeply-felt responsibility was resting.

The one consideration to which Mr. Madison seems to have given no weight whatever was the fact, plain enough afterward, that the United States needed a foreign war. They had no position abroad, no influence, no respect ; their commerce was plundered at will, and their protests were treated with contempt so long as other nations believed them so feeble and so disunited that they would not and dared not risk a fight. The need of such a war was even greater at home to bind together the jarring sections and factions. In buying Louisiana and in borrowing money, and in several other important matters, the United States had acted as a nation, as one people pulling together ; but the effect of these upon the popular heart had not been like that of a

war, with sacrifices of blood and treasure for the
common good, and with one common interest in
every glory or disaster. No army had marched
under the new flag except against the Indians. No
squadron had sailed under it except against the
Algerine pirates. The affair of the Chesapeake and
Leopard had been felt by all the nation as a sting.
It had also left a stain which was now to be wiped
out in a manner which had an important bearing
upon the result. The Chesapeake had been altogether unprepared for action, and as helpless as a
merchantman. The British sloop-of-war Little Belt
had eighteen guns, was much too ready for a fight,
and had been sent, with others, to break up the
commerce between the United States and France.
She was met not far from Sandy Hook, in May,
1811, by the American frigate President, of forty-
four guns. There was some dispute afterward as to
who fired first, but in a few minutes the Little Belt
gave up the fight, with thirty men killed or wounded,
while one man only on the President was reported
slightly hurt. Mr. Madison wrote about the encounter that just such things were likely to occur
again, from time to time, and would " probably end
in an open rupture or a better understanding, as the
calculations of the British Government may prompt
or dissuade from war." He had watched the working of those calculations year after year, and knew
their purpose to be that the United States should
never rival England on the sea. Whether by European blockades, commercial restrictions, an American embargo, or a destructive war, there was to be

no realization, if England could prevent, of the dream of John Adams when, a boy of nineteen, he wrote, in 1755 : "We have, I may say, all the naval stores of the nation in our hands ; it will be easy to obtain the mastery of the seas ; and then the united force of all Europe will not be able to subdue us." The "nation" he then wrote of included England with America, and the English part of it had now lost control of the naval stores.

Negotiations abroad and political agitation at home drifted on through what seemed uncertainty and confusion, but was not, for hardly anything could have been more sure than the war which at last came. There was an abundance of sage counsel in the Cabinet of Mr. Madison at the first, but it contained no military element. He needed at least one thorough soldier, and on November 25th, 1811, Mr. Smith, as Secretary of State, was succeeded by Colonel James Monroe, a scarred veteran of the Revolution. The appointment of a man who had been under fire so very often, and who was known to be anything rather than a non-resistant, was a distinct indication of what was in the mind of Mr. Madison and of his adviser, Thomas Jefferson.

The war party in and out of Congress grew stronger month by month, and before spring it was evident that it could carry the country with it, while current events more surely narrowed the conflict to a war with Great Britain alone. On April 1st, 1812, the President sent to Congress a very brief message, recommending the immediate imposition of "a

general embargo on all vessels now in port or hereafter arriving for the period of sixty days."

Congress made it ninety days, and everybody
understood that it was one of the preliminary pre-
cautions taken before announcing open hostilities.
A few weeks later, June 1st, the President sent in
his expected message recommending a declaration
of war. In the House of Representatives the Committee on Foreign Relations, through its chairman,
John C. Calhoun, reported in favor of " an immediate appeal to arms," and were sustained by a vote
of seventy-nine to forty-nine.

The more conservative Senate, on June 17th,
1812, decided for war by a majority of six only, but
this was enough to show the correctness of Mr.
Madison's political calculations.   His critics could
have learned something from the vote in the Senate
on the declaration, and more from the subsequent
legislation relating to the army and the navy.

The country was soon to enter upon a Presidential election canvass, and Mr. Madison was already
a candidate for re-election.   He went before the
people, therefore, for an approval or disapproval of
his policy as a whole, including the war, and they
sustained him.   If he had adopted the reverse policy
and had refused to declare war, some other man,
a war man, would surely have been nominated and
elected, for the new men of the country, all the rising
generation able to vote, except in a few localities,
were bent upon having the fight with Great Britain.

The politicians in Congress continually practised
false economies with reference to the war, and did

and said many unwise things. The navy won many honors, and the land forces not so many. The blunders committed and the disasters sustained were every way as important and as profitable to the United States, for the real uses of the war, as were any of the victories gained by sea or land. The record of all these does not belong to the biography of Mr. Madison, but it is worth while, in view of many criticisms which have been written and printed and will still be read, to quote the language used at this time by Thomas Jefferson, writing from Monticello to Thomas Flournoy about the re-election and the war. It should be borne in mind how long and patiently and earnestly Mr. Jefferson himself had striven to keep the peace with England. He wrote :

"Servile inertness is not what is wanted to save our country. The conduct of a war requires the vigor and enterprise of younger heads, and therefore all such undertakings are out of the question with me, and I say so with the greater satisfaction when I contemplate the person to whom the powers are handed over. You probably may not know Mr. Madison personally, or at least intimately, as I do. I have known him from 1779, when he first came into the public councils ; and from three-and-thirty years' trials I can say conscientiously that I do not know a man in the world of purer integrity, more disinterested and devoted to genuine republicanism than himself ; nor could I, in the whole scope of Europe and America, point out an abler head. He may be illy seconded by others, betrayed by the Hulls and Arnolds of our country, for such there are everywhere, we know only too well. But what man can do will be done by Mr. Madison. I hope, therefore, there will be no difference among Republicans as to his re-election, for we shall only appreciate his true value when we have to give him up and look for his successor."

The next four years of the life of Mr. Madison were little more than the history of the war.

CHAPTER XV.

The Raid upon the Capital—Burning of the White House and Other Public Buildings—A very Dismal Night—A Timely Hurricane—A Party Funeral —Peace Negotiations—Peace and the Battle of New Orleans.

AT the outbreak of the War of 1812 Mr. Madison's administration was confronted by a powerful anti-war party with strong and popular leaders. His opponents were able to sustain their position by plausible arguments, many of which, viewed by themselves, were entirely sound and rational. They were able to show, then and afterward, that the war was costly, useless, a diplomatic blunder, and a military failure. What they did not see or concealed were the facts that it was unavoidable and indispensable to the growth, honor, unity, and life of the nation. So surely are there two strong sides to every great political case.

In the management of the war and of the negotiations with which it closed Mr. Madison did what man could do, as Jefferson predicted, and the subsequent growth of the nation took charge of the incomplete result. The entire country was touched by the course of war events. There were fights all along the Canadian border. There were flurries of Indian hostilities on the Western frontier. The last

battle was fought at the extreme southern limit of
the new land which Jefferson had purchased of
Napoleon. Not even the battle of New Orleans,
however, was so grotesquely, piratically dramatic as
was the one British attack upon the centre of the
long American sea-coast line.

In the summer of 1814 an American squadron,
under Commodore Barney, cruising off the Virginia
coast, found itself confronted by a fleet of twenty-
one British war ships, under Admiral Cockburn.
No attempt was made to oppose a force so over-
powering, and the British admiral sailed on into
Chesapeake Bay. He had brought with him about
four thousand British veterans, under General Ross,
who proposed to strike a sudden blow with them at
either Baltimore or Washington. No definite military advantage could so have been gained, but it
was possible for General Ross to land wherever he
might please, and impossible to rally any sufficient
force against him. Commodore Barney went ashore
with some marines and sailors, gathered a few regu-
lars and some raw militia, and undertook to check
the British advance toward Washington. There
was a fight at Bladensburg, the Americans were
routed, the commodore was taken prisoner, and
General Ross and his troops marched on. It was
said that one object proposed for the expedition
was the capture of the State papers at Washington,
particularly those of the President, but all were put
into bags and carted away to Leesburg, Virginia, in
good season. This was done by order of the Secretary of State. The President, whom the anti-war

party were at this time assailing with peculiar bitterness, remained in the city, while Mr. Monroe rode
out to watch the progress of events.   He went as
far as a village near the shore, from which he could
observe the landing of the British, and kept the
President advised of their subsequent movements
and of the retreat of Commodore Barney's beaten
militia from Bladensburg.

The destructive purposes of the invaders were
sufficiently indicated by a message sent to the
White House by the officer commanding their advance, warning Mrs. Madison that she must leave
or the house would be burned over her head.   There
was already a panic in the city, and the wooden
Long Bridge over the Potomac was crowded with
fugitive women and children.   It had begun with a
note from James Monroe to the President : " The
enemy has advanced six miles along the road to the
wood-yard, and our troops are retreating.   You had
better make all preparations to leave."

His soldier judgment was correct, but so small
had been the fear of an enemy's arrival until near
the last that Mrs. Madison had invited guests to a
dinner-party for that very day, although a little in a
spirit of feminine bravado, as the alarmed replies of
some of her friends indicated.   The British arrived
in time to eat up the dinner which she had provided.

Mr. Madison crossed the Potomac early in the
afternoon of August 24th, accompanied by the
Secretary of the Navy and some friends—the only
President of the United States who has ever been
compelled to flee from the capital.   Mrs. Madison's

retreat was otherwise provided for, and the British Army might possibly not have regarded her as a proper prisoner of war. She lingered until the very last, securing papers, packing trunks, superintending the loading of wagons with furniture and other valuables, all the while in a fever of nervous apprehension concerning her husband. She secured, among other public papers, the Declaration of Independence, and her last exploit, as the British drew near, was to insist upon waiting until a valuable portrait of Washington, which was one of the few ornaments of the White House, was taken from its frame and rolled up for transportation. When at last she consented to get into a carriage and escape, the doomed building she was leaving still contained about twelve thousand dollars' worth of property belonging to herself and Mr. Madison, besides a large part of his private library.

The destruction of the Navy Yard was entirely legitimate as an act of war, but not so was the wanton burning of the Capitol, the Executive Mansion, and other public buildings; and the public press of England, as well as some of her leading statesmen, characterized the proceeding in very appropriate terms, leaving few hard words for Americans to use in addition.

More mischief would have been done at the time but that the day was nearly gone, and that there were signs of a coming storm. When this came it was a hurricane of two hours' duration, and of a violence not often paralleled. Two cannon stationed on a rising ground were lifted and blown several yards to the rear. Roofs were torn off like paper, and many houses were blown down altogether, burying men and women in the ruins. Among the victims were thirty British soldiers.

Mrs. Madison's first refuge appears to have been with a friend near Georgetown, Maryland, and her next at a tavern sixteen miles from Washington, in Virginia, where Mr. Madison had appointed to meet her. The road to it was difficult and circuitous, the rain drenched her and her companions as they toiled dejectedly through the mud, and when they reached the tavern it was already crowded with angry fugitives who refused to admit her, reproaching her and her husband as the causes of the war and of their misfortunes. The approach of another terrible thunder-storm made them relent, and they permitted the shivering lady of the White House to come under the same roof with themselves. Mr. Madison made his appearance at last, dejected and careworn. His wife prevailed upon him to eat such a meal as could be had and to lie down and go to sleep. About midnight, however, a weary courier came in haste with an erroneous warning that the enemy had discovered the President's hiding-place and were on their way to capture him. His friends joined their entreaties to those of Mrs. Madison, and he consented to seek another refuge, passing the remainder of the night in a cabin in the woods.

The alarm had been needless, for the British troops had moved away from all that remained of the city of Washington. They had suffered loss and much discomfort from the storm, and had been further

disturbed by reports that American forces were
approaching. The news of their departure overtook
Mrs. Madison shortly after she had set out in a
small wagon, attended only by one soldier and a
Mr. Duvall, in search of greater safety. She started
at daybreak, leaving her carriage to her friends, for
she went in disguise. On learning that the British
had retreated she turned again toward Washington,
but on reaching the Long Bridge over the Potomac,
found that both ends of it had been burned away.
There was a boat on the Virginia side, but the
officer in charge of it refused to ferry an unknown
woman into the city. He hesitated even after disguise was put aside and he was asked to take over
the wife of the President, but he finally consented,
and she was permitted to go and take a look at the
fire-blackened remnants of the White House and its
contents. She obtained a carriage and drove to the
house of her sister, Mrs. Cutts, through a very
gloomy, silent, and deserted national village. Later
in the day the President received the news, and he
also returned at once.

The remnant of the Federal Party made a desperate effort to rally as the anti-war party. They
called and held a Convention at Hartford, Connecticut, which may be fully described, though briefly,
as the most complete funeral ceremony ever performed for itself by a political organization. The
anti-war element in the New England States was
by no means all Federalist, and still less was it disloyal, for New England furnished more soldiers in
the War of 1812 than did all the States south of the

Potomac. The politicians did not correctly read the minds of the people, as they were to discover at the next election. As to one point, they were entirely correct : Mr. Madison was not a particularly good war President, and had added nothing whatever to his reputation as a statesman by his conduct of affairs, which, both before and after the declaration of war, demanded a man of action, a man of stronger will, a man more by nature a ruler if equally a good legislator. Such a man might, nevertheless, have won greater praise for himself at greater cost to the country.

So far as mere fighting was concerned, by land or sea, Napoleon Bonaparte had already done all that was necessary, year by year, to prepare the taxpaying people of Great Britain for peace negotiations. He had all but exhausted their capacity to pay taxes, and the war with the United States was a burden which they were very willing to get rid of. Their rulers felt differently, but the aspect of continental European affairs was threatening, and they reluctantly consented to talk about a peace. In the spring of 1814 John Quincy Adams, James A. Bayard, Henry Clay, Jonathan Russell, and Albert Gallatin, well representing the old and the new in American politics, went to Ghent, in Belgium, on behalf of the United States, to meet British commissioners and negotiate a treaty. Month after month passed by, during which there was no cessation of hostilities, nor any apparent willingness on either side to give up the main points upon which the war had nominally been begun. A treaty was at last signed, December 24th, 1814, and the British journals declared that their Government had made a diplomatic surrender. On the other hand, the United States seemed, to Americans, to have gained very little, for England did not surrender her claim to the right of search. All that was really gained in that direction was a silent understanding that American commerce should no more be molested and restricted and plundered as before. The war itself established in the minds of European diplomatists the idea that the protests of an American minister or ambassador might have ships and guns behind them, and were not any more to be brushed aside with indifference.

Since that day even sober historians of high rank have charged that Mr. Madison assented to the War of 1812 in a bargain made to secure his re-election to the Presidency, sacrificing the lives and the property of his countrymen to his own personal ambition. If this charge were true, his name should go down in history beside that of Benedict Arnold ; but it is simply partisan and untrue.

The war closed with a remarkable illustration of the fact that Great Britain had not expected it to close so soon. The treaty of Ghent was signed December 24th, 1814, was ratified by the Senate of the United States on February 18th, 1815, and between those dates, on January 8th, 1815, the British Army under Sir Edward Packenham, to which had been assigned the mission of seizing the Louisiana territory and the future navigation of the Mississippi, was disastrously defeated by the Americans under Jackson at the battle of New Orleans. Ten days later peace was formally proclaimed, and all the blood shed in that battle had been wasted ; but it answered one purpose, that of lifting into fame and bearing forward to power one of the most remarkable men in American history, Andrew Jackson.

JAMES MADISON'S MONUMENT.

CHAPTER XVI.

Peace and Prosperity—Election of Mr. Monroe and Retirement of Mr. Madison—Life at Montpellier —Visits at Monticello—A Venerable Old Age— End of a Useful Life.

MR. AND MRS. MADISON spent several weeks of the summer of 1814 in a vacation at Montpellier. The city of Washington needed many repairs before it again became a pleasant place of residence or furnished proper accommodations for Congress and the departments. When the President returned he rented for a year a private residence known as the "Octagon." It was here that the treaty of peace was signed, and the White House repairs were not completed until nearly the end of Mr. Madison's term of office.

Now peace had returned, an era of conciliation set in, for with peace had come prosperity, such as had been impossible at any time before the war. A long confusion, preceded by a long oppression, was at an end forever. The nation had entered upon a new career. Ships could come and go, and home industries could thrive under a government which had given a necessary token of vitality. Mr. Madison and his administration were not to be accredited with this result any more than they were to be charged with the previous evils or with the war itself, but a popularity, a general kindly feeling, came to them from all parties in a land which was so very much relieved.

The tariff question, including not only revenue but protection, was before Congress, and Mr. Madison could cordially approve measures which must have reminded him of his earliest perplexities and labors in the old Continental Congress. He also assented to a national bank against his often-expressed opinion that it was not provided for in the Constitution, of which he was termed the father.

James Monroe had been conspicuously the war member of Mr. Madison's Cabinet from the hour in which he entered it. From September 27th, 1814, to March 2d, 1815, he had added the duties of Secretary of War to those of Secretary of State. When, therefore, his party nominated him for President in 1816, the nation was asked to approve or disapprove of the war policy. They gave Mr. Monroe one hundred and eighty-three electoral votes against thirty-four given to the Federal candidate, Mr. Rufus King, and Mr. Madison had a right to accept the result as a popular rejection of partisan criticisms upon himself. A sarcasm current at the time described the Federal Party as disappearing from the political stage with the remark : " There ! Thomas Jefferson's political family have been provided for. James Monroe is the last of them."

After the inauguration of Mr. Monroe, March 4th, 1817, Mr. and Mrs. Madison retired to their Montpellier home. He was sixty-six years of age and she but forty-five. Pure life, regular habits, had preserved to them excellent health. The death of Mr. Madison's father and of his brother Ambrose had left the ex-President sole owner of the Montpellier estate, twenty-five hundred acres of land, with over a hundred slaves. The very good condition of the property at this time was largely due to the increase of wealth brought to her husband by Mrs. Madison. The new house had been built without destroying the old, and the original family homestead was still occupied by Mr. Madison's mother. Here she kept up the old-fashioned ways of housekeeping, waited upon by servants who grew old and faded away with her. She divided her time between her Bible and her knitting, all undisturbed by the modern hours, the changed customs, or the elegant hospitalities of the mansion-house itself. She was a central point in the life of her distinguished son, and the object of his most devoted care to the end of her days. These were long, for she passed away at ninety-eight.

The Montpellier home was admirably situated. Its long, wide, pillared portico looked out upon a pleasant slope, and beyond in the distance were the rugged ranges of the Blue Ridge. Much had been done for ornament all around the house, and the lawns, the trees, the shrubbery received much attention from Mr. Madison, who now returned to his daily habit of taking long walks for exercise, such as he had written about to Jefferson long years before. He retained his interest in natural history, and rare seeds and plants were sent him from abroad. There is a tradition that one package of seeds sent by Lafayette was marked "very rare," and contained only thistle-seed, from which all the thistles in Virginia trace their ancestry.

In the house itself there was nearly all that wealth and culture could add to the hearty, open-handed life of a Virginia planter. There were many pictures, mostly portraits, and one room set apart to the purpose contained more than fifty statues and busts. There were medallions and other mementoes presented by foreign powers to Mr. Madison when President, and Mrs. Madison's collection of curious things in furniture and china had been made with good taste. His own sitting-room contained furniture, high-post bed and all, brought to him by James Monroe from among the wreck of the mob-dismantled palace of the Tuileries. The library was large, for the elder Madison had purchased the collection of Lord Dunmore, the last royal governor of Virginia, and added it to his own, to be now increased by that of his son, less such books as had perished when the British marauders burned the libraries of the Capitol and the White House.

Mr. Madison continued to take a deep interest in public affairs, but he was not Thomas Jefferson, and no party made a shrine and insisted upon finding a director at Montpellier as at Monticello. There were to be long years, not of obscurity, or of neglect, or of entirely vanished influence, but of a retirement which grew more and more venerable as time went by. He studied much, thought much, and he wrote much, especially concerning the political history in which he had been an active participator. He had long since recorded his opinion of chattel slavery, and he gave the subject more attention now as a slaveholder honestly wishing that there were no slaves. Whatever he and others then predicted of its evil consequences fell sadly short of the truth. He prepared a paper, "Advice to My Country," to be opened and read after his death, and in this also was a lesson drawn from his entire experience as a statesman: "The advice nearest my heart and deepest in my convictions is, that the Union of the States be cherished and perpetuated. Let the open enemy to it be regarded as a Pandora, with her box opened, and the disguised one as the serpent creeping with his deadly wiles into Paradise."

His attendance upon the convention for revising the Constitution of Virginia can hardly be called a break in his retirement. It was precisely like the attendance of John Adams at the convention held to remodel the constitution he himself had drawn up for Massachusetts. Both of the old patriots were now constitutional grandfathers, and were entitled to be invited and to be given the seat of honor.

A cordial and liberal hospitality much in excess of what the estate could afford was maintained at Montpellier, and guests came from far. Lafayette made quite a visit there in 1825, and made great friends of the negroes in their cabins, going among them alone or in company with Mrs. Madison, and enjoying their quaint talk and ways and odd ideas.

Camp-meetings and political barbecues in the neighborhood often filled the house to overflowing,

for people who came to the open-air preachings or
the rude feastings were sure to take the opportunity
for a word with a man who seemed to them a living
part of the history of their country.

Monticello was no farther away than Shadwell had
been when the boy James Madison went to ask the
young lawyer Thomas Jefferson just what and how
much he must read to become a scholar and know
everything.   So now, in their old age, the two ex-
Presidents frequently overcame the thirty miles of
bad roads between them, even when servants on
horseback had to come along to occasionally pry a
carriage out of an unreasonably deep mud-hole.

Mrs. Madison had been a sort of American queen
in Washington society during sixteen years, but had
hardly appeared to better advantage in her most
brilliant " drawing-rooms" at the Executive Mansion than she now did as the mistress of Montpellier.
All who crossed her threshold praised her, and old
Mrs. Madison, slowly withering into feebleness, said
of her : " Dolly is my mother now, and cares most
tenderly for all my wants."

The time came when Mr. Madison himself required of her the same tender and minute attention,
for old age crept upon him, and with it disabling
rheumatic complaints.   He was first confined to the
house, then to his chair, then to his bed, suffering
with patience and cheerfulness, and retaining full
possession of his faculties to the very last.   In the
early summer of 1836 it became evident that the
end was drawing near, and the physicians in attendance had a hope that it might not come before the

Fourth of July. The calm good sense of Mr. Madison refused to sympathize with the hope or the wish, and he refused to make any effort or take any merely stimulating nostrums. The time for his departure had come, June 28th, 1836. He was ready to go, and he passed away.

THE END.

PORTRAIT OF JAMES MONROE.

JAMES MONROE.

FIFTH PRESIDENT.

By WILLIAM O. STODDARD.

CHAPTER I.

Birthplace and Ancestry of James Monroe—Boyhood on a Plantation—Stirring Times in the Colonies—Going to College—Virginia Arming for the War of Independence—Bunker Hill—From College to Camp—Monroe a Lieutenant in the Continental Army.

THERE are a great many readers to whom the department of biography is like a dim gallery of old portraits. The men and the women on the wall may have been living once, and may have been interesting, but they look so cold now in their frames! In the gallery of American biography, however, all the chill passes away when the picture of James Monroe is reached. There was no frost about him, but very much that was warm and human and that attracted all other men who knew him. Descended from Scotch cavaliers who had fought for church and king, he inherited certain fiery traits of character which were of value, or the reverse, according to circumstances. Such men yield to quick, hot impulses ; they make blunders ; they incur censure ; but there is a sound of something stirring, living, vigorous, wherever they are known to be, and the world would be badly off without them.

Colonel Spence Monroe belonged to the old colonial aristocracy of Virginia. He owned a fine estate in Westmoreland County, along Monroe's Creek, on the right bank of the Potomac River. His wife's maiden name had been Eliza Jones, of King George County. All around them, up and down the river and for a very long ride into the interior, were the hospitable homes of other planters. They were an honorable, open-handed, high-spirited race of men, fond of social enjoyments, much given to field sports, horsemanship, and vigorous exercise in the open air. There was nothing in their way of life which permitted effeminacy, and in the middle of the eighteenth century they were raising among them a generation of young men fitted to do good service in the council or on the battle-field. The first President of the United States, and the third, fourth, and fifth, came from Virginia farms, and all were born within a moderate distance from the head of Monroe's Creek. Here, on the 28th day of April, in the year 1758, was born James Monroe, who was to be the fifth upon the list of Presidents.

At this precise date Colonel George Washington, aged twenty-six, was in command of the Virginia troops defending the frontier from the Indians, and was at his headquarters at Fort Loudoun. John

Adams, whose one term was to be the only break in the Virginia line of succession during thirty-six years, was teaching school and studying law at Worcester, Massachusetts, and writing letters about the necessity for union among the colonies.

The colonies all along the coast were entering upon an era of agitation, leading on to revolution and to independence, and no man among them yet dreamed of the treasonable doctrines he was so soon to adopt in place of his born duty of loyalty to the King of England.

The childhood and boyhood of James Monroe passed very much as did those of other sons of wealthy planters, except that more than ordinary attention was paid to his education, as well as to his morals and his manners. Thomas Jefferson had but just completed a four years' course of study under the Rev. William Douglass, who had come over from Scotland to be a tutor in the family of Colonel Monroe, and had then opened a larger school on his own account. Without knowing who were his successors during the later years when James required a tutor, the fact of the employment of such an instructor indicates the value set upon education in the household upon Monroe's Creek. There seems to be no record existing of the school-days, the employments, the adventures of those first few years of a life which was to be so very busy and so full of excitements and undertakings. The boy was sufficiently faithful to his books, for he was early prepared for college. .He went to Thomas Jefferson for advice, and received nearly such as that hard student gave to James Madison and others. He grew strong in body also, as well as in mind, developing his physical resources for the brilliant career before him.   Political education kept even pace with every other, for the Monroe family and their neighbors and connections were intensely patriotic.   James Monroe was only nine years old, in 1767, when his father and other gentlemen along the Potomac joined in a written protest against the Stamp Act.   A year later they sent to London £76 8s. to be expended for a portrait of Lord High Chancellor Camden, in token of their appreciation of his opposition to the hated stamp impost.   They failed to get it, but obtained a good likeness of Lord Chatham, which reached them in 1769.   The Jones family were also prominent in opposing ministerial tyranny, and Mrs. Monroe's brother, Judge Joseph Jones, was afterward twice a member of the Continental Congress.

Nearly all the news which came to the rural homes of Virginia during the years after James Monroe was old enough to understand the conversation among his father's guests and in the home circle related to the troubled condition of the western frontier or to the increasing oppressiveness of British domination.   No boy was likely to forget whatever account he might hear of the doings of the red men, or of any official insolence or aggression. Men who uttered in his presence heated words about a war for liberty made a deeper and more lasting impression upon him than any who expressed a vain hope of more wisdom and better manners for English statesmen and for their agents in America.

The year 1774 came at last, with its plain promises of an open rupture with England. It began with the rejection of the taxed tea and with the Boston Harbor tea-party. Next came the passage of the act of Parliament revengefully closing Boston Harbor, and then the Virginia House of Burgesses was dissolved by Governor Dunmore for naming as a day of public fasting and prayer June 1st, upon which the Boston Port Bill was to go into operation. The summoning of the first Continental Congress followed, and its election and its assembling at Philadelphia. Before it adjourned and afterward the Committees of Safety were raising and drilling independent companies in every county in Virginia; but James Monroe was only sixteen, and could not have been accepted as a recruit in the Westmoreland company. He was a school-boy, ready for the college of William and Mary, at Williamsburg, and not for the army. Whatever was the precise date of his arrival at that old colonial capital, he was not destined to pore there over the list of heavy books furnished him by Thomas Jefferson, for he found more political excitement in the atmosphere than love of learning. Williamsburg was almost as fiercely rebellious as was Boston itself. Its main street, three quarters of a mile in length, was terminated at one end by the Capitol, and at the other by the college buildings. In another part of the town was the old Raleigh Tavern, and in this was the great ball-room, the Apollo, to which the dismissed House of Burgesses had resorted to complete the debates and the votings which had been cut

short in the Capitol by the royal governor. When
they were all there the Apollo probably did not contain a greater amount of patriotic enthusiasm, man
for man, than did the dingy college buildings. In
one room of these, in the room of the young student
Thomas Jefferson, the raw country lawyer Patrick
Henry had drawn his famous resolutions and had
prepared himself to electrify the Assembly by his
first great speech in behalf of liberty. The college
politics had grown more and more fiercely American
ever since. All the news received by the students
during the winter of 1774–75 was calculated to keep
their zeal as nearly as might be at the boiling-point.
When spring came the Legislature, now in another
form as the Convention, did not return to Williamsburg, to be within reach of Lord Dunmore and the
marines he might obtain from British ships of war.
It had adjourned from the Apollo to meet at Richmond, farther up the James River, in March, 1775.
It was there, on the 23d of the month, after a burst
of prophetic eloquence from Patrick Henry, that the
Virginia Colony decided to arm itself for a fight
which was plainly seen close at hand, and Colonel
George Washington consented to superintend the
process of arming.

Less than a month later, April 20th, Williamsburg
was in an uproar on account of the seizure of the
powder in its magazine by Lord Dunmore, and all
the college boys were in the mob from which the
governor fled in haste on board the ship-of-war
Fowey. Later still, as the slow mails travelled, by
sea or land, came news incomparably more thrilling,

for it was a voice from the bloody road between Boston and Lexington calling the young men of America to arms. The battle of Bunker Hill soon followed, and the appointment of General Washington to the command of the Continental Army.

James Monroe was now seventeen years of age. Like nearly all Virginia planters' sons, he was a good horseman and familiar with the use of weapons. He felt that any longer poring over books was unendurable, with, as Patrick Henry might have expressed it, "every gale from the north bringing to his ears the clash of resounding arms." He seems to have remained at William and Mary until the close of the college year, but not to have returned after the summer vacation. Three of the professors and twenty-five or thirty of the students in like manner decided that their duty was with the army. One pretty good authority states that Monroe reached the camp at Cambridge, before Boston, in the course of the year 1775. If so, he served as a cadet, without any commission, until the following year, and witnessed the trying scenes of Washington's first winter camp, as well as the departure of the discomfited British Army and the triumphant entry of the Continentals into Boston as the winter closed. The first commission known to have been issued to him was as a lieutenant in the Third Virginia Regiment, commanded by Colonel (soon afterward General) Hugh Mercer. He received it in 1776, after Washington, in April, had removed his headquarters to New York.

CHAPTER II. .

The New York Campaign—Declaration of Independence—Battle of Long Island—Lieutenant Monroe Under Fire at Harlem—Again at the Battle of White Plains—The Movement Across the Hudson —Fall of Fort Washington.

THE summer of the year 1776 brought to General Washington duties whose performance called for uttermost exertion of every good quality he possessed of mind or body.

The army with which he had driven General Howe out of Boston had been a miscellaneous body of men, who came and went under short enlistments. They organized very patriotically behind the Cambridge intrenchments, fought and suffered awhile, and then for the greater part marched home again. A large body of them had followed him to New York, but of these the terms of enlistment were fast expiring, and Washington had obtained the necessary Congressional legislation for the organization of a new army. While the difficult processes of enlistment, assignment, equipment, and drill were going forward he was compelled to fight a losing campaign against a superior force of the best troops in the world, supported in all their movements by a powerful fleet.

It was during this reorganization that James

Monroe received his commission in the Virginia line. He was very young, but he had in him the very kind of courage which was to be required by the long trial before him and his comrades. On June 29th, 1776, a British fleet of forty sail appeared off Staten Island. They brought ten thousand of the old Boston garrison and a strong re-enforcement of Highlanders. Other ships followed, with further detachments of regular troops and of Hessians, while Washington's new recruits came in but slowly. When the British forces landed on Staten Island thirty thousand strong he had but twenty thousand, most of whom were raw, undisciplined, untried. The bilious fever raged in his camps and disabled nearly a quarter of his army. All the wisdom he exercised in making his appointments and his assignments to duty failed to prevent sectional and personal jealousies from interfering with his plans. He knew that the country expected him to hold the city of New York, but he also knew that it would soon be almost out of his power to do so. All the inhabitants able to seek refuge elsewhere had gone or were going, and such as remained added seriously to the perplexities of the commander-in-chief.

On July 4th, 1776, the independence of the United States was declared, and Lieutenant Monroe was therefore no longer a young colonial Englishman, but an officer in the army of a new Republic. He was also, by British law and in the eyes of British soldiers and American Tories, a rebel, a traitor to his king, liable to death by hanging and to the confiscation of his property, in case the Continental

Army should finally fail to make good the Declaration.

There were negotiations of various kinds, but there was no fighting until August 27th, when the record of disaster began with the terrible defeat on Long Island. The Third Virginia was not engaged, and its exact whereabouts have not been recorded. If with General Mercer in the " flying camp," Lieutenant Monroe must have been with a detachment he about this time sent to New York.

Washington effected his masterly retreat from Long Island on August 28th and 29th. There was a lull after that, for the British commander made another attempt at negotiation, not yet convinced that the time for anything of that sort which did not secure American independence had gone by. All the while it became more and more evident that at the first pressure from the enemy the island of Manhattan, with the exception of the heights on its north-western extremity, must be abandoned.

The British general began to press, on August 14th, by landing a strong force on the islands at the mouth of the Harlem River, with a manifest intention of cutting off the retreat of the American Army to the Westchester mainland. The evacuation of New York, already going on, was urged with great rapidity as soon as Washington heard of this threatening movement, but he was almost too late. He had a strong force at the Harlem River, and he had caused breastworks to be constructed at Turtle and Kip's bays. There were no Virginia troops at either of these points, and the men behind the breastworks were mostly militia who had been broken in courage by the share they had taken in the defeat on Long Island. They had been cannonaded severely on the 13th by four ships-of-war in the East River, and were ready to run at the first fire. They did so on the 15th. Six more war ships came in from the Sound, and under cover of so many guns a division of Hessians under Count Donop, and another of British under Sir Henry Clinton, were boated across from Long Island to the New York shore. The militia broke so disgracefully that General Washington, who strove to rally them, lost his temper entirely, as well as his hat, and would have been captured or killed if an aide had not seized his bridle and forced him to ride away. The retreating rear division of the Continental Army was under Putnam, and made a forced march under a hot sun, taking with it as much as it could of the remaining military stores and baggage. The enemy's ships were pushing up the Hudson also, but for some reason General Clinton failed to take advantage of his opportunity to strike the American flank.

Manhattan Island terminates, on its western side, in a long, narrow neck of rocky heights, bounded on the west by the Hudson, on the north by Spuyten Duyvil Creek, and easterly by Harlem River. On one of the heights stood Fort Washington. A mile and a half below the fort General Washington had now drawn a double row of lines, about a quarter of a mile apart, reaching from the Harlem to the Hudson, and strengthened by bat-

teries. He said of them : " Here I should hope
the enemy, in case of attack, will meet a defeat if
the generality of our troops would behave with
tolerable bravery ; but experience, to my extreme
affliction, has convinced me that it is rather to be
wished than expected. However, I trust there are
many who will act like men worthy of the blessings
of freedom."

His faint trust was about to be more than justified, and that, too, by just such men as had broken
at Kip's Bay. On the morning of September 16th
the British lines, two miles in length, extended
across from the Hudson to Horen's Hook, on the
East River, each flank protected by their war ships.
Strong columns were sent forward from them to feel
the American front, and there was a sharp skirmish
at an outpost held by Connecticut men under Lieutenant-Colonel Knowlton. The Americans were
outnumbered and driven, and Washington sent them
re-enforcements, first some Virginians under Major
Leitch, then some Marylanders, and then other
troops from New England. It was a hot action,
hardly large enough to be called a battle, but the
enemy were driven back to their own lines, and the
effect upon the spirits of the Continentals was of
great value. Among the Virginians engaged was
Lieutenant James Monroe, under fire for the first
time. He escaped unhurt, but he had seen Knowlton and Leitch go down, and many another, while
their comrades, himself among them, fought on
until the British veterans gave way. He was no
longer a college-boy, but a soldier.

The subsequent movements of the enemy rendered necessary a transfer of the entire army, except the garrison. of Fort Washington, to the Westchester mainland. That garrison ought also to have been removed and the fort abandoned, but Washington had been a general only a short time, and allowed his better judgment to be overruled. On October 23d his headquarters were at White Plains, near which he had temporarily established a fortified camp. The enemy pressed his retreat closely, and there were many skirmishes, in which the "ragged rebels," as Howe's men contemptuously called them, exhibited a great deal of stubborn courage.

By the afternoon of October 25th the advance of the British Army under General Howe was only four miles from the American lines, but hesitation threw away another British opportunity, for it was two days later before Washington's rear division arrived, under General Lee. On the morning of October 28th, 1776, Washington and Lee and several other generals rode out to reconnoitre a better place for a camp, and while they were so engaged a trooper came galloping hard to shout to the commander-in-chief, "The British are in the camp, sir!" He was somewhat over-hasty. Howe's attack had begun, and the American pickets had been driven in, but there had been no disaster. The generals rode back again, and the battle of White Plains followed. The entire American loss was less than four hundred men, killed, wounded, and prisoners, and that of the enemy was about the same. Washington was forced to fall back, but in doing it took a position so strong that General Howe refused to assail it.

This was the second battle in which Lieutenant Monroe is recorded as having been personally engaged. He had now before him a very different test of his soldierly qualities and of his devotion to the cause of freedom. Badly as the army had hitherto been supplied with food and clothing, matters were fast growing worse, while the weather demanded tents and blankets. A British officer wrote : " The rebel army are in so wretched a condition as to clothing and accoutrements that I believe no nation ever saw such a set of tatterdemalions." General George Clinton, of New York, wrote to his wife : " Our lines were manned all night ; . . . a most horrid night it was to lie in cold trenches. Uncovered as we are, daily on fatigue, making redoubts, fleches, abatis, and retreating from them and the little temporary huts made for our comfort before they are all finished, I fear will ultimately destroy our army without fighting."

On the night of November 4th General Howe gave up his attempts to strike a blow at the American lines, and retreated with his whole army. Washington at once determined to leave a sufficient force in Westchester, another in charge of the passes of the Hudson, and to take the remainder with him into New Jersey. Among the regiments selected for his own immediate command was the Third Virginia. British ships patrolled the lower Hudson or lay threateningly at anchor as high up as the Tappan Sea and Haverstraw Bay. The Maryland

and Virginia regiments crossed at Peekskill before November 10th, and the rest followed on the 12th under Washington's supervision. He then hurried forward, to be a witness of the fall of Fort Washington and the loss of more than three thousand of his best men on the 15th, while his army struggled slowly after him through the narrow and rugged passes of the Catskill Mountains. It was dreary work in the bitter November weather, but the officers toiled with the men. None of them were working for pay, for profit, or reward.

CHAPTER III.

The Retreat through New Jersey—Beyond the Delaware—Battle of Trenton—Monroe Wounded while Leading the Advance—Commissioned a Captain for Bravery—Aide to General Stirling—Major—Battles of the Brandywine and Germantown—Valley Forge—Monmouth Court-House—Monroe's Return to Virginia.

THE movements of the British Army after the fall of Fort Washington rendered necessary an immediate retreat of the scanty forces under the American commander-in-chief. Invaluable military stores had been lost with the fort, and nearly all he had left were sacrificed now. He reached the Hackensack River only to find that he was in as much danger as before, and his army seemed to be melting away around him while he retreated to the Raritan. The terms of enlistment of some of his men had expired, and there were many so discouraged that they deserted what seemed a lost cause and a ruined commander. He had not lost heart or hope, for it was after crossing the Delaware in the December frost that he said to General Mercer:

" What think you, if we should retreat to the back parts of Pennsylvania, would the Pennsylvanians support us ?"

" If the lower counties give up, the back counties will do the same," said Mercer.

" We must then retire to Augusta County, in Virginia. Numbers will repair to us. for safety, and we will try a predatory war. If overpowered, we must cross the Alleghanies," replied Washington.

Among the men who would surely have followed him was James Monroe, as he was about to prove.

General Howe deemed a winter campaign unnecessary, now that the thoroughly-beaten Americans were driven beyond the Delaware. He established strong detachments, mostly of Hessians, at several points along the river, and returned to comfortable winter quarters in New York.

The moment Washington was sufficiently reenforced to justify him in making any movement he planned a series of blows at Howe's outposts. The first was to be struck at Trenton, where there were fifteen hundred Hessians and some cavalry under Colonel Rahl. On Christmas Day, 1776, twenty-four hundred men and twenty small field-pieces were gathered near McKonkey's Ferry under Washington in person. An officer bringing him despatches traced the march to the river-bank for miles by the blood on the snow from the frost-cracked feet of shoeless men. Only two brave fellows were actually frozen to death that night, but the river was full of floating ice which threatened the boats with destruction, and the extreme cold added materially to the difficulties and hardships of the seemingly desperate undertaking.

Other movements were progressing, but this was deemed the most important of all.

The weather aided somewhat in convincing the Hessian commander that no attack would be made upon him during such a night, although he had received positive warnings.

Washington had hoped to cross the river before midnight of December 25th, but it was three o'clock next morning before all his cannon were over. He formed his men in two columns, one led by himself and one by General Sullivan, to advance by separate roads to the outskirts of Trenton and attack in concert. Through a storm of driving hail and sleet the march was pressed, and Sullivan reached at daylight the cross-roads where he had been ordered to halt and wait the arrival of the other column. The muskets of his men were found to be wet and useless, and he reported the fact to Washington by a messenger, with an anxious inquiry as to what he should do. General St. Clair had already told him : " You have nothing to do but to push on and use the bayonet," and Washington's response was a stormy order to " Advance and charge !"

It was eight o'clock in the morning when all was ready. There had been a false alarm calling out the garrison during the night, and it made them all the more willing now to yield to the storm and remain within doors. Even the pickets and sentries got under cover and were taken by surprise when the attack was made.

The American advance was headed by some brave

fellows under Captain William Washington and Lieutenant James Monroe. The Hessian drums began to beat to arms, the cavalry trumpets sounded the alarm, sharp firing began from windows and from behind houses. An attempt was made by some of the fast-rallying garrison to form in the main street and to train upon the charging Continentals a couple of cannon which had been stationed there.

It might have resulted in a serious check, endangering the complete success of Washington's plan, but for the headlong rush of the few half frozen men led on by William Washington and James Monroe. Before the artillerists could use their guns they were driven from them. Captain Washington was disabled by a bullet wound in the wrist, and Lieutenant Monroe went down with a ball in his shoulder ; but the cannon were captured, and the American column swept on without being raked by what would have been a destructive fire at short range. The victory was complete, and the prisoners taken numbered nearly a thousand. The dash upon Trenton had not been the whole of Washington's plan, but the weather had interfered with it seriously at other points, so that he was compelled at once to recross the Delaware. Badly wounded men like young Monroe were boated over, like the rest, under care of the Marblehead fishermen, who attended to all of Washington's army ferriage. A few days later he struck another blow, at Princeton, and here fell General Hugh Mercer, who had been the first colonel of the Third Virginia Regiment.

The Hessian cannon in the main street of Trenton had been charged and captured under the eyes of Washington, for the general was at the head of his men that winter morning.   The promotion of James Monroe " for bravery" came directly from the commander-in-chief.   He had himself been appointed a major at nineteen, before he had ever seen a shot fired or a full regiment paraded.   Monroe was a year younger when he won the much higher honor of a captain's commission to command such iron men as had followed him through that winter night until he fell at their head beside the captured guns.

By a comparison of dates and military movements it appears that the Third Virginia, or what remained of it, must have first crossed the Delaware in the gloomy retreat before Howe's advance, on or about December 5th, 1776.   On that day some of the undergraduates of William and Mary College met in the Apollo room of the Raleigh Tavern at Williamsburg, to organize a chapter of the Phi Beta Kappa Society.   No doubt they enjoyed themselves, and among them were some who afterward rendered good service to their country.   They did well, and all young students could not be in the Continental army.   Nevertheless, the contrast is very striking between the scene in the Apollo, where James Monroe's name was not called with those of his fellow-collegians, and the other scene on the icy river-bank, in the darkness and the storm, yet so brilliant with courage, endurance, and self-sacrificing patriotism.

The captain's commission was to have given its

recipient a company in one of the new regiments which Washington was trying to form, but the exhausted state of the patriot finances prevented the fulfilment of the general's purpose, and Monroe was transferred to the staff of General Lord Stirling, as a volunteer aide, with the rank of major. He soon recovered from his wound and was ready for the active duties sure to come to any man who served with Stirling.

The brief winter campaign was over, and the army went into camp at Morristown, New Jersey, to contend as best it might with cold and hunger and epidemic small-pox. Every effort was made to obtain, equip, and drill recruits, and to re-enlist as many as possible of men who had already served. By the end of May Washington moved out of his winter quarters with seven thousand three hundred men fit for duty, and with a difficult and harassing campaign before him. There were protracted and fatiguing military manœuvres and marches and many skirmishes, until at last the British and American armies came together at the Brandywine, September 11th, 1777. General Stirling's division was one of the first brought into action, and behaved well, although shattered, and his aide, Major Monroe, is said to have been with Lafayette when the brave Frenchman was wounded.

The battle of the Brandywine was a defeat for the Americans, and so was that of Germantown, on October 4th, where Major Monroe was again under fire. The remainder of the campaign consisted of skirmishes more or less severe, and of a cautious

generalship on Washington's part, rendered necessary by the condition of his army.   Sad indeed was
the last march, in December, to the winter camp at
Valley Forge, for again the feet of the Continental
soldiers left bloody marks in the snow.   The story
of their sufferings during the succeeding months
must never be forgotten.   It should be read in the
letters which Washington himself wrote pleading
for his army.

Drill went on under Baron Steuben in spite of all
hardships, and in the spring all was ready for a trial
of strength with the British under Howe.   It did
not come until June 28th, 1778, at Monmouth
Court-House, and here Lord Stirling commanded
the American left wing, and Major Monroe was
with him.

The young soldier had seen an abundance of hard
service, and had earned the warm approval of his
comrades and superiors ; but there was something
unreal and tantalizing about the rank he held as
volunteer aide to General Stirling.   It cut him off
from all hope of genuine promotion, and lost him
his regular place in the Continental line.   Congress
was not providing for the formation of any new regiments, and Major Monroe went home to Virginia
to try and secure a State commission.   Patrick
Henry's term as governor of that State was about
to expire.   Thomas Jefferson, elected in January,
became governor June 2d, 1779, and the testi-
monials his young friend was able to lay before him
seemed to give the latter a right to hope for the
success of his application.   General Stirling strongly

urged the claims of his gallant aide-de-camp, while Washington himself wrote zealously on his behalf. Part of the recommendation from the commander-in-chief is as follows :

" The zeal he discovered by entering the service at an early period, the character he supported in his regiment, and the manner in which he received a wound, induced me to appoint him to a captaincy in one of the additional regiments. This regiment failing, from the difficulty of recruiting, he entered into Lord Stirling's family, and has served two campaigns as a volunteer aide to his lordship. He has in every instance maintained the reputation of a brave, active, and sensible officer. As we cannot introduce him into the Continental line, it were to be wished that the State could do something for him."

CHAPTER IV.

*Monroe a Law Student and Aide to Governor Jeffer-
son—Virginia Harassed—Defeat of the Army
under General Gates—Lieutenant-Colonel Monroe
a Military Commissioner—Elected a Member of the
State Legislature—Delegate to the Continental Congress.*

ON April 28th, 1779, James Monroe became
twenty-one years of age. His brief but highly honorable military career was ended, for he was not
only shut out from his place in the regular line of
Continental promotion, but no suitable staff appointment could be given him. John Adams, chairman
of the Board of War and at the head of all military
affairs in Congress, testified that the resources of the
Confederation were too much exhausted to organize
another regular regiment. The country contained
thousands of young and eager patriots like Monroe,
to whom neither arms nor food could be supplied as
soldiers. The State of Virginia was almost as badly
off with reference to its own militia and its empty
treasury, and its governor was vainly attempting to
borrow money in Italy and elsewhere.

Thomas Jefferson retired from the practice of the
law in 1774, but he was still quite willing to direct
the studies of some of his young friends precisely as
if he were still at the bar and they reading in his

office preparatory to admission. At the same time
it was manifest that such a pupil as James Monroe
would become, to all intents and purposes, a military
aide to his preceptor the governor of Virginia upon
every emergency calling for war work rather than
for law-book work. Such occasions came speedily,
and they were of the most pressing and exciting
nature. The boundaries of the State of Virginia,
as understood by its legislators and people at that
time, included all of what is now described on maps
as Virginia, West Virginia, Kentucky, and nearly
all of Ohio, Indiana, and Illinois. There was a
bloody war going on with the red men, who disputed
all pale-face control of the region west of the mountains. The leading chiefs and tribes were willing,
however, to receive presents and arms as allies of
the British king. The fleets and marauding parties
of the same king were harassing the altogether un-
fortified Virginia seaboard. Only three weeks prior
to Jefferson's inauguration some ships-of-war had
sailed into the James River, landed two thousand
men without opposition, and these had ravaged and
robbed and burned during several days before the
fiery governor could rally force enough to frighten
them away. Men answered his call abundantly,
courageously, but he could not furnish so much as
one man in four with a musket. It aids the reports
of Washington upon the condition of his army in
explaining the fact that James Monroe read law instead of leading soldiers in the darkest days of the
war of independence.

· The State capital, and with it the governor, the

Legislature, and Thomas Jefferson's law pupils, removed to Richmond on April 1st, 1780. The rav-
ages upon the coast had been partly compensated
by successes against the Indians on the west, but all
the news from the North was gloomy, and that from
the South included the fall of Charleston, South
Carolina.

The British Army which had broken in through
that gate was believed to have begun a march which
would lead it through North Carolina into Virginia,
unless checked upon the way. General Gates came
down from the North in July, 1780, bringing with
him a few veteran troops, and prepared to take
command of all Southern levies and oppose Lord
Cornwallis. He also brought with him the glory he
had won at the surrender of Burgoyne, and a private
letter from General Lee warning him that he was
going South to lose it. He lost it all, and a large
part of his army, at the battle of Sanders Creek,
August 16th, 1780, leaving the road to Virginia
open before Cornwallis. While the forces Gates
was to command were gathering, the governor and
people of Virginia taxed their last resources to
equip and supply the brave recruits who came forward. Ladies gave their jewels, and farmers their
cattle, horses, and wagons. The first important
detachment of Continentals came down from Washington's camp under Baron De Kalb in the early
part of the year 1780, and the true nature of James
Monroe's position in Jefferson's law office received
a striking illustration. He was appointed military
commissioner for the State, with the rank of lieu-

tenant-colonel, with orders from the governor to attend to State matters in connection with De Kalb's command. It is plainly a matter of course that other duties were included and accomplished, but there is no record of them, save that he performed well whatever was intrusted to him.

The northward march of Cornwallis was one half of a larger plan. On October 22d, 1780, sixty British vessels entered Hampton Roads and began landing troops near Portsmouth. A campaign for the subjection of the State had begun which was only to terminate with the surrender at Yorktown. The law studies of a young Virginian like James Monroe, who was also military commissioner and an ex-officer of the Continental line, were likely to be pursued under difficulties at such a time, with many warlike interruptions and stirring episodes. The British remained on land a month, put to sea again, and returned on the last day of the year 1780 to sail up the Chesapeake and into the James River. By the fourth day of the new year they were landing troops at Westover, only twenty-five miles from Richmond, and it was known that they were led by Arnold the traitor. The governor toiled with desperate eagerness from the moment the first sail was reported to him. Council and Legislature fled, caring for their families, for public property and papers, and he was left almost alone. He summoned militia, dashed hither and thither directing all things, until he rode one horse to death and wearied others ; yet only a faint trace remains of the assistance given him by his military law student, who must inevitably have been as busy as himself. The life of such a man as James Monroe can be neither understood nor appreciated without a mental effort to look behind the curtain of the defective record. His half-seen figure is as interesting as is that of the hard-riding governor. The enemy held Richmond only a few days, did much harm there and in the vicinity, and then returned on board their ships ; but, whether afloat or ashore, they had come to stay.

Again and again during the spring of 1781 sudden alarms interrupted the sessions of the Virginia Legislature at Richmond, and at last they adjourned to meet at Charlottesville, not far from Monticello. Mr. Jefferson's term of office was to expire on June 1st, and it was needful that he or another should receive a proper election. No quorum came to Charlottesville, but the British cavalry under Tarleton did come there and to Monticello as well. Virginia was left for twelve days without any new governor, and the old barely escaped being captured in his own house. One of his two law students was with him when the enemy came near, and helped him remove his family and gather and carry off his papers ; but James Monroe is reported as being absent "in the field." The British Army under Cornwallis came over the border into Virginia, and pressed forward to unite with the troops the fleet had landed on the bank of the James River. They made a fortified camp at Yorktown, and what became of them and it belongs to the history of the war. James Monroe had little more part in the re-

mainder of the decisive Virginia campaign than that
of a chafed and dissatisfied looker-on who longed to
be in action. He fell into a depressed and gloomy
state of mind, which was afterward embittered by
yet another defeat, the particulars of which he kept
to himself. Jefferson was disappointed in his first
love, and so was Madison ; and in September, 1782,
Monroe wrote to his old commander, General Lord
Stirling : " Till lately I have been a recluse. Chagrined with my disappointment in not attaining the
rank and command I sought, chagrined with some
disappointments in a private line, I retired from
society with almost a resolution never to return to
it again."

This disappointment must have been peculiarly
severe to have produced so deep an effect, for he
had not returned to Virginia from the army in an
unhealthy state of mind. He had undertaken his
law studies in sober earnest. He at first had been
in some doubt as to whether he had not better read
law in connection with instructions to be given by
George Wythe, with whom Jefferson himself had
studied, rather than to become the pupil of the
latter, a man who was evidently more statesman
than jurist. That was what he himself was to become, but he did not know it, and he consulted his
mother's brother, Judge Joseph Jones. The following extracts from the reply sent him March 7th,
1780, contain the advice, which was followed with
important results :

" Charles Lewis, going down to the college, gives me an opportunity of answering by him your inquiry respecting your removal

with the governor, or attending Mr. Wythe's lectures. If Mr. Wythe means to pursue Mr. Blackstone's method, I should think you ought to attend him from the commencement of his course, if at all, and to judge of this, for want of proper information, is difficult."

After commenting upon the uncertainties and perplexities attending law lectures and law studies at a time when an old system was passing away, through a process of legislative revision and reconstruction, the letter goes on :

"I have no intimate acquaintance with Mr. Jefferson, but from the knowledge I have of him, he is as proper a man as can be put into the office [of governor], having the requisites of ability, firmness, and diligence. You do well to cultivate his friendship, and cannot fail to entertain a grateful sense of the favors he has conferred upon you ; and while you continue to deserve his esteem he will not withdraw his countenance. If, therefore, upon conferring with him upon the subject, he wishes or shows a desire that you go with him, I would gratify him. Should you remain to attend Mr. Wythe, I would do it with his approbation, and under the expectation that when you come to Richmond you shall hope for the continuance of his friendship and assistance. There is likelihood the campaign will this year be to the South, and in the course of it events may require the exertions of the militia of this State ; in which case, should a considerable body be called for, I hope Mr. Jefferson will head them himself ; and you, no doubt, will be ready cheerfully to give him your company and assistance, as well to make some return of civility to him as to satisfy your own feelings for the common good."

Monroe went with Jefferson. The prediction of Judge Jones as to the campaign at the South was fulfilled, and the governor and his pupil had many duties in connection with the army, and especially with the Virginia militia. Nevertheless, the summer of 1781 found Mr. Jefferson under an unde-

served cloud of public censure which prevented his
re-election as governor, and his law student and
military commissioner was in so soured a state of
mind that he wished to become a sort of hermit.
Whether or not the hidden part of Monroe's distresses
had then entirely fallen upon him, he was not so
disgusted with life as was his older and more sensitive friend. The outburst of unjust criticism died
away like a bursting bubble, and Jefferson's constituents unanimously elected him to the State Assembly in the fall of 1781. Cornwallis surrendered on
November 19th, and the State and the nation went
wild with joy; but one month later the author of the
Declaration of Independence arose in his place in
the Assembly to declare his readiness to meet all
charges. None were made, and a unanimous vote
of thanks to him for his services as governor was
passed instead. Nevertheless, he went home so
melancholy and sore-hearted that he refused to
attend the next session. He remained gloomily at
Monticello until James Monroe wrote to him a
strong remonstrance, appealing to him to return to
his public duties, and representing that the public
mind would not fail to blame him for shunning his
share of the general burden in such an hour of need.
He replied to Monroe at much length, setting forth
his loss of personal ambition, the length of his
public service, which entitled him to withdraw to
private life, the demands of his family and estate,
and the depths of the wrongs done him by the hasty
reflections made upon his acts as governor. Of
these he said : " I felt that these injuries, for such

they have since been acknowledged, had inflicted a wound upon my spirit which will only be cured by the all-healing grave." He added more concerning his plans for his retirement, and invited Monroe to come and visit him at Monticello.

The remonstrance and the reply indicate the nature and intimacy of the friendship which had been formed. Jefferson recovered his interest in public affairs for a time, only to have that and almost his hold on reason and life temporarily shattered by the loss of his wife, on September 6th, 1782.

Monroe's military ambition had been thwarted and his law studies had been injuriously interrupted, but his services in camp and field, and afterward during the invasion of Virginia, had not escaped the notice of his old Westmoreland County neighbors. In 1782 they elected him a member of the Legislature, and he took his seat ; but he was not to occupy it long. He had that in him which attracted other men besides Jefferson. He possessed a vitality, a force of character, an inherent energy, which carried him to the front rank in civil life as surely as in a charge through the main street of Trenton. It was not long before he was chosen a member of the Executive Council. In June of the following year, 1783, he was elected a delegate to Congress, and so was Jefferson. They were to take their seats in November, while James Madison was preparing to return to private life, as he supposed. His own disappointment had come to him toward the end of his term in Congress, and Jefferson wrote him consoling letters. In one of these, dated February 20th, 1784, he said : " Monroe is buying land almost adjoining me. Short will do the same. What would I not give if you could fall into the circle !"

He painted a dreamy sort of scholarly and agricultural retirement, but the circle they were all really falling into was of a very different sort altogether. He was himself to go to France as one of the American commissioners the following spring, and to take Short with him as Secretary of Legation ; Madison was to be chosen a member of the Assembly and go there to perform great services and win great fame ; while Monroe was to remain in Congress, one of its most active and well-known workers, giving such satisfaction to his constituents that at the end of the Fourth Congress (old Confederation) they re-elected him to serve them in the Fifth, and again in the Sixth.

CHAPTER V.

A Tour Through a New Country—A Pen Portrait of James Monroe—Courtship and Marriage—Law Practice—A New Home—Children.

MR. MONROE'S first election to the old Congress, in 1783, made him a member at the early age of twenty-five. Around him were older men with well-earned fames, and he was not prepared by nature or experience to shine at once among them as either a legislator or an orator. They overshadowed him, and the position assigned to him on the records of the time is necessarily secondary to that of some others. Distinct political parties did not yet exist, and men were hardly able to define their own tendencies. Those of Monroe may be indicated as strongly opposed to the ideas of John Adams, Alexander Hamilton, and James Madison, and to their propositions for giving greater power to the central government. He was as yet a State Rights man, of the jealous school represented by Patrick Henry, as was soon to appear in the course of political events. At the same time he earnestly advocated a firm and permanent union of the States, with what he deemed needful protection to these against tyrannical Federal supremacy.

In March, 1784, the Virginia delegation delivered to Congress, on behalf of their State, the first of the five great quit-claim deeds of land known to American history. This parchment relinquished Virginia's claim to the north-west territory ; the next of the series was to surrender that of France to Louisiana ; then one from Spain was to transfer the Floridas ; later still was to come a deed from Mexico giving up Texas, New Mexico, Arizona, and California, and of this the Gadsden purchase was a sort of adjunct, to round it off ; the last, from Russia, gave us Alaska and its many islands.

On the first occasion the central figure was deservedly that of Thomas Jefferson, but Mr. Monroe, with others, was associated with him in the transaction, and was immediately aroused to a statesman-like interest in the future of the region described by the great Virginia parchment. He employed his summer vacation, after the adjournment of Congress, in a tour of observation through the Northwest. He wrote to Jefferson, then in Paris, that the purpose of his journey was " to acquire a better knowledge of the posts we should occupy, the cause of the delay of the evacuation by British troops, the temper of the Indians toward us, as well as of the soil, waters, and, in general, the natural view of the country." He returned late in the autumn with a mass of information which he could not so well have collected in any other way.

Low water in the Ohio cut short an attempt which he afterward made to attend a great council of the Shawnee tribe at the mouth of the Great Miami River, but for the first time in his life he crossed the Alleghanies to the site of old Fort Duquesne, then

Fort Pitt, now Pittsburg. He gained new ideas of the future of the Great West, and it was upon his motion that Congress appointed a committee to report upon the proper division of the territory acquired. There were many committees and many reports and many long debates before, July 13th, 1787, after Mr. Monroe had ceased to be a member of Congress, the great ordinance was adopted by which the question of slavery was for a time compromised, and its northern boundary fixed at the Ohio River.

Before going to the Virginia Assembly Monroe had had a dream of travel in Europe, and had even gone so far as to provide himself with letters of introduction ; but he had given it up to enter upon his new career. Now he had another such dream, and corresponded about it, among other matters, with Jefferson. The latter wrote to him in June, 1785 : "The pleasure of the trip will be less than you expect, but the utility greater. It will make you adore your own country—its soil, its climate, its equality, liberty, laws, people, and manners. My God ! how little do my countrymen know what precious blessings they are in possession of, and which no other people on earth enjoy ! I confess I had no idea of it myself."

The horrible evils of all kinds which led him to the use of language so vehement were the causes which made the French Revolution inevitable and the Reign of Terror possible.

The responsibilities pressed upon Mr. Monroe during the year 1784 were not altogether legislative.

There was a dispute between the States of New York and Massachusetts concerning a boundary line, and he was selected one of a board of nine men to whom, as judges, the decision of the matter was referred. He hesitated, accepted, then resigned, another man was appointed in his place, and the cause of his refusal to act was said to have been little more than his own hot temper, aroused in a controversy over the question of the navigation of the Mississippi. If this is the truth, it was also an early indication of the position of political hostility he was soon to assume toward a group of men who were taking rank as the leaders of the Federal Party.

He was now twenty-eight years of age, and in order to obtain an idea of the impression he made in the brilliant and very aristocratic society of New York, it is only necessary to subtract thirteen years from the pen picture drawn by William Wirt of his personal appearance in 1799.

"In his stature he is about the middle height of men, rather firmly set, with nothing further remarkable in his person, except his muscular compactness and apparent ability to endure labor. His countenance, when grave, has rather the expression of sternness and irascibility; a smile, however (and a smile is not unusual with him in a social circle), lights it up to very high advantage, and gives it a most impressive and engaging air of suavity and benevolence.

"His dress and personal appearance are those of a plain and modest gentleman. He is a man of soft, polite, and assiduous attentions; but these, although they are always well-timed, judicious, and evidently the offspring of an obliging and philanthropic temper, are never performed with the striking and captivating graces of a Marlborough or a Bolingbroke. To be plain, there is often in his manner an inartificial and even an awkward simplicity, which, while it provokes the smile of a more polished person,

forces him to the opinion that Mr. Monroe is a man of most sincere
and artless soul."

He had a very important use to make of all the
" soft, polite, and assiduous attentions" at his command during his last term in Congress.   Miss Eliza
Kortwright, daughter of Lawrence Kortwright,
Esq., of New York, was a young lady of more than
ordinary personal attractions and of good social
position.   When the young Congressman first found
himself drawn toward her he wrote to his uncle,
Judge Jones, asking his advice concerning the important subject of marriage.   Very sage advice was
returned, as was to have been expected ; but James
Monroe was all the while taking counsel with Miss
Kortwright, and she with him, and they finally
came to a decision.   They were married in the
spring of 1786, and just before the wedding Monroe
wrote to Madison : " If you visit this place shortly
I will present you to a young lady who will be
adopted a citizen of Virginia in the course of this
week."   He did not announce his purpose to Jefferson, for distances were long in those days, but he
wrote to him three months later :

"You will be surprised to hear that I have formed the most interesting connection in human life with a young lady in this town,
as you know my plan was to visit you before I settled myself ;
but having formed an attachment to this young lady—a Miss
Kortwright, the daughter of a gentleman of respectable character
and connections in this State, though injured in his fortunes by
the late war—I have found that I must relinquish all other objects
not connected with her.   We were married about three months
since.   I remain here until the fall, at which time we remove to
Fredericksburg in Virginia, where I shall settle for the present in

a house prepared for me by Mr. Jones, to enter into the practice of the law."

The intended visit to Monticello had reference to the old-time plan of the two friends for becoming near neighbors, and this was only temporarily put aside. On August 19th, 1786, another letter to Jefferson told him :

" I shall leave this about October 1st for Virginia—Fredericks-burg. Believe me, I have not relinquished the prospect of being your neighbor. The house for which I have requested a plan may possibly be erected near Monticello ; to fix there, and to have yourself in particular, with what friends we can collect around, for society, is my chief object ; or rather the only one which promises to me, with the connection I have formed, real and substantial pleasure, if, indeed, by the name of pleasure it may be called."

Jefferson's enthusiasm for architecture was almost a passion, and he drew plans for many buildings, public and private. When, however, the house he planned for Monroe was built near Monticello, the nails also were supplied by him, and were in part, at least, manufactured by the African blacksmiths among his own slaves.

Two children came to the first home provided by Monroe for his Northern bride, and both were daughters. In default of sons he afterward extended his almost paternal affection to his wife's kindred. He did all in his power for his nephews, with the single and honorable exception that he steadily refused to employ any of his official powers for their preferment.

CHAPTER VI.

*Monroe again in the Legislature of Virginia—The
Year 1787—The New Constitution of the United
States—The Virginia Convention—James Monroe
Defeated for Congress by James Madison—Monroe
Sent to the Senate of the United States at Thirty-two.*

DURING Mr. Monroe's repeated terms of service
in the old Congress the radical defects of the existing Confederation became more and more apparent,
year after year. That he discerned them as clearly
as did other public men appears manifestly in his
letters and speeches. No man could be more patriotic, and only a very few sought more eagerly for
adequate measures of relief ; but he was not a deep-
thinking, philosophic statesman like Jefferson or
Madison. He was fully prepared to regard the
territory of the United States as one country, and
to love it all as his own, but he was not quite ready
to say that the country was occupied by one people.
They were cut up into thirteen separate peoples,
who were parts of the whole only through their
several State organizations. Every plan for a better
central government capable of paying its debts and
expenses, and of defending itself at home or abroad,
must therefore, to meet his views, be the creation
of the States, and not of the people as a whole acting directly.

In the year 1786 his plan for practising law after the expiration of his term in Congress was nipped in the bud, for he was once more elected a member of the Virginia Legislature. There was much important work before that body, but the thoughts and hearts of all men were turned toward national politics. The year 1787 came, the great initial year of American political history. In July Congress passed the great statute already referred to, known ever afterward as "the Ordinance of 1787." The convention of delegates from all the States to devise a new Constitution for the United States was summoned to meet in Philadelphia on Monday, May 14th, and actually began its labors on the 25th, to finish them on September 17th.

When the ordinance limiting the territorial area of human slavery came to the Virginia Legislature for its action, Mr. Monroe was a member of the committee to whom it was referred, and which promptly reported in favor of the ratification of the ordinance by the State.

When the Constitutional Convention, through Congressional action, sent out to the several States the plan of national government which they had matured, Mr. Monroe wrote to Mr. Madison, October 13th, 1787:

"There are, in my opinion, some strong objections against the project, which I will not weary you with a detail of; but under the predicament in which the Union now stands, and in this State in particular, with respect to this business, they are overbalanced by the arguments in its favor."

The great battle of tongues and pens for and

against the Constitution began at once in every State. Had a vote been taken at the outset an overwhelming rejection would have resulted, for its friends were lukewarm. James Monroe, after faintly favoring it, drifted rapidly into vigorous opposition. Even Madison and Hamilton were deeply dissatisfied with several features of the Constitution to which, as compromises, they had been forced to yield their assent in the Convention. In Virginia the tide of dissent was so strong that Washington and others urged Madison to come home and take charge of the contest in his own State. He was the " Father of the Constitution," but only his personal popularity secured him an election by his own county as a delegate to the Virginia Convention which was to pass judgment upon his work, amended as it had been by other men to his dissatisfaction. It came first before the Legislature, of which Monroe was a member, and there the process of taking sides was narrowly watched, for the political parties of the future were beginning to show themselves. The Legislature contained a majority who were favorably disposed, and Washington wrote to Madison, October 22d, 1787 : " The sentiments of the members are infinitely more favorable to the Constitution than the most zealous advocates for it could have expected. I have not met with one in all my inquiries (and I have made them with great diligence) opposed to it except Mr. Henry, who, I have heard, is so, but could only conjecture it from a conversation with him on the subject."

Washington probably had not conversed with

James Monroe, and he lost sight of the fact that none of his reverent fellow-citizens were willing to engage in a conversational controversy with himself. Even Patrick Henry's ready tongue seems to have been held still by its owner while he was face to face with the best-beloved man in America. It was loosened the moment the Legislature adjourned, January 8th, 1788, after providing for a State Convention, to be held at Richmond on the first Monday in June. The leaders of the opposition to the Constitution were Patrick Henry, George Mason, and Richard Henry Lee, followed closely by younger men like James Monroe. They made an active canvass, and when the Convention came together in June they controlled an apparent majority of its membership. Patrick Henry's own influence throughout the State was such that there was more than a mere jest in the title " King of Virginia," thrown at him by his critics. Mr. Monroe's opposition related not so much to what was in the Constitution. as to the fact that certain important safeguards which he deemed needful were not there. He was elected to the Convention, and took his position at the beginning as a moderate member of the opposition, but grew warmer and more positive as the debates proceeded.

The first speech of Patrick Henry went to the root of the whole matter, for in it he said, speaking of the Virginia delegates to the Constitutional Convention at Philadelphia :

" I have the highest veneration for those gentlemen ; but, sir, give me leave to demand what right had they to say, 'We, the people,' instead of, ' We, the States ' ? States are the characteristic and soul of a confederation. If the States be not the agents of this compact, it is one great consolidated, national government of the people of all the States."

Governor Henry's voice was that of James Monroe, and formulated the political creed of what was yet to be the extreme faction of the Anti-Federal Party.

Mr. Monroe took part in the debates of the Convention, but the leadership fell to others, perhaps because their views were more radical than his own, for he declared his willingness to assent to the Constitution on condition of its being improved by certain amendments. The Convention finally ratified it, by a narrow majority, without proposing conditions, and the desired amendments were afterward obtained substantially.

James Madison had been the leader of the Constitutional side in the Convention, and he had led it in a masterly manner. Against him, therefore, the wrath of Governor Henry was especially directed. In the Legislature his name was proposed as one of the two United States Senators to be chosen under the new form of government, and he was defeated by Patrick Henry's opposition. At the same time the State was so partitioned into Congressional districts that Mr. Madison's local strength in Orange County was supposed to be buried under the adverse vote of the other counties attached to it. The district so arranged to defeat Madison also contained James Monroe, and he was nominated as the candidate of the opposition. An active canvass followed,

without any disturbance of personal friendship between the two candidates, and Monroe was defeated.

In conducting that campaign, however, he had
placed the party which nominated him, and Govern-
or Henry in particular, under obligations. The two
leaders of the Anti-Constitutional Party in the Convention who had first been elected United States
Senators under the Constitution they had opposed
were Richard Henry Lee and William Grayson. On
the death of the latter, James Monroe was chosen
to fill the vacancy, and took his seat in the year 1790.
His course until the close of his term, in 1794, was
that of an opponent of the part of the Washington
administration which was represented by the Secretary of the Treasury, Alexander Hamilton, but not
of the other part represented by the Secretary of
State, Thomas Jefferson.

CHAPTER VII.

Federalists and Republicans—Monroe Appointed Minister to France—A Remarkably Dramatic Reception—A Success and yet a Failure—Mr. Monroe Censured and Recalled — A Pamphlet War — More Praise than Blame.

CARE should be taken to do full justice to the patriotism of the guardians of State rights in the formation era of the republic. They believed in and purposed a strong and enduring Union of States. Jefferson wrote to Monroe from Paris, in 1786, in urging the construction of a navy with which to strike a blow at the Algerine pirates : " It will be said there is no money in the Treasury. There never will be money in the Treasury till the Confederacy shows its teeth. The States must see the rod ; perhaps it must be felt by one of them. I am persuaded all of them would be rejoiced to see every one obliged to furnish its contributions."

Monroe was the very man to accept the doctrine that the nation must show its teeth in order to be respected at home or abroad. He was afterward to join Madison in acting upon it, at Jefferson's advice, in the year 1812.

For the present and permanent good of the country all the best features of Hamilton's financial policy, so little understood by his opponents, were

MONROE BEFORE THE FRENCH ASSEMBLY.

triumphantly carried through Congress. There had been nothing whatever in Monroe's education or career to give him sound ideas concerning finance, and he was prepared to scrutinize closely, with a strong probability of opposing, any machine whatever invented by Alexander Hamilton. The political and personal breach between the latter and Jefferson grew wider from year to year, until both ceased to be members of Washington's Cabinet without ceasing to be the unquestioned leaders of their respective parties. Their friends in Congress looked to them as before for advice and direction, and, what is more remarkable, their personal relations to Washington himself and those of their adherents underwent no change whatever, for he represented the whole country, as they represented parties in it. James Monroe, for instance, yet carried in his shoulder the bullet Washington had seen him receive at Trenton ; and when Gouverneur Morris ceased to be Minister to France there was no reason in Washington's mind why Monroe should not be appointed in his place. There were many men in Congress who were quite willing to have some less resolute anti-Federalist sent to the Senate from Virginia ; his confirmation followed his nomination, and he was commissioned on May 28th, 1794.

There were especial reasons why he seemed a proper person to represent the United States in France. Like all other sensible Americans, he had condemned the remarkably erratic course of the French envoy Genet, but it was well understood that his warm sympathies from the first signs of the re-

volt against tyranny had been with the French people.   He belonged to what was known as the French
party in the current politics of his own country, and
was more likely to be received in a friendly manner
by the people to whom he was sent than any member
of the opposite faction could have been.   They
actually received him only too well.

   The two nations were at variance upon questions
of vast importance, and not the smallest of the difficulties in the way of a settlement was the shifting,
uncertain, irresponsible character of the something-
or-other which officiated as a government in France.
There was a continually recurring peril of needless,
fruitless, disastrous war between the two republics,
for the very demon of war had taken possession of
the French people.   The first and most important
duty of an American envoy would be to prevent an
open rupture, and steer the interests of his own
country safely through a period of mad excitement.
His second duty, hardly less important, was that
the first should be accomplished without sacrificing the dignity of the United States, and without
compromising their relations with other European
powers, enemies of France or of the existing state
of things in France.   Mr. Monroe had before him,
therefore, an utter impossibility, and went to certain failure.   He failed in such a manner, however,
that something like success resulted.   His career in
France is one of the curiosities of American diplomatic history.   He was censured, and his acts were
repudiated by his own Government ; he was covered
with abuse and ridicule both in Europe and Amer-

ica. At the same time he accomplished the main
object of his mission, and received praises for it almost as unstinted as were the criticisms. He came
out of the long controversy which followed a man
much better known, more admired by the masses of
the people, and decidedly more a leader of his own
party.

Mr. Monroe's course in France cannot be understood without taking into consideration his intense
sincerity. His heart and soul were genuinely with
the French crusade against the kings. He hated
monarchy so bitterly that he dreaded even the restricted power of an American President. He hated
aristocracy in its every development, including the
Federal Party. He hated England with a zeal
which contained memories of Valley Forge.

The instructions received by Mr. Monroe from
Mr. Randolph, the Secretary of State, were intended
to cover the entire field of perplexing duties assigned, but were also in their tone such as might
have been given to an envoy from whose declared
opinions and known impetuosity of character something like excessive zeal could fairly be anticipated.
The concluding passages were regarded by Mr.
Monroe as justifying him in the position he assumed
among the French people, but were not so construed
by Mr. Randolph. They were as follows :

"You go, sir, to France to strengthen our friendship with that
country ; and you are well acquainted with the line of freedom and
ease to which you may advance without betraying the dignity of the
United States. You will show our confidence in the French Republic
without betraying the most remote mark of undue complaisance.
You will let it be seen that, in case of war with any nation on

earth, we shall consider France as our first and natural ally.
You may dwell upon the sense we entertain of past services, and
for the more recent interposition in our behalf with the Dey of Al-
giers.   Among the great events with which the world is now teem-
ing, there may be an opening for France to become instrumental in
securing to us the free navigation of the Mississippi.   Spain may,
perhaps, negotiate a peace, separate from Great Britain, with
France.   If she does, the Mississippi may be acquired through this
channel, especially if you contrive to have our mediation in any
manner solicited."

Napoleon Bonaparte was one of the great events
unconsciously alluded to, and became, as ruler of
France, the channel through which, upon Mr. Mon-
roe's second visit to France, the navigation of the
Mississippi was more perfectly obtained than Mr.
Randolph then imagined possible.

Mr. Monroe was in Paris early in August, to
find Robespierre fallen and an undefined executive
authority lodged in the hands of a Committee of
Public Safety, while the real power was jealously
retained and exercised by the National Convention.
All Europe held aloof, not one power being represented diplomatically at Paris.   A Swiss envoy, it
is true, had been striving for several weeks to obtain
recognition, but he had failed.   Mr. Monroe tried
to reach the Committee of Public Safety, but they
held him at arm's length.   As he afterward wrote,
" I waited eight or ten days without progressing an
iota."

He was constitutionally opposed to long delays,
and determined upon a method of severing the
knot before him which was altogether characteristic.
Whoever sent him to the front of any fight was re-

sponsible for the known fact that he would certainly charge and lead the charge himself. He wrote a letter to the President of the National Convention setting forth the difficult position in which he found himself, "not knowing the competent department nor the forms established by law for my reception." Nobody else in all the French chaos knew any more than he did, but a decree was passed August 14th, 1794, that the Minister of the United States should "be introduced into the bosom of the Convention to-morrow, at 2 P.M."

The occasion was made one of especial ceremony. Mr. Monroe appeared before the Convention at the hour appointed, and the *procès verbal*, or journal of that body, for August 15th, 1794, contains the following record of the proceedings :

"The Citizen James Monroe, Minister Plenipotentiary of the United States of America near the French Republic, is admitted in the hall of the sitting of the National Convention. He takes his place in the midst of the representatives of the people, and remits to the President with his letters of credence a translation of a discourse addressed to the National Convention ; it is read by one of the secretaries. The expressions of fraternity, of union between the two peoples, and the interest which the people of the United States take in the success of the French Republic, are heard with the liveliest sensibility, and covered with applause.

"Reading is also given to the letters of credence of Citizen Monroe, as well as to those inscribed by the American Congress and President to the National Convention and to the Committee of Public Safety.

"In witness of the fraternity which unites the two peoples, the President gives the fraternal embrace to Citizen Monroe.

"Afterward, upon the proposition of many members, the National Convention passes with unanimity the following decree :

"*Article I.* The reading and verification being had of the powers of Citizen James Monroe, he is recognized and proclaimed Minister Plenipotentiary of the United States of America near the French Republic.

"*Article II.* The letters of credence of Citizen James Monroe, Minister Plenipotentiary of the United States of America, those which he has remitted on the part of the American Congress and President, addressed to the National Convention and to the Committee of Public Safety, the discourse of Citizen Monroe, the response of the President of the Convention, shall be printed in the two languages, French and American, and inserted in the bulletin of correspondence.

"*Article III.* The flags of the United States of America shall be joined to those of France, and displayed in the hall of the sittings of the Convention, in sign of the union and eternal fraternity of the two peoples."

Paris did not contain an American flag, and the French authorities were ignorant of its proper pattern ; but on application to Mr. Monroe he supplied them with one, presenting it to the Convention through Captain Barney, commander of the American frigate which had brought him to France.

His own address was overflowing with enthusiasm, and concluded with the following paragraph :

"In discharging the duties of the office which I am now called to execute I promise myself the highest satisfaction, because I well know that, while I pursue the dictates of my own heart in wishing the liberty and happiness of the French nation, and which I most sincerely do, I speak the sentiments of my own country ; and that, by doing everything in my power to preserve and perpetuate the harmony so happily subsisting between the two republics, I shall promote the interest of both. To this great object, therefore, all my efforts will be directed. If I can be so fortunate as to succeed in such manner as to merit the approbation of both republics, I shall deem it the happiest event of my life, and retire hereafter with a consolation which those who mean well and have served the cause of liberty alone can feel."

He meant well, and he had apparently won a diplomatic victory, for it looked as if he had swept away at one blow whatever had imperilled peace between France and America. The latter was regarded as the one friend of the French people among the nations of the earth, and at the funeral of Rousseau the American Minister and his suite were the only persons permitted to enter the Pantheon with the members of the National Convention.

It was but a burst of sentimental and fleeting enthusiasm, with little effect upon the future drift of national policy. The men who received the zealous envoy, and voted the decrees, and twined the flags, and refused even to recognize the American language as English, were jealously ready to take offence at any American action otherwise than in accord with their view of the predominant interests of the French Republic. At the same time, Mr. Monroe had permitted his view of the relations of the United States to Europe to be narrowed to the one idea of an alliance with France. His address to the Convention and all accounts of his other activities were read by Washington and his counsellors with a distinct perception of the possible or probable effect thereby produced upon the minds of the statesmen of England and of other powers, to whom the French Republic was a political wolf which they were about to hunt down and destroy.

The Secretary of State at once wrote in terms of severe censure, and Mr. Monroe defended himself with ability. He took hold of all the perplexing duties of his post with energy, and proved himself a capable and zealous public servant, but his lot had fallen among evil times. He was not at all in accord with the foreign policy of the administration which he represented. The American people as a whole, and particularly the political party he belonged to, were very nearly with him, but Mr. Randolph and the Federal Party were not. The new Secretary of State, Mr. Pickering, who finally succeeded Mr. Randolph, was a Federalist of the extreme faction, denounced by its opponents as " the British Party." Matters grew worse as time went on. The French Government, now the Directory, grew more and more arrogant and difficult to deal with. Early in 1796 they declared the alliance between the United States and France to have been terminated by the ratification of the treaty negotiated with Great Britain by Mr. Jay. They were about to send a special envoy to the United States to set forth their condemnation, and it seemed as if war was at hand. Mr. Monroe succeeded in preventing extreme measures, but even in doing so he incurred further censure. He was accused of yielding altogether too much, and of failing to maintain the honor and the rights of his country. Some bitter partisans even went to the absurd excess of charging him with accepting bribes from the French Directory. The corrupt junto misruling France were shamelessly ready to accept bribes themselves, but had no money to waste in buying Americans. Mr. Pickering's official denunciations ended in a peremptory recall of Mr. Monroe, dated August 22d, 1796, and Mr. C. C. Pinckney was appointed in his place. On the arrival of the latter Mr. Monroe duly presented him to the Directory, and they not only refused to recognize him, but forbade him to remain in Paris. He went, by permission, to the South of France, and a sort of civil coolness with which Mr. Monroe had for some time been treated changed suddenly into a demonstrative extreme of official politeness. It was one way of expressing ill-will toward the administration which had recalled him.

He wrote to his uncle, Mr. Jones, that he should not cross the Atlantic in winter, but would return home in the spring of 1797 ; but he did not fail to send in advance his own written view of the manner in which he had been treated. The opposite view can be best and most moderately summed up in the language of Washington himself, who wrote : " The truth is, Mr. Monroe was cajoled, flattered, and made to believe strange things. In return he did, or was disposed to do, whatever was pleasing to that nation, reluctantly urging the rights of his own."

Washington may have failed to give due consideration to the views held by Mr. Monroe before he went to France or had been at all flattered by Frenchmen, and neither he nor either of his Secretaries of State had had any personal dealings with the French political magnates of the day. Thomas Jefferson knew them better, and did not fail to sympathize with his very angry friend on his return.

A fierce war of newspapers and pamphlets followed, and Mr. Monroe published, in 1798, an octavo volume containing the entire diplomatic correspondence and a hundred pages of commentary by him-

self.   Hardly any review at all is required to ascertain the fact that his views of the situation had been
at open war with those of his superiors, and that
they were justified in recalling a man who did not
represent them.   It is equally true that he made
out a strong case for himself, and carried the majority of the American people heartily with him.

CHAPTER VIII.

James Monroe Governor of Virginia—The Negro Conspiracy—Jefferson President—The Louisiana Purchase—Monroe Sent to Paris—A Notable School-girl Friendship—Monroe Appointed Minister to England —Home again—Member of the Assembly and Governor of Virginia.

PARTISAN feeling and prejudice had a great share in forming the judgments passed upon Mr. Monroe's management of the French mission. It is also true that his defence of himself and his vigorous arraignment of the administration did much in the way of arousing and directing party feeling. Some of his friends urged him to re-enter Congress, where a seat was assured and a career ready ; but he had another field before him. The time was drawing near for the election of a governor of the State of Virginia, and he determined to strike for the higher prize. His success, by a vote in the Legislature of one hundred and one votes to sixty-six given for his Federalist competitor, John Breckinridge, was Virginia's verdict upon his career in France. It was also a very plain indication of the waning strength of the old Federal Party, which had done its uttermost to defeat the result. Concerning this its leading journal in that State, the Richmond *Federalist*, declared that the day of election was a day of mourning, and that Virginia's " misfortunes may be comprised in

one short sentence, ' Monroe-is elected governor.' "
He entered upon the duties of his office in 1799,
and discharged them during the three years following in a manner which received the entire approval
of his constituents, especially that large majority of
them which now belonged to his own party.

In the following year, 1800, came the great political struggle which resulted in the election of Thomas
Jefferson to be President of the United States.

The only other memorable excitement which
marked Mr. Monroe's term as governor was a dangerous conspiracy among the negro slaves. In great
secrecy they formed an oath-bound league, and a
plan they concocted for a rising and a war of ex-
termination against the whites ripened very nearly
to its hour of execution. It was defeated by the
fact that, while the great mass of the colored people
of Virginia had no taste for murder, the few exceptional savages who proposed bloodshed admitted one
conscientious man to their secrets. He was a slave,
but neither he nor the other slaves of Virginia planters had been so treated as to justify horrible vengeance. He broke away from his associates, and
gave timely warning. It was only just in time, but
Governor Monroe acted with characteristic vigor.
The militia were called out, the insurrection was
crushed at its beginning, and its most guilty members were punished.

The first two years of Jefferson's administration
were crowded with anxieties and vexations relating
to foreign affairs. Through them all a great transaction, vitally affecting the future of the United

States, grew to maturity through a series of startling changes in the relations of European powers to each other. On March 29th, 1801, a few weeks after Mr. Jefferson's inauguration, the American Minister to England, Mr. Rufus King, sent to the State Department a dispatch reporting a rumor in diplomatic circles that Spain had ceded Louisiana and Florida to France. The rumor was a truth, although for a long time the French Government denied it, concealing the treaty of transfer as a State secret until their plans were ripe. These included the creation of a French Empire in the Mississippi Valley, for Napoleon was First Consul and ruler of France, and he was capable of reading the future of America. So were many Americans, and particularly the man whom they had elected President. From the hour in which the Secretary of State, Mr. Madison, came to Mr. Jefferson with Mr. King's dispatch, the Louisiana question, in its new shape, outweighed all others. Mr. R. R. Livingston, Minister of the United States to France, received instructions accordingly, but did not at first understand their full meaning. It was a year before any trustworthy assurance was obtained that the mouth of the Mississippi was really French property. Through all the year 1801 a deepening interest in Louisiana was taken by the people of the United States, especially those of the South and West. It swelled to a fierce excitement in 1802, after Congress received in December, 1801, a message from the President announcing the ascertained fact that Louisiana had passed to Napoleon. Congress began to take action by appropriating two millions of dollars toward the purchase from France of the outlet of the great river, but this was only a beginning.

From the outset of Mr. Livingston's attempts to negotiate, he was hindered by two great obstacles. One was the fact that other causes of dispute between the two nations required adjustment. The other was the ambitious pride of Napoleon.

Little or no progress seemed to be made during 1802, but the American position was thus clearly stated in a letter from Mr. Jefferson to Mr. Livingston :

" There is on the globe one single spot, the possessor of which is our natural and habitual enemy. It is New Orleans, through which the produce of three eighths of our territory must pass to market ; and from its fertility it will erelong yield more than half of our whole produce, and contain more than half our inhabitants. France, placing herself in that door, assumes to us the attitude of defiance. Spain might have retained it quietly for years. Her pacific dispositions, her feeble state, would induce her to increase our facilities there, so that her possession of the place would hardly be felt by us ; and it would not, perhaps, be very long before some circumstance might arise which might make the cession of it to us the price of something of more worth to her."

The remainder of the letter was like a promise of a declaration of war in case of actual French occupation of New Orleans, but Napoleon went steadily on with his purpose. He prepared a colonizing expedition, comprising two ships of the line, several frigates, three thousand soldiers, and as many workingmen. Rumors of what was going on were continually in circulation in the United States, and the excitement nearly reached the boiling-point. The riflemen of Kentucky made unconcealed preparations to march down and meet any French troops they might find along the Lower Mississippi. In November, 1802, Mr. Livingston wrote to Mr. Madison that the French expedition would surely sail in a few days, and added : " Fortify Natchez, strengthen the upper posts." On December 19th, 1802, Lieutenant-General Victor, appointed governor of the new colony, was ordered by Napoleon to send one of his staff officers to notify the French Minister in Washington of the coming event.

The popular excitement in America was the precise power which Jefferson required to carry him through a course of executive action for which the Constitution seemed to give no warrant, and for which he had no adequate Congressional authority. He watched it with unsurpassed sagacity until it swept in the Federal Party, and his old enemies began to make political capital of his apparent inaction. Then, on January 10th, 1803, he wrote to James Monroe :

" I have but a moment—I shall to-morrow nominate you to the Senate for an extraordinary mission to France.—Pray work night and day to arrange your affairs for a temporary absence, perhaps for a long one."

Monroe had served his time as Governor of Virginia, and had nothing to keep him there. This summons was something like an order to lead a sudden attack, and it was obeyed with enthusiasm. He was the one American whose nomination would

carry the deepest meaning to the minds of his own
countrymen, owing to the idea they held of his relations to the French people.   Napoleon was likely
to give an especially cordial reception to so pronounced a friend of France.   One little memory
of the Monroe family, of no political bearing, is
nevertheless worth mentioning by way of illustration.
Mrs. Monroe accompanied her husband during his
residence in France as minister, and she was known
in French society as "*la belle Americaine.*"   Her
little daughter Eliza, who afterward married Judge
George Hay, of Virginia, went to a school in Paris
kept by the celebrated Madame Campan.   Here she
formed an intimate friendship with another little
girl named Hortense Beauharnais, and it lasted after
the mother of Hortense became the Empress Jo-
sephine and she herself the Queen of Holland.   A
daughter of Mrs. Eliza Monroe Hay in due time
was named Hortensia, and received as presents from
the queen after whom she was named oil-portraits
of herself and of her brother Eugene and of Madame
Campan.   All of this, except the friendship of the
two children, was yet to come ; but unquestionably
Mr. Monroe's known French affiliations added much
to the fitness and effect of his selection as a special
envoy to that country at a critical juncture.

His affairs at home were quickly arranged, and
within two months Mr. Monroe had crossed the
ocean, landed in France, and was riding post-haste
to Paris.   There had been a great change in European affairs, however, since his nomination as envoy.   Napoleon himself had made all things ready

for a sale of Louisiana to the United States, for he had declared war with England, and had countermanded the sailing of General Victor and his expedition. He had made up his own mind to surrender forever his idea of a French empire in America. Just before Mr. Monroe's arrival he said to one of his ministers :

"Irresolution and deliberation are no longer in reason. I renounce Louisiana. It is not only New Orleans that I will cede—it is the whole colony, without any reservation. I renounce it with the greatest regret. To attempt obstinately to retain it would be folly. I direct you to negotiate this affair with the envoys of the United States. Do not even await the arrival of Mr. Monroe ; have an interview this very day with Mr. Livingston. But I require a great deal of money for this [English] war, and I would not like to commence it with new contributions. If I should regulate my terms according to the value of those vast regions to the United States, the indemnity would have no limits. I will be moderate, in consideration of the necessity in which I am of making a sale ; but keep this to yourself. I want fifty millions of francs, and for less than that sum I will not treat ; I would rather make a desperate attempt to keep those fine countries. To-morrow you shall have your full powers."

The interview with Mr. Livingston was had in pursuance of Napoleon's orders, and he was asked for a hundred millions of francs, with the important addition that the United States should assume the payment of large claims held by Americans against France. After some chaffering the hundred millions came down to sixty millions, and that sum seemed to Mr. Livingston equally impossible. He also was troubled with an idea that his own Government would be satisfied with a purchase of New Orleans and Florida. He had been in France two years, and did not appreciate the change in the will of the American people, or the intense determination of the President. Mr. Monroe arrived two days later, thoroughly aware of and perfectly expressing both. There was no undue haste, but after eighteen days of propositions and counter-propositions the bargain was completed at sixty millions of francs for Louisiana, twenty millions more being added for the payment of the claims. Napoleon was satisfied, in spite of his comprehension of the value of the property he was selling. He needed the money very much ; he had rescued Louisiana from any danger of its capture by Great Britain, and, as he said, he had "given to England a maritime rival which will sooner or later humble all her pride."

The plenipotentiaries signed the first draft of the treaty on May 2d, 1803, and a ratified copy was forwarded to Mr. Madison on the 13th.

The credentials of Mr. Monroe included England and Spain as well as France. The first part of his mission had been admirably prepared for him before his arrival, and was now triumphantly accomplished. His next errand was to London, and on June 24th he was presented to the First Consul, for the purpose of taking leave, explaining that the American Minister to England had resigned, and that orders from President Jefferson required him to proceed at once. He declared the friendly feeling of the United States for France, and was somewhat frankly informed by Napoleon that " the cession he had made was not so much on account of the price given as from motives of policy, and that he wished for friendship between the republics.''

Spain still retained ownership of Florida, and there was much dispute and uncertainty as to the precise boundary-line between her land and that which France had now sold to the United States. Mr. Monroe had expected to go to Madrid and open negotiations, but found that Mr. Livingston had already made a beginning. It was afterward discovered that Congress, in making the Louisiana appropriation, had exhausted its willingness to spend money upon additional territory. The remaining negotiations with Spain related mainly to the boundary-line, and Mr. Monroe had no occasion to go to Madrid.

On arriving in London, and continuously afterward, he found that failure had been as completely laid out for him here as success had been in Paris. Great Britain claimed excessive rights of blockade in her wars with other nations, from the enforced exercise of which great losses and hardships had been inflicted upon American merchants and seamen. She claimed the right of her ships of war to stop all American vessels, private or national, upon the high seas ; to search them for possible British sailors on board ; to make her naval officers judges of any man's birthplace, disregarding any subsequent naturalization under American laws, with authority to impress him as a marine slave on board her own vessels. Her absolute determination not to yield either of these claims was the real cause of Mr. Monroe's failure then and of the War of 1812

afterward. Soon after he reached London he received from home a draft of a proposed treaty between the United States and England, containing
provisions for the protection of American ships and
seamen. It was very much such a treaty as England refused to make even at the end of the War of
1812, and neither Mr. Monroe nor any other man
living could have procured its signature in 1804–06.
He worked hard, was in poor health, had suffered
pecuniary losses, and became low-spirited. He
wrote to his uncle, Judge Jones, that he could live
better in Richmond on two thousand dollars a year
than in London on two thousand pounds. His purpose was to return home and practice law, bringing
a library with him. He also had some ambition
connected with the government of Louisiana. It
was a blue time for an American Minister to Great
Britain. Two years dragged by with changes in
British administrations, but with none in England's
policy toward her former colonies. On May 17th,
1806, a new commission was issued to James Monroe and William Pinkney jointly, giving increased
authority, but not adding an ounce of power for
making such a treaty as was wished for. Month
after month of delay and vexation followed, until
the year was gone, and a treaty was made at last,
subject to ratification by the United States, but containing no provision against impressment and no
indemnity for past injuries. British statesmen then
and afterward roundly declared it a good enough
treaty, and there is no doubt but that it offered as
much as they were then ready to yield. They were

surprised at the impertinence of so weak a power as the United States in presuming to demand equal rights with England upon the sea. Mr. Monroe and Mr. Pinkney had done their best, but President Jefferson quietly took the responsibility of rejecting the treaty, without reference to the Senate. Fresh instructions were sent out and fresh negotiations were undertaken, rendered more difficult from time, to time by additional British aggressions, notably the outrageous attack of the British frigate Leopard upon the American frigate Chesapeake, June 23d, 1807. All this baffling, harassing, fruitless diplomacy was precisely the kind of work calculated to wear out the patience of such a man as James Monroe. He gave it up at the end of that year, and early in 1808 he was once more in the United States, defending himself to the State Department and in the public press against criticisms upon the management of his mission. Once more, also, it was generally well understood by the people that the fault had been that of Great Britain and not that of the envoy she had so completely tired out. His own party thought so well of him that he narrowly missed becoming its nominee for President of the United States in that very year, 1808. Any temporary coolness between him and either Jefferson or the Secretary of State, his old friend Madison, soon disappeared. The latter was nominated and elected, and was inaugurated on March 4th, 1809, while Monroe took up law practice for a time. His neighbors sent him to the Assembly in 1810, and the State of Virginia made him its governor again in

1811.   He accepted the honor, but a very different and much wider field of action had been steadily getting ready for him, and he now had only a few short months to wait for it.

CHAPTER IX.

Monroe Appointed Secretary of State—The War of 1812—New Government Machinery—War Lessons —The City of Washington Captured by British Raiders—The Treaty of Peace—Battle of New Orleans.

IN the year 1811 the great majority of European public men had but a faint belief in the United States as a permanent member of the family of nations. They hardly knew what was to become of her, but would not have been at all surprised any day to hear that the experimental republic had disappeared altogether. American politicians rather than the American people had also clear perceptions of their country's naval, military, financial, and commercial weakness. Few of them understood, however, that this weakness was largely occasioned by lack of what is called character when individuals are spoken of. The masses of the people felt this rather than reasoned, and a party in favor of a war with England at any hazard or cost was now growing rapidly. Of this party not even Henry Clay in Congress was so distinct a personal representative and index as was Governor James Monroe, of Virginia. President Madison was not ready for war nor sure of a sufficient popular support in the spring and summer of 1811, but when, on November 25th, he appointed

Mr. Monroe Secretary of State in place of Robert Smith, resigned, he gave all men a clear indication of what was coming.

There was no precipitation even after that, and six months more were consumed in diplomatic efforts to induce England to concede what America considered only a moderate measure of justice. It is true that the American statesmen who opposed the war were able to present a powerful array of arguments, and were fully justified in their opposition. What they desired was peace, and they believed that it could be obtained, and with it prosperity, without paying blood or money for it. Their fundamental error was in believing that any real peace with England existed. They failed to see that, under a thin disguise of peace, a war destructive of American commerce, rights, and national self-respect had been going on for years.

When war was formally declared on June 18th, 1812, the task of drawing up the act of declaration fell to William Pinkney, late Minister to England, now a member of Madison's Cabinet. It was communicated to the British ministry by James Monroe, Secretary of State.

One of the first discoveries made by the United States soon after the beginning of hostilities was that its people and their representatives in Congress were unmilitary. They knew nothing about war. There was no properly organized War Department. The Continental Army had disbanded thirty years before, and the living generation of able-bodied men, brave enough individually, had never seen a gun fired, with the exception of a few small squads of men who had served against the Indians. Very valuable lessons were rapidly learned when half-drilled troops, whose officers for the greater part were destitute of military training, came into collision with British veterans. Disasters came over which the nation boiled with rage, while it looked around for somebody upon whom it could lay the blame. The commanding officer of each unsuccess- ful detachment was sure to receive his full share of censure, and the leader of every partial success was awarded at least his full due of praise. Many men poured out unstinted condemnation upon President Madison as the author and mismanager of the war, and the Anti-War Party believed itself to be grow- ing stronger, but it was not. Only the Anti-Defeat Party increased in numbers, and the course of events at sea gave it much encouragement.

The jealousy of England had been aroused by the enterprise of American merchants, the energy and skill of American sailors, and the genius of Ameri- can shipbuilders for designing the best models and launching the swiftest vessels afloat. Ships of war designed and built and manned and handled by the same men, provided, as one sailor remarked, "with not so many guns, but with more ruin in each gun," now met the old-fashioned British cruisers with marked success. Swift-sailing merchantmen turned readily into dangerous privateers, and it was dis- covered abroad that war with the United States was a very disagreeable affair, as soon as the arbitrary seizures of ships ceased to be all on one side. Up

to this time they had been so, to the value of many
millions of dollars ; but the wickedness and waste of
piracies committed by a strong nation had not before appeared so clearly.

Mr. Monroe's military experience had been that
of a soldier, not of a commander. He knew little or
nothing of the great science of war, but he was a
man of energy and executive ability, and he saw
that the defeats of the first campaigns began at
Washington. He and others severely criticised the
management of army affairs by Dr. Eustis, the Secretary of War, and that gentleman resigned ; but the
defective system and the absence of trained staff
officers did not resign with him. Mr. Monroe acted
as Secretary of War, *ad interim*, until the appointment of General Armstrong, but effected no changes,
and the new Secretary of War fell heir to the old
disorder of things, including the criticisms. The
President, the Secretary of State, and all the other
chiefs of the Republican Party sought for remedies,
and did not quite understand the nature of the defects they were sorrowfully finding. The Republican was also the Anti-Federal Party, opposed to
centralization ; but it was now discovered that a
leading idea of Federalism—that of a strong, well-
organized, efficient, central national Government,
with wide-reaching authority and good machinery—
must be rescued from the political wreck which was
disappearing, and be adopted by the great party of
the future. Many men soon saw that the Republican
Party was becoming sufficiently Federal for the uses
of the country. That it did so was one of the good

results obtained through the varied experiences of the War of 1812.

A curious illustration of the yet undefined, unsettled condition of the national governmental machinery is to be found in the fact that General Armstrong, who believed himself to have military ability, believed also that he could at the same time act as Secretary of War and as general-in-chief, commanding the forces in the field. When he undertook to do so Mr. Monroe rightly took action against it, and wrote to Mr. Madison a long letter, setting forth the views which have ever since governed the distribution of the duties involved. He declared himself "convinced that the duties of Secretary of War and military commander were not only incompatible under our Government, but that they could not be exercised by the same person. The Secretary of War could not perform, in his character as Secretary, the duties of general of the army."

In the same letter, dated July 25th, 1813, his own state of mind with reference to the course of events on land appears very plainly. He wrote :

"I cannot close these remarks without adding something in relation to myself. Stimulated by a deep sense of the misfortunes of our country, as well as its disgrace by the surrender of Hull, the misconduct of Van Rensselaer and Smyth, and by the total want of character in the Northern campaign, and dreading its effects on your own administration, on the Republican Party and cause, I have repeatedly offered my services in a military station, not that I wished to take it by preference to my present one, which to all others I prefer, but from a dread of the consequences above mentioned. I was willing to take the Department of War permanently, if, in leaving my present station, I thought I might be

more useful there than in a military command.   I thought otherwise."

He had much more to say, very patriotically, but
Mr. Madison evidently agreed with him that his post
of greatest usefulness was in the State Department.
Six months later he wrote to the President another
letter concerning General Armstrong, and used the
following earnest language :

> "It is painful to me to make this communication to you, nor
> should I do it if I did not most conscientiously believe that this
> man, if continued in office, will ruin not you and the administra-
> tion only, but the whole Republican Party and cause.   He has al-
> ready gone far to do it, and it is my opinion, if he is not promptly
> removed, he will soon accomplish it."

Neither the country nor the party nor the Madison administration was going to ruin, but precisely
one year from that day a detachment of British
troops occupied the city of Washington, after brush-
ing aside a mob of hastily gathered Americans
at Bladensburg, and after burning the President's
house, the Capitol, and other public buildings.   A
full week of confusion and bad management preceded the arrival of the British and illustrated the
perpetual unreadiness which had caused nearly every
disgrace of the war, including the one important
disaster at sea, the loss of the Chesapeake.   Even
the accounts afterward written are confused and
contradictory, but Mr. Monroe's head was clear and
his conduct steady from first to last.   To prevent
any misunderstanding, it should be added that he
was steadily angry.   He went to Benedict, a place
on the Patuxent, near enough to the shore of

Chesapeake Bay to observe the landing and subsequent movements of the British force. This consisted of nearly four thousand soldiers under General Ross, and some sailors and marines under Admiral Cockburn. Commodore Barney, in command of some American ships which had retreated up the bay, came on shore also, and a few regular soldiers, with the marines and sailors he landed, formed the nucleus of the force beaten at Bladensburg.

Mr. Monroe was attended by a small mounted escort, and continued to watch the movements of the invaders. During ten successive days and nights he did not undress himself, and was on horseback most of the time. On the 22d he sent a message to Mr. Madison which contained the following ominous warning : "You had better make all preparations to leave." There was a terrible panic and flight of the people of Washington, while the officials were removing papers and documents, and the British drew hourly nearer. The latter were but moderately delayed by the fighting at Bladensburg, and were in Washington on the 24th. Before night the public buildings were all on fire.

The demoralized militia retreated through Washington and Georgetown from the Bladensburg disgrace, and were rallied by Colonel Winder at Montgomery Court-House. They were disposed to believe that more of them should have been on hand, better supported and better handled, and their feeling against the Secretary of War was so bitter that he might have suffered personal harm had he gone among them. Mr. Monroe agreed with them entirely as to the person upon whom blame should fall.   Two days later, August 27th, when Mr. Madison returned to the city, the duties of the War Office were added to those of the State Department, and Mr. Monroe continued to act as Secretary of War, *ad interim*, until March 2d, 1815, after the war had ended.

The raid upon the city of Washington was no sudden affair, nor any unauthorized freak of an erratic military commander.   It had been planned in English official circles, and Albert Gallatin, then in London, had sent to Mr. Madison written warning two months before the fleet under Admiral Cockburn sailed into the Chesapeake.   All things should have been ready for the defence of the capital.

Another expedition on a larger scale for the seizure and occupation of the mouth of the Mississippi was also planned by the British Ministry, and its purpose was known in America.

Both operations are to be studied with reference to the fact that British and American plenipotentiaries were at Ghent all the while discussing terms of peace between the two countries.   No agreement was reached until December 24th, 1814, three months after the blow at Washington, but during that time the necessary preparations for meeting the British at New Orleans were in different hands from those which had supinely left the American capital defenceless.

Mr. Monroe's measures for the further protection of Washington and Baltimore were promptly and effectively made.   The entire administration of army matters underwent a change, and he himself recovered his lost good spirits in his work. He did his uttermost to strengthen the hands of General Jackson, strenuously urging the governors of the States nearest the scene of the coming conflict to do the same. He wrote to them : " Hasten your militia to New Orleans ; do not wait for this Government to arm them ; put all the arms you can find into their hands ; let every man bring his rifle with him ; we shall see you paid." Nearly every man in the Southwest owned a rifle and knew how to use it. The sharpshooters rallied fast, and General Jackson gained his victory. The Senate of the United States confirmed the treaty, and it is now mere matter of speculation whether or not any new complication would have arisen if Jackson had lost the day.

CHAPTER X.

*James Monroe Elected President of the United States
—The Era of Good Feeling—A Grand Northern
Tour—Purchase of Florida—A Southern Tour—
The Missouri Compromise.*

THE people of the United States had good reason
for their great joy over the peace of Ghent. It did
not in terms relinquish the asserted British right of
search, but the impression upon the public mind
was general and entirely correct that the arrogant
exercise of that right had been abandoned. The
American flag carried more meaning with it and
conferred better security than ever before. The
peace had come to stay.

Whatever had been gained by or through the war
had been dearly paid for. One thousand six hundred and eighty-three vessels of all sorts, carrying
over eighteen thousand sailors, were reported lost.
Seaports had been blockaded ; coasts and bays had
been infested and harassed by the enemy's cruisers ;
the Western and Northern frontiers had been almost
continually disturbed ; while the financial burdens
of the war had pressed heavily. Many industries
had suffered, but there were also many which had
been fostered or even created by the necessity of
manufacturing in America articles which could no
longer be imported.

Glad as were all men that the war was over, there was very little disposition to condemn the party or the statesmen who had been compelled to assume its responsibilities. To Mr. Monroe, in particular, an increased popularity came as a sort of reflection from the successes of the army during his brief term as Secretary of War. His dispatches to General Jackson and the governors were very good political reading during the remainder of the year 1815, and when, in 1816, a caucus of his party was called to select a candidate for President, no stronger name could be suggested, and a moderate exertion of Thomas Jefferson's influence gave him a unanimous nomination. In the canvass which followed skilful use was made by opponents of every fact of his political record, but a great many people liked him for the very characteristics condemned by others.

In the Electoral College he received one hundred and eighty-three votes against thirty-four given to the Federalist candidate, Rufus King. Daniel D. Tompkins, of New York, was elected Vice-President.

The oath of office was taken on March 4th, 1817, but long before that day arrived a pleasant change had come over the minds of the long-harassed and weary-hearted nation. The effects of returning prosperity showed themselves in the heartiness of manner with which old-time political foes met each other at the brilliant drawing-rooms given at the White House by Mrs. Dolly Madison. It was the dawn of what was afterward happily termed "the era of good feeling."

The change had other causes and effects. Old parties and party leaders were passing away, and the masses were taking a long political vacation before again dividing upon new issues.

Jefferson was at Monticello, Madison at Montpellier, John Adams at Quincy, and the field was open to a new generation, among whom Clay, Webster, Calhoun, and others had already risen to prominence.

Mr. Monroe appointed John C. Calhoun, Secretary of War ; W. H. Crawford, Secretary of the Treasury ; William Wirt, Attorney-General ; R. J. Meigs, Postmaster-General, and left Mr. Madison's Secretary of the Navy, Benjamin W. Crowninshield, in office.

The most important post of all, with reference not only to foreign affairs but to American politics, was that of Secretary of State. When Mr. Monroe appointed John Quincy Adams it was, to the minds of many men, nearly equivalent to naming him as next in succession to the Presidency. He was then Minister to England, and the news of his nomination and confirmation did not reach him until April 16th. It was September before he entered upon the duties of his office, and it was not long before Mr. Monroe discovered that the Federal doctrine of a strong Executive had come in with him, inherited from sturdy old John Adams.

All things looked very sunny in the spring of 1817. Congress had adjourned, and Mr. Monroe had no sooner put the several Departments in working order than he set out in May upon a tour of inspection of the Northern States, with special reference

to the defences of the Canada frontier. He left the
members of his Cabinet behind him at their work,
and took with him General Joseph G. Swift, Chief
Engineer of the Army. The tour became a series
of ovations. From city to city along the Atlantic
coast as far north as Portland, Maine, the people
were glad to see their President. By far the greater
number of them had never before looked upon the
face of one. From Portland the route turned westward, across New England and through New York,
to Detroit, Michigan, then a Western frontier village
with an unpleasant war memory. The return to
Washington was by way of Ohio and Pennsylvania.
At every place and point the people knew that the
President was coming and made ready for him, re-
hearsing all the good things they had ever heard of
him, from the Harlem fight to the day of his election. The record of the tour made an octavo volume when it was printed, and Mr. Monroe was the
most popular man the country had possessed since
the death of George Washington. The journey also
had a very beneficial effect upon his health, which
had suffered somewhat from prolonged confinement
in the discharge of official duties.

Mr. Monroe reached the capital in November,
1817, to find one of the most important political
events of his Presidential career very nearly ready.
It grew out of the fact that Spain still owned
Florida, and that the Spanish governors had little
power and even less disposition to hold in check the
Seminole Indians. The savages made raids across
the Georgia border, and then retired to Spanish ter-

ritory as to a secure place of refuge. The President ordered General Jackson to Georgia, with instructions to put an end to the inroads of the Seminoles. The entire story of the manner in which he carried out his instructions belongs to General Jackson's biography, but the general gave his views in writing January 8th, 1818, to Mr. Monroe before he went. He took command of the Georgia militia and other troops, and a full report of his subsequent proceedings did not reach the President until July. Then it was known that he had chased the Seminoles back into Florida, followed them across the line, stormed the Spanish post of Pensacola, captured the Barrancas, and approved of the execution of two Englishmen named Ambrister and Arbuthnot, accused of inciting the Indians against the Georgia white people. This latter act would have made serious trouble with Great Britain at any date prior to 1812, but was more easily prevented from resulting badly in 1818. The main difficulty was likely to be with Spain, and it appeared that General Jackson, by exceeding his instructions, had placed his country in peril of a foreign war, and at the same time had put the administration into the serious dilemma of having begun that war without Congressional sanction.

The President could only moderately disapprove of General Jackson's course, for it was very much what he would have taken if he himself had been following the Seminoles. It was also necessary, in the opinion of every member of the Cabinet but one, to disavow to Spain diplomatically and to the coun-

try generally a series of acts so dangerously energetic. It was supposed that an alarmed nation and
a jealous Congress would condemn the general, but
the two best and shrewdest politicians in the land
knew better. John Quincy Adams, in the Cabinet,
vigorously defended Jackson, though compelled to
yield a silent assent to the decision of his colleagues,
and when he afterward wrote and printed his views,
Jefferson at Monticello declared his wish that the
argument of Mr. Adams might be translated into
French and sent to every court in Europe as the
voice of America. When Congress came together a
majority there also sustained the general, and the
whole affair was thrown forward into future political
discussions.

There was no real danger of war with Spain, and
the Seminoles may have aided Mr. Monroe in the
negotiation he was carrying on for the purchase of
the entire country containing them. The treaty
was concluded on February 22d, 1819, and Florida
became part of the United States. It was afterward
sourly said by political opponents that the Republican Party had purchased the Seminole War.

After the adjournment of Congress in the spring
of 1819, the President undertook another tour of
observation. This time he travelled southward to
Augusta, Georgia ; thence westward through what
was then the Cherokee Country as far as Nashville,
Tennessee, and north through Kentucky to the
Ohio River at Louisville.

During the winter session of Congress of 1818–19,
the political question which for forty years following

was to overshadow all others first came in definite shape before Congress. Missouri applied for admission into the Union as a State, and failed temporarily for the reason declared by a vote of the House of Representatives, that the clause in its Constitution permitting slavery came in conflict with the great Ordinance of 1789. The great debates which resulted in the Missouri Compromise did not begin until Congress came together again for the winter session of 1819-20. The struggle was severe. In the Senate, where each State had two votes, the majority was in favor of admitting Missouri with slavery. In the House, representing population, the majority was against admission, but grew weaker until March 1st, 1820, when committees of both Houses agreed upon a compromise. Missouri was to be a slave State, but slavery was not to exist north of latitude thirty-six degrees, thirty minutes. This result was reached by the votes of anti-slavery men, who were convinced that disunion and civil war would follow rejection, and it was regarded as a settlement forever, taking the slavery question out of current politics. Mr. Monroe looked at the slave question as one purely of the local or individual rights of white men under the Constitution. He wrote prior to the settlement: "As to the part which I may act in all circumstances in which I may be placed I have not made up my mind, nor shall I until the period arrives when it will be my duty to act, and then I shall weigh well the injunctions of the Constitution, which, when clear and distinct to my mind, will be conclusive with me. The next consideration will be a fixed and an unalterable attachment to the Union.''

He was, therefore, to be recorded as favoring the Missouri Compromise, in common with all but a very small number of his fellow-citizens North and South.

CHAPTER XI.

Mr. Monroe's Second Election as President—A New Political Era—The Monroe Doctrine—Visit of Lafayette—John Quincy Adams Elected President.

IN the year 1820 the great sea of American politics was without a perceptible tide. Old questions had ebbed away, and the Presidential election took place at slack water. Washington's second unanimous election had been the people's eager, half-frightened request for the continued services of the one man who was able, in their opinion, to conduct national affairs successfully under existing difficulties. The all but unanimous second election of James Monroe was nothing of the kind. It was simply a popular record of the fact that there was no known reason why he should not be accorded the compliment of another term. Not to have given it to him would have been a gross national impropriety. In the Electoral College he received two hundred and thirty-one votes, one solitary elector recording his preference for John Quincy Adams. Mr. Tompkins was re-elected Vice-President. The admission of Missouri as a State had not yet been perfected, but the counting of her three votes was permitted as a small matter not affecting the result.

With the second inauguration of Mr. Monroe the " era of good feeling" definitely ended, and with it went the cohesiveness of the great national party which had elected him. Before the end of his second term new parties had arisen, each claiming to be the heir of that old Republican Party which was passing away as completely as had its Federal predecessor.

In the political questions which agitated Congress and the country, that of internal improvements received, perhaps, most attention from the President. . He believed in a system by which improvements of national rank and importance might be undertaken by the nation, leaving all lesser works to States, corporations, and individuals, and he favored an amendment to the Constitution giving Congress power, which he believed it did not already possess, to spend the national money upon such undertakings as the public good might seem to require.

The slavery question had not been entirely wiped away by the admission of Missouri. Questions relating to the National Bank, the tariff, the bankrupt law, and other great subjects were before Congress, and were under discussion by the press and people. All were in the hands of a new generation of statesmen upon whom Mr. Monroe could exercise but moderate influence. Some of them were intellectually stronger men than he, and there were other reasons for his lack of political control. He belonged now to the history of his country and to an era which was passing away, while they were of the present and the future. He was not a philosophical thinker, a scientific statesman like Thomas Jefferson or James Madison. To the very last he looked to them, especially to the former, for counsel and direction, frankly conscious that he needed it.   He was never at any time an originator or leader of public thought or feeling or action.   He sometimes appeared to be so, because he was so perfect an index and so energetic an expression of the great national ideas and impulses which he accepted as his own.   He was not in the least degree a demagogue, for he was thoroughly sincere, and when he went forward with apparent rashness and calm, wise men said he had blundered, they were apt to find that a majority of the nation had blundered with him.

No better illustration could be given of Mr. Monroe's place in American political history than the fact that his name has become inseparably attached to what is called "the Monroe doctrine." So much of that doctrine as was formulated by Mr. Monroe is to be found in his annual message to Congress, December 2d, 1823.

He wrote :

"At the proposal of the Russian imperial government, made through the minister of the emperor residing here, a full power and instructions have been transmitted to the Minister of the United States at St. Petersburg to arrange, by amicable negotiation, the respective rights and interests of the two nations on the north-west coast of this continent.   A similar proposal has been made by his Imperial Majesty to the Government of Great Britain, which has likewise been acceded to.   The Government of the United States has been desirous, by this friendly proceeding, of manifesting the great value which they have invariably attached to the friendship of the emperor, and their solicitude to cultivate the best understanding with his Government.   In the discussions to which this interest has given rise, and in the arrangements by which they may terminate, the occasion has been judged proper for asserting, as a principle in which the rights and interests of the United States are involved, that the American continents, by the free and independent condition which they have assumed and maintain, are henceforth not to be considered as subjects for future colonization by any European powers."

After stating the policy of the United States, of non-interference in European affairs, the message proceeds :

"With the movements on this hemisphere we are, of necessity, more immediately connected, and by causes which must be obvious to all enlightened and impartial observers. The political system of the allied powers is essentially different in this respect from that of America. This difference proceeds from that which exists in their respective governments. . . . We owe it, therefore, to candor and to the amicable relations existing between the United States and those powers to declare that we should consider any attempt on their part to extend their system to any portion of this hemisphere as dangerous to our peace and safety. With the existing colonies or dependencies of any European power we have not interfered, and shall not interfere. But with the governments [American] who have declared their independence and maintained it, and whose independence we have, on great considerations and on just principles, acknowledged, we could not view any interposition for the purpose of oppressing them, or controlling in any other manner their destiny, by any European power, in any other light than as the manifestation of an unfriendly disposition toward the United States. . . . It is impossible that the allied powers should extend their political system to any portion of either [American] continent without endangering our peace and happiness ; nor can any one believe that our southern brethren [republics], if left to themselves, would adopt it of their own accord. It is equally impossible, therefore, that we should behold such interposition in any form with indifference."

Before ending this important message to Congress the President was well aware that his Cabinet was a unit in its approval. The idea that he had invented

anything or was announcing for the first time a new
basis for American diplomacy did not enter his
mind. American jealousy of European interference
attained full strength through the processes which
led to the war of independence. It was expressed
in a further development in Washington's advice
against entangling alliances with European powers. It was set forth more clearly than by Monroe
when Jefferson told Napoleon that France, assuming the ownership of New Orleans, would become " the natural enemy of the United States,"
compelling the latter to a war and an alliance with
England. It had been the soul of Alexander Hamilton's great dream of leading an army to help the
South American rebels against Spain. It had purchased Louisiana and Florida. It had grown with
the growth of American national life and thought,
and it was as a man fully in accord with the heart
and brain of the American people that James Monroe put it upon paper for them as a declaration from
their President to their Congress. How completely
they were with him was to be afterward declared by
a long succession of orators, writers, and statesmen.

One of the pleasantest features of the second term
of Mr. Monroe was the visit paid by Lafayette to
the United States, as the guest of the nation, on
invitation by Congress. The personal relations between the marquis and the President had been of
the most friendly nature since the days when they
were enthusiastic young soldiers of the Continental
Army. When Monroe was Minister of the United
States to France and Lafayette a prisoner at Ol-

mutz, the former made efforts for his friend's release, and the money sent to the prisoner by Washington had passed through Monroe's willing hands.
They now met again on the old, kindly, and familiar
basis, and after Lafayette's return to France many
letters passed between them.

In the year 1824 the country took up the business
of selecting a successor to President Monroe, and
it was at once discovered that the great Republican
Party, organized and for so long a time directed by
Thomas Jefferson, had broken up. When the votes
of the Electoral College were counted, the total
number being two hundred and sixty-one, John
C. Calhoun received one hundred and eighty votes for
Vice-President and was elected, but the votes for
President were divided as follows : Andrew Jackson, ninety-nine ; John Quincy Adams, eighty-four ;
William H. Crawford, forty-one, and Henry Clay,
thirty-seven. This result threw the decision into
the House of Representatives, where Henry Clay,
lowest on the list of candidates, ceased to be a candidate, but became master of the situation. The
condition of Mr. Crawford's health removed him
from the field. Mr. Clay was already a pronounced
opponent of General Jackson, and Mr. Adams was
elected.

CHAPTER XII.

*Retirement of Mr. Monroe—Planter Life at Oak Hill
—Regent of the University of Virginia—Last Days
and Occupations—The End.*

THE hospitalities of the White House were well
maintained by Mr. and Mrs. Monroe, with an effect
upon their private fortunes much like that experienced by Jefferson and Madison. A lady, Mrs.
Tuley, of Virginia, who attended the New Year's
Day reception at the White House, 1825, described
Mrs. Monroe as "a regal-looking lady." Mrs.
Hortensia Hay and Mrs. Maria Gouverneur, her
daughters, were with her on that occasion. Both
were attractive, dignified, and accomplished.

Soon after the inauguration of his successor Mr.
Monroe retired to his country-seat, Oak Hill, in
Loudoun County, Virginia. It became, like Monticello and Montpellier, although to a lesser degree,
a centre of social and political pilgrimages. The
financial affairs of its owner were seriously embarrassed from the first, and he labored in vain to obtain justice from the country he had served so long
and so well, at heavy pecuniary cost and loss. His
old friend Lafayette, now once more prosperous,
sent an offer of assistance with a delicacy and gen-
erosity which did him honor. A little was done at
last by Congress, but not enough, and the day
came when Oak Hill was advertised for sale.

The post of Regent of the University of Virginia was accepted by Mr. Monroe as not inconsistent with his view of the entire retirement from public life becoming an ex-President. Associated with him in the discharge of his duties as regent, as in so many long years of patriotic toil, were Jefferson and Madison.

When the State of Virginia called a convention for the revision of her Constitution, Mr. Monroe consented to become a member. He took an active interest in the affairs of his own neighborhood, discharging the duties of a local magistrate. He had a large correspondence to attend to, and he watched with deep interest the course of public events, but his mind dwelt mostly upon the events of the great past in which he had been an actor. He had always been sensitive to criticisms upon his official conduct, and was little less so now, when hardly any person living required from him any defence or explanation. He wrote much, but only part of the work he performed has been preserved. The most important part, never finished or printed, is thus described by him in a letter to his son-in-law, Mr. Gouverneur, in 1830 :

"I am engaged in a work which will be entitled 'a biographical and historical view of the great events to which Mr. Monroe was a party, and of which he was a spectator in the course of his public service '—commencing with my services in the army, in the Legislature and council of the State, in the Revolutionary Congress, and in the Senate. I have brought it to the conclusion of my first mission to France, which would, if printed, make about one hundred and twenty pages, and with the appendix, should it be thought advisable to add one, perhaps as many more."

There were to be additional features of correspondence, of record and of comment, but the health of the writer was at that time failing fast, and the work was never done. Even a sprained wrist, occasioned by his horse falling with him, interfered seriously.

During Mr. Monroe's retirement at Oak Hill it was his daily custom, the weather and other circumstances permitting, to take morning and evening horseback rides, and his friend Judge Watson records of him that during these excursions " it was his habit to bow and speak to the humblest slave whom he passed as respectfully as if he had been the first gentleman of the neighborhood."

He lived more and more in the past as the short years went by, but it was a grand past for any man's memory to dwell in, full of heroic men and noble women and great events, of camps and battle-fields, of legislative halls and council chambers and the audience rooms of kings, of high offices well filled and of widely important duties well performed. As to his own reputation, he need have had little anxiety when Thomas Jefferson declared of him : " He is a man whose soul might be turned inside out without discovering a blemish to the world." The old-time friendship with Madison continued to the end, and Monroe seemed never quite so contented as in his frequent visits at Montpellier. There are not many more attractive home pictures in American history than are furnished by the fireside and piazza talks of those two old men. Madison said of him : " His understanding has been much underrated ; his judgment was particularly good ; few men have made more of what may be called sacrifices in the service of the public.'' They were his personal friends, but John Quincy Adams, Calhoun, Benton, Webster, and others of the new school of political leaders, passing deliberate judgment upon his career and services, grew warmly eloquent in their tributes to his ability, integrity, and stainless patriotism. He was a man not brilliant, not learned, not polished, not eloquent, and yet a man of more than common strength of character, vastly useful to his country and well beloved by his countrymen. With him passed away the generation of statesmen, and died the political parties of the first era of the Republic.

Mrs. Monroe died at Oak Hill on September 23d, 1830, and after her departure the old man found his lonely farm life insupportable. He had previously visited much with his daughters, and he now went to live with Mrs. Gouverneur, in New York. He wrote to Mr. Madison, April 11th, 1831 :

" It is the wish of both my daughters, and of the whole connection, that I should remain here and receive their good offices, which I have decided to do. I do not wish to burden them. It is my intention to rent a house near Mr. Gouverneur, and to live within my own resources, so far as I am able. . . . The accounting officers have made no decision on my claims, and have given me much trouble. I have written them that I would make out no account adapted to the act [of Congress], which fell far short of making me a just reparation, and that I would rather lose the whole sum than give to it any sanction, be the consequences what they may. I never recovered from the losses of the first mission, to which those of the second added considerably.

" It is very distressing to me to sell my property in Loudoun, for besides parting with all I have in the State, I indulged a hope, if

I could retain it, that I might be able occasionally to visit it, and meet my friends, or many of them, there. But ill health and advanced years prescribe a course which we must pursue. I deeply regret that there is no prospect of our ever meeting again, since so long have we been connected, and in the most friendly intercourse, in public and private life, that a final separation is among the most distressing incidents which could occur. . . . I beg you to assure Mrs. Madison that I never can forget the friendly relation which has existed between her and my family."

The two old friends were, indeed, never to meet again. Less than three months more went by, and then, on July 4th, 1831, the warm heart of old James Monroe ceased to beat.

The remains of the ex-President received burial in New York, but twenty-seven years later, in 1858, on the one hundredth anniversary of his birthday, they were re-entombed at Richmond, Virginia.

THE END.

PORTRAIT OF JOHN QUINCY ADAMS.

JOHN QUINCY ADAMS.

SIXTH PRESIDENT.

By WILLIAM O. STODDARD.

CHAPTER I.

*Parentage and Birth—School-days—A Boston Boy—
Birds and Animals—Battles of Lexington and
Bunker Hill—A Small Post-boy.*

A PART of the town of Quincy, in the State of
Massachusetts, was known, in the year 1767, only
as the North Parish of Braintree, in the British
colony of Massachusetts Bay. All the people of
Braintree village were ready to declare themselves
loyal subjects of King George III. of England, and
all of them were disposed to exercise their born
rights as Englishmen and to strenuously oppose the
colonial policy then and afterward pursued by the
King's ministers. Their leader and representative
in this opposition was a young and poor but rising
lawyer named John Adams. His father had been
a small farmer of Braintree, and he had married
Abigail Smith, daughter of the minister of the First
Congregational Church of Weymouth. Her mater-

nal grandfather, Colonel John Quincy, had been
for a long time Speaker of the Colonial House of
Representatives, and a member of the Colonial
Council. When, therefore, on July 11th, 1767, a
son was born in the home of the Braintree lawyer,
the baby was named John Quincy, at the special request of his grandmother.

John Quincy Adams was born into an atmosphere
already warm, and which rapidly grew warmer with
colonial patriotism, love of freedom, and hatred of
British oppression. From the hour in which he
learned to talk and to understand the talk of others
around him, his mental activities received in this
atmosphere an unintentional but uncommon stimu-
lus. He also obtained a premature knowledge of
public affairs, and the intense excitements of a
stormy time continually aided in moulding his character.

John Adams was devoted to his family, but he
was deeply engrossed by professional and political
duties, and his absences from home were many and
long. Mrs. Adams was an admirable woman in
mind and character, well prepared for the earlier
training of a young life which was yet to be of so
great a value.

As soon as little John Quincy was old enough he
went to the village school provided by the wisdom
of the lawgivers of the colony, and learned to read.
From that time forward he was well disposed to
learn whatever books could teach him, his quick
mind grasping ideas easily and retaining the driest
facts with a firm, clear memory. Being taught at

home to love his country, he did it literally, and learned to love not only the hills and rocks and trees, but the birds and animals. He was fond of studying the habits of his furred or feathered neighbors, and of listening to every sound they made.

It was concerning this boyhood time that he wrote, in Europe, long years afterward :

" Penn's Hill and Braintree North Common Rocks never looked to me and never felt to me like any other hill or any other rocks ; because every rock and every pebble upon them associates itself with the first consciousness of my existence. If there is a Bostonian who ever sailed from his own harbor for distant lands, or returned to it from them, without feelings, at the sight of the Blue Hills, which he is unable to express, his heart is differently constituted from mine."

It was well that his love of his native land should be so firmly anchored, for a very large part of his life was to be spent abroad, and no American—at least not one sent out in the service of his country—ought to be able to see another land fairer than his own.

John Adams removed to Boston in 1768 and lived there three years, returning to his old home in 1771. One year later he again removed to Boston, and bought a house there. It follows that John Quincy Adams learned his letters at the Braintree village school when he was four years old, in 1771. After that he was for more than two years a Boston boy, and, as a British officer remarked at the time, " The very children here breathe the air of liberty." The streets were full of red-coated soldiers, regiments of whom paraded daily in the public squares to overawe the rebellious town, and the Sons of Liberty often came in the evening to give patriotic serenades under the windows of John Adams.   On June 17th, 1774, John Quincy knew that his father was presiding over a crowded meeting of patriots in Faneuil Hall. The next day all the family knew that it must go again to Braintree, for its head had been elected a member of the first Continental Congress, and would ever afterward be in much peril of being hung for treason.   He left Braintree for Philadelphia on August 10th, 1774 ; he was at home through the winter, and before he set out again, in the spring of 1775, the Adams' household had been near neighbors of the bloody fight along the road from Lexington. From that day onward, as is testified by the letters of Mrs. Adams to her husband after he returned in May to his work in Congress, the house was a scene of continual excitement.   Fugitives from Boston rested there for days or weeks.   Hungry patriot soldiers came freely in for refreshments.   There were repeated alarms of raids by the British troops. Children receive deep and lasting impressions under such circumstances, but John Quincy Adams was very soon to see a picture he could never forget. On Sunday, June 18th, 1775, Mrs. Adams wrote to her husband :

" Charlestown is laid in ashes.   The battle began upon our intrenchments upon Bunker Hill Saturday morning, about three
o'clock, and has not ceased yet, and it is now three o'clock Sabbath
afternoon.   It is expected they will come out over the Neck to-
night, and a dreadful battle must ensue.   Almighty God, cover the
heads of our dear countrymen, and be a shield to our dear friends !
How many have fallen we know not.   The constant roar of the
cannon is so distressing that we cannot eat, drink, or sleep."

She had been a witness. Taking with her little John Quincy, eight years old, she had gone out to the summit of Penn's Hill, and they went there again, for from it they could see the smoke and flame of the burning houses and hear the musket rattle and the booming cannon of the battle of Bunker Hill. Afterward, during the long siege of Boston, he used to climb there alone to stare at the lines of the Continental Army, to watch the rockets and the bursting shells, and hear the cannonading.

He was a witness of other terrible things during the siege. The pestilence so apt to come with war had raged all around him, he being the only member of his own family who escaped seizure. He had lost his maternal grandmother, an uncle, brother of his father, and one of the household servants, while Mrs. Adams and her two other children recovered slowly and with difficulty.

The British Army evacuated Boston early in the spring of 1776, and after that Mrs. Adams frequently sent her nine-year-old boy to town on horseback after the latest news, a ride of twenty-two miles, going and coming.

CHAPTER II.

*Perilous Voyages—An American School-boy in Europe
—Spain, France, Holland, Germany, Russia, Swe-
den, Denmark, and England for Schools—A Very
Young Diplomatist—Returning to America.*

ON July 4th, 1776, by the Declaration of Independence, John Quincy Adams legally ceased to be
an English boy ; but he saw very little of his father,
busy with Congressional duties during that year and
the next. Near the close of 1777 John Adams was
appointed, with Benjamin Franklin and Arthur Lee,
a Commissioner of the United States to France.
He and his wife decided that it was best for her and
the two younger children to remain at Braintree,
but that so good an opportunity for giving their eldest son a better education ought not to be thrown
away. Only an armed ship and very swift could at
that time have much hope of getting across the
ocean under the rebel American flag, and Congress
ordered the Boston, as good a vessel as it had, to
carry its Commissioner. She was two months in
getting ready, and her movements were so closely
watched that her passengers were under serious risks
in getting on board.

Mount Wollaston is a headland of the Braintree
coast, and was then a part of the property of Nor-
ton Quincy, uncle of Mrs. Adams. At his house, on
the morning of February 13th, 1778, John Quincy

Adams and his father waited and watched the coming ashore of a small boat from the Boston, lying in Nantasket Roads. The weather was boisterous and the sea was rough, but the boat carried them safely on board, and then their real perils began. Imprisonment if not death would surely have been the portion of John Adams if captured, for his name had already been excepted by the King from his offers of pardon to his American subjects guilty of treason. His son was only ten years of age, but was well aware of the danger. After they entered the Gulf Stream the ship had an encounter of three days with " a furious hurricane and a storm of thunder and lightning," as John Adams afterward wrote, " which struck down our men upon deck and cracked our mainmast ; when the oldest officers and stoutest seamen stood aghast at their last prayers, dreading every moment that a butt would start and all perish."

Other experiences came to the boy passenger when the Boston was attacked by a privateer, which she captured, and when only her fast sailing enabled her to escape from British cruisers on the lookout for her, and when she dodged her way among enemies in the British Channel until she reached safe anchorage in the harbor of Bordeaux.

Diplomatic work for the father began as soon as they arrived at Paris, April 8th, 1778, and so did school work, in ancient and modern languages, for the son. At the end of a year Mr. Adams was called home at his own request, the studies were interrupted, and week after week was spent at French seaports, waiting for the frigate which was to sail for America. On June 17th, 1779, John Quincy Adams began in the Sensible his second voyage across the Atlantic. The French frigate, like the Boston, was compelled to run the gauntlet of British cruisers, and did not reach Boston Harbor until August 2d. This was the first opportunity the Braintree schoolboy had of knowing how he would feel looking at the Blue Hills while sailing in through the Bay. His visit to his mother was to be little more than three months long, for his father was soon appointed upon another foreign mission. On November 13th John Quincy and his younger brother Charles were on the deck of the Sensible, sailing for France. Several other American boys were with them, going to Europe, under the charge of Mr. Adams, to obtain the educational advantages their own country could not then give. Mr. Marbois, a French diplomatist who was a passenger on the Sensible on the first voyage, had acquired a high opinion of the promise of John Quincy, and had urgently advised that every opportunity for improvement should be given him.

With so many young fellows together for company it looked as if a few weeks at sea might be only a sort of good time, but it turned out otherwise. There were war perils, as before, but worse by far was a leak sprung by the Sensible. There were, wrote Mr. Adams, "perhaps four hundred men on board who were scarcely able, with two large pumps going all the twenty-four hours, to keep water from filling the hold, in hourly danger, for twenty days together, of foundering at sea."

They were compelled to make for the nearest neutral port, and this proved to be that of Ferrol, in Spain, where the long and tedious voyage ended early in December. Weeks more were consumed in a fatiguing journey through the mountain ranges of Spain, amid snow and ice, part of the way on foot and part of it on mule-back. There was less hardship after France was reached, but it was February 5th, 1780, before they were safe in Paris. John Quincy Adams was only twelve years of age, but he had made three voyages across the Atlantic, each under circumstances of extraordinary trial and excitement, and his father wrote to his mother that he had behaved very well indeed. It was during the last of these voyages, November 12th, 1779, that he began to keep a diary, which he continued year after year.

The interrupted studies were taken up again, and could not possibly be confined to printed books, with Paris all around like a great theatre, full of things never looked upon by other American boys. He had taken a winter glimpse of Spain, and now to study Paris was almost to read France. At the end of little more than two years John Adams was appointed Minister of the United States to the Netherlands, and his son went with him in July, 1780, to enter the schools of Amsterdam and to study the Dutch people and their country. From thence he went shortly to the University of Leyden, and remained there until July, 1781.

Americans possessed of any knowledge of foreign lands and languages were very rare at that time.

There were almost none who had received any diplomatic training or were acquainted at all with European official ways and usages. Therefore, when Francis Dana, in 1781, was appointed Minister Plenipotentiary of the United States to Russia, and needed a private secretary, he sent to Leyden for John Quincy Adams. They travelled through Germany together on their way to St. Petersburg. Here the young diplomatist continued his studies of Latin, French, German, and other books, including a general course of English history, and he spent a year at a court and among a people with whom it was exceedingly important for an American statesman of the future to be acquainted.

In September, 1782, having performed his official duties to the satisfaction of Mr. Dana, he left St. Petersburg for Stockholm, Sweden. A winter of study here was followed, when the return of warm weather permitted, by a tour of the Swedish interior and by visits to Copenhagen and Hamburg.

In the early spring of 1782 John Adams achieved a great diplomatic triumph in obtaining official recognition as an envoy from the United States to the Government of Holland. It was a sort of formal admission of the young western republic as a known member of the family of nations. Another commission received from home then required his presence in Paris, and his son joined him at the Hague to accompany him.

They made it a pleasure trip, taking their own time and seeing all that they could find worth seeing on their way to Paris. Here negotiations were pend-

ing for a treaty of peace between the United States
and England. Month after month went by, during
which young Adams, acting as a secretary to his
father, had better opportunities than formerly for
obtaining a knowledge of affairs and of men. Not
only was he older, old beyond his years, and with
much experience already acquired, but he and his
father and their fellow-citizens and the land they
represented had now attained a position, social and
political, which before had been denied them. The
treaty was signed on January 21st, 1783, and John
Quincy Adams was present at the signing. Hardly
was the great State paper on its way to the United
States for ratification before the elder Adams was
prostrated by a long and dangerous illness. As soon
as he was able to travel he set out, October 20th,
1783, for England, and his son went with him.

American diplomatic relations with the British
Government had not yet been established, and the
main business in hand was sightseeing. Nothing
within reach of any interest in art, manufactures,
commerce, or historical association was permitted to
escape unexamined. Mr. Adams was still in feeble
health, but in the midst of his English diplomatic
perplexities and his sightseeing important public
business compelled him to undertake, at the peril of
his life, a winter journey to Holland. His son accompanied him, of course, and a dangerous and dole-
ful trip they made of it. John Adams afterward
wrote, after specifying the other worst experiences
of his eventful life, " I never suffered so much in
any of these situations as in that jaunt from Bath

to Amsterdam in January, 1784. . . . My young companion was in fine spirits ; his gayety, activity, and attention to me increased as difficulties multiplied."

The public errand at Amsterdam was duly accomplished, and John Quincy Adams once more went to Paris to pursue his studies. At the end of one more year he was called upon to make a decision with reference to his course in life. His father had been appointed Minister to England, and the family were to reside in London, and the young man's question and decision are thus recorded by himself :

"I have been seven years in Europe, seeing the world, and in its society. If I return to the United States I must be subject, one or two years, to the rules of a college, pass three more in the tedious study of the law, before I can hope to bring myself into professional notice. The prospect is discouraging. If I accompany my father to London, my satisfaction would possibly be greater than by returning to the United States ; but I shall loiter away my precious time, and not go home until I am forced to it. My father has been all his lifetime occupied by the interests of the public. His own fortune has suffered. His children must provide for themselves. I am determined to get my own living, and to be independent and free. Rather than live otherwise, I should wish to die before my time."

CHAPTER III.

Harvard College—Admitted to the Bar—Writing on Politics—Minister to Holland—Appointed to Portugal—A Question of Honor—Opinion of George Washington—An Important Visit to England.

In May, 1785, John Quincy Adams sailed for the United States. He was not yet eighteen years of age, but he had travelled in England, France, Spain, Germany, Holland, Russia, Sweden, and Denmark, and this was his fourth voyage across the Atlantic. He had seen kings and great men, and had watched the progress of important affairs. Under all excitements and in spite of all interruptions, he had pursued his studies so diligently that he was now prepared, after some months of reviewing under proper direction, to enter the Junior Class in Harvard University in March, 1786. He was graduated, in 1787, with the second honors of his class, and the oration he delivered on Commencement Day on the "Importance of Public Faith to the Well-being of a Community," was thought worth printing and publishing. Perhaps his own deepest impressions of the importance of public faith had been gained during his winter journey with his father from England to Holland, rendered needful by the defects of the United States Treasury.

The three years following were spent in the study

of the law at Newburyport, Massachusetts, under
Theophilus Parsons, afterward Chief Justice of that
State.   On admission to the bar, in 1790, Mr. Adams
opened an office in Boston.   In an address to the
bar of Cincinnati, in 1843, he thus described some
of his early experiences as a lawyer :

"I went, therefore, as a volunteer, an adventurer, to Boston ; . . .
I was without support of any kind.   I may say I was a stranger in
that city, although almost a native of that spot.   I say I can hardly
call it practice, because for the space of one year from that time it
would be difficult for me to name any practice which I had to do.
For two years, indeed, I can recall nothing in which I was engaged
that may be termed practice, though during the second year there
were some symptoms that by persevering patience practice might
come in time.   The third year I continued this patience and per-
severance, and having little to do, occupied my time as well as I
could in the study of those laws and institutions which I have since
been called upon to administer.   At the end of the third year I
had obtained something which might be called practice.   The fourth
year I found it swelling to such an extent that I no longer felt any
concern as to my future destiny as a member of that profession."

The indication given by the topic of his college
oration must be followed through the years of study
and of patient waiting.   He was a student of American institutions and politics, who was provided with
experiences and mental training which enabled him
to look at them in perspective.   He was an American, thoroughly aware of the position the United
States held in the minds of European public men.
He was a son of John Adams, and as such had a
political rank and association.   The father was already Vice-President when the son was admitted to
the bar, and hardly anything can be more sure than
that the young man's cold reserve of manner, belong-

ing to an intense pride of character, had much to do with the prolonged scarcity of clients of which he afterward complained. With all his abilities, including his faculty for studying America from the outside, John Quincy Adams had a born, natural gift for making himself needlessly unpopular.

His next known printed publication after the college oration was a well-written series of essays, which appeared in the *Columbian Sentinel* in 1791. They were commentaries upon and refutations of an unsound pamphlet, a digest of French radicalism, written by Thomas Paine and too hastily approved by the extreme school of American Republicans. Mr. Adams wrote under the signature of " Publicola," and there were those who said that they recognized the work of the Vice-President.

The views advanced were those of Washington and his Cabinet, not altogether omitting Thomas Jefferson, and the young lawyer's next series of papers drew their attention to him more forcibly. Great Britain and France were at war in 1793, and there were many reasons why the French sympathies and anti-British feelings of the American people got the better of their prudence and duty of neutrality. Once more the young lawyer without many clients, this time as " Marcellus," appeared in the *Sentinel*, declaring, in a series of able arguments, that " impartial and unequivocal neutrality was the imperative duty of the United States." He showed that a disregard of that duty was the sure road to ruin.

In November, 1793, as " Columbus," in the *Senti-*

nel, the course of the Administration with reference to the arrogant and reckless conduct of the French envoy, Genet, was vigorously sustained and defended.

In all these essays appeared an acquaintance with and an understanding of both American and European affairs, an insight, a capacity, a ripeness of thinking power, too rare and too valuable to be left without public employment. The country needed such a man as the writer in its diplomatic service. On May 29th, 1794, President Washington nominated John Quincy Adams United States Minister Resident at the Hague, and the Senate next day unanimously confirmed the appointment. It was a high honor to come to a man only twenty-seven years of age.

He went at once to Philadelphia, then the seat of Government, and three months were consumed in the preparatory steps of his mission. He sailed from Boston in September, and his fifth Atlantic passage was in a leaky, badly handled ship, so that peril came to him, as usual. He spent two weeks in London, where Jay and Pinckney were negotiating a treaty with England which was afterward badly received in the United States, but which Mr. Adams defended. He reached the Hague on October 31st, 1794, and presented his credentials. He was officially recognized by the Stadtholder and States-General of Holland, just before they were compelled to fly from the invading French army under Pichegru. What was called the Batavian Republic was proclaimed, and the old order of things was nominally abolished. Extreme French Radicalism violently controlled France, but there was nothing pre-cisely like it in Holland. Conquest of the Dutch people by no means implied their transformation, but Mr. Adams began the discharge of his duties under difficulties which presented an extraordinary test of his prudence, tact, and good judgment. He made no blunders. When the French authorities recognized him as the representative of another free nation and declared fraternity with America, his re-sponse assured them of the good-will and grateful memories with which the people of the United States regarded those of France. At the same time he requested protection for American property and persons in Holland, the Batavian Republic. When, however, he was asked to join one of the popular societies which the French military missionaries were organizing for the political conversion of the Dutch, he politely declined as a stranger and a dip-lomatic agent. He wrote about it :

" It was unnecessary for me to look out for motives to justify my refusal. I have an aversion to political popular societies in general. To destroy an established power they are undoubtedly an effica-cious instrument, but in their nature they are fit for nothing else. The reign of Robespierre has shown what use they make of power when they obtain it."

At the end of his first year in Holland, October, 1795, Mr. Adams received from the Secretary of State an order to proceed to England. He reached London in November, and found himself loaded with important matters, both public and private. The former related to the exchange of ratifications of the Jay treaty and to other diplomatic business, all of which he performed to the entire satisfaction of the Department of State.   The other and to him personally the more interesting part of his temporary mission to Great Britain related to Miss Louisa Catharine Johnson, with whom he became acquainted shortly after his arrival.   She was the daughter of Joshua Johnson, American Consul at London, and a niece of Governor Johnson of Maryland, one of the signers of the Declaration of Independence.   A courtship followed and then betrothal, the wedding being postponed until a more convenient season.

In May, 1796, Mr. Adams was once more at the Hague, after an extended and valuable intercourse with English statesmen and society.   The duties of his position in Holland were not onerous, and left him time to continue his studies in ancient and modern languages and varied law and literature. His diary testifies how careful an account he kept with himself of the use he made of his time and opportunities.

In August, 1796, he received a notification from the Secretary of State that he had been appointed Minister Plenipotentiary to Portugal, but was to remain in the discharge of his duties at the Hague until further instructions should be sent to him. Nearly a year went by before these arrived, and there was a noteworthy reason for it.   The Presidency of George Washington was drawing toward its close. All men expected that John Adams would succeed the Father of his Country, and he did so.   Both before and after taking the oath of office, however, the idea of conferring public station and honor upon his own son was to him exceedingly repugnant. Still more sensitive was the son about receiving official favors from his father. His private letters home, especially to his mother, witness how keenly his independence and sense of honor reacted from the possible suggestion of favoritism. That he consented to remain in office was due to Washington himself, who wrote to John Adams, February 20th, 1797, just before the inauguration of the latter as President :

"I have a strong hope that you will not withhold merited promotion to Mr. John Quincy Adams because he is your son. For without intending to compliment the father or the mother, or to censure any others, I give it as my decided opinion that Mr. Adams is the most valuable public character we have abroad, and that he will prove himself to be the ablest of all our diplomatic corps. If he was now to be brought into that line, or into any other public walk, I would not, on the principles which have regulated my own conduct, disapprove the caution hinted at in the letter. But he is already entered ; the public, more and more as he is known, are appreciating his talents and worth ; and his country would sustain a loss if these are checked by over-delicacy on your part."

Mrs. Adams sent this letter to her son, and his reply to her expressed his appreciation of a testimonial so extraordinary. It induced him to continue in the public service. The appointment to Portugal was changed to one at Berlin, and, on accepting it, he wrote to his father :

"I cannot and ought not to discuss with you *the propriety* of the measure. I have undertaken the duty, and will discharge it to the best of my ability, and will complain no further. But I most earnestly entreat that whenever there shall be deemed no further occasion for a minister at Berlin I may be recalled, and that no nomination of me to any other public office whatever may ever again proceed from the present chief magistrate."

CHAPTER IV.

*Marriage—Minister to Prussia—Home again—Law-
yer—State Senator—Orator—United States Senator
—Harvard College Professor—A Very Independent
Politician.*

MR. MURRAY, who succeeded Mr. Adams at the
Hague, did not arrive until July, 1797. Sooner than
that a very interesting visit to London could not be
undertaken. The 26th of July, however, was made
the wedding day of John Quincy Adams and Louisa
Catharine Johnson, and their subsequent journey to
Berlin, where they arrived on October 26th, was a
bridal tour. At the gate of the Prussian capital, it
is related, they were delayed by the officer of the
guard until he could be properly informed who and
what were the United States of America mentioned
by these travellers as the country from which they
came.

The main purpose of the mission to Berlin was the
negotiation of a treaty between the United States
and Prussia. It was signed, after many delays, on
July 11th, 1799, and was afterward ratified unanimously by the Senate of the United States. There
had been more society than hard work for the
American Minister in Berlin, and now that all the
work was done he wrote home asking to be recalled.
He was a diplomatist without anything to do, and

so he and Mrs. Adams made a tour through Saxony and Bohemia. The next summer they made another tour in Silesia, for the recall was delayed, and the Berlin mission was very nearly a sinecure.

During that year, however—the year 1800—there had been a great change in American politics. The Federal Party, and with it John Adams, had passed out of power. A new party, with Thomas Jefferson at its head, had taken their place. One of the last official acts of the retiring President was the long-delayed recall of his son, and there is no doubt of either its wisdom or propriety. John Quincy Adams once more landed in the United States on September 4th, 1801, bringing with him a reputation for uncommon ability that was a sure guarantee of a successful career.

The fallen Federal Party was composed at this time of two factions, whose relative strength no man knew. One approved of the course of John Adams as President, while the other, led by Alexander Hamilton, strongly condemned it. United the party was political master of the State of Massachusetts.

John Quincy Adams returned home a very independent Federalist, not at all a partisan, and having peculiar views as to the rights of minorities under a republican form of government, and upon some other questions not yet brought before the public mind. He was appointed by the District Court a Register in Bankruptcy, but was somewhat unexpectedly removed by President Jefferson under a change in the law governing such offices. His party position was somewhat helped by such a removal, but he at first proposed to himself to withdraw from political life and devote himself to law practice. There had been much revision of statutes and many other changes during his residence abroad, calling upon him for a severe course of law study and review. To this he at once directed his well-trained and vigorous power of application, after opening a law office in Boston. Such pecuniary resources as he had been able to accumulate had suffered by the failure of European bankers, and he was entirely dependent upon his own exertions for support. If he had been permitted he would speedily have over-come all difficulties and would have risen to emi-nence at the bar, for his genius was pre-eminently adapted to success in his chosen profession. There was but one obstacle in the way, and that was the great need in which the Federal Party stood of pre-cisely such a man. The very bitterness of the per-sonal animosities which divided the old leaders tended to push them all aside, and younger men of name and fame were very scarce. It was largely owing to this that the Federalists of Boston left Mr. Adams in his law office less than six months. On April 5th, 1802, they elected him to the State Senate. He took his seat and, two days afterward, astonished all kinds of party men by a proposition that the Republican minority should be given a fair numerical representation in the State Council. It was negatived, of course, as chimerical, but years afterward he wrote of it : " It was the first act of my legislative life, and it marked the principle by which my whole public life has been governed from that day to this." It was the reverse of a bid for popularity, but had its influence upon his political career. His subsequent course in the State Senate and the Senate of the United States was in like manner marked by a devotion to principle and not to party. There was really not enough left of Federalism to call upon any man for much enthusiasm. In the following November this was finely illustrated. Mr. Adams was induced to run for Congress in the Boston district. Thirty-seven hundred votes only were cast, and the opposition candidate, William Eustis, was elected by a majority of fifty-nine.

The newspapers were probably right in saying that the result would have been different if the weather had been good, and Mr. Adams himself caustically remarked : " This is among the thousand proofs how large a portion of Federalism is a mere fair-weather principle, too weak to overcome a shower of rain." He might have added that the principles for which the party in its prime had contended had been solidified in the Constitution of the United States, and required no further partisan work. The house was built, and the scaffoldings of the builders could be knocked away. They were so.

Mr. Adams had already given some public evidences of his oratorical power, and now found himself beginning to be sought for to deliver occasional addresses, as, for instance, one in December of 1803, at Plymouth, commemorating the Pilgrim Fathers. The old liking of the Massachusetts people for John Adams began to rally fast around his son and heir.

He was a strong, young tree of a family well rooted
in the history of the Commonwealth, and nowhere
else could such a fact be of greater importance. In
February, 1803, after three preliminary ballots to
clear the way, the State Senate elected him to the
Senate of the United States. His competitor,
Timothy Pickering, an ex-member of Washington's
Cabinet and leader of the Hamilton Federalists in
Massachusetts, was chosen to fill a vacancy which
occurred a few weeks later, and they both, the old-
time and the new-time, went on to Washington, to
separate there politically more completely.

Mr. Adams removed his family to the national
capital, a remarkably just-begun and ragged-looking
settlement on the bank of the Potomac, in October,
1803. His first vote in the Senate was given, with
those of other Federal senators, against the bill en-
abling the President to take possession of Louisiana.
Power was obviously expressed in the bill beyond
any which Congress could constitutionally confer
upon the President. Only one week later Mr.
Adams voted with the Republican senators and
against his own party in favor of the appropriation
of eleven millions of dollars to pay for Louisiana.
Both of these votes were given upon principle, for
clearly-stated reasons, and struck the key-note of a
legislative career unsurpassed for independence,
ability, and spotless integrity. At the same time
they aided other circumstances in placing the young
Senator from Massachusetts in a sort of senatorial
solitude. He could make no advances to the Republican opposition, and they were not yet suffi-

ciently accustomed to the exercise of political power
to understand independence or tolerate criticism.
His Federal colleagues were sour with defeat, and
looked upon any concurrence with their old party
enemies, upon any matter whatever, as a species of
treason. There were, therefore, three parties in the
Senate—the Republicans, the Federalists, and John
Quincy Adams. He recorded in his diary that the
situation called upon him for " firmness, persever-
ance, patience, coolness, and forbearance. The
prospect is not promising ; yet the part to act may
be as honorably performed as if success could attend
it." He fought his way admirably, winning respect
and influence but not popularity, and was able, at
the close of his term, to record that he had voted
with the Republicans somewhat more frequently
than with the Federalists.

Mr. Adams had yet one more claim to the respect
of the people of Massachusetts. From the foundation of the colony they had set a high value upon
scholarship, and they were now well pleased to be
represented by a man of scholarly attainments.
Even the cold reserve of his manner, so much complained of by some, became of less consequence in
the minds of his constituents when they considered
that he was a bookish person, entitled to be somewhat externally like a college professor. The
strength of this idea was manifested, in 1805, when
the corporation of Harvard College elected him
Boylston Professor of Rhetoric and Oratory. He
asked for some statutory modifications of the re-
quirements of the position and then accepted it, at

once beginning a preparatory course of reading among Greek, Latin, French, and English authors. The actual discharge of his duties began with the college year of 1806, his professorship dating from Commencement in June.

There was one central feature of the politics of the maritime world of special importance to the United States as a rising commercial power of the first class concerning which Mr. Adams entertained strong views. Great Britain claimed to be mistress of the seas, hardly admitting that any other nation could have rights conflicting with her own interests. Upon this doctrine she acted with reference to neutral powers in time of war and all weak powers in time of nominal peace. The result was a persistent policy of arrogance, oppression, and spoliation. Mr. Adams had obtained a clear understanding of this policy in all its bearings during his residence abroad, and his uncompromising condemnation of it grew stronger year by year after his return. He had expressed his opinions so plainly, from time to time, that no man need have been surprised at any yet more vehement expression upon any proper occasion. This was given June 27th, 1807, by the British man-of-war Leopard, when she made her outrageous attack upon the American frigate Chesapeake. It was during the recess of Congress, but Mr. Adams, in opposition to Federal party leaders, attended indignation meetings in Boston, at the State House, and at Faneuil Hall, and drew up and advocated patriotic resolutions. Such occasions as these then and afterward aided a great many people to understand how much real fire there was in him, but the men who attended the meetings were for the greater part Republicans, not Federalists.

President Jefferson called a special meeting of Congress October 27th, 1807, and when that body came together his message related mainly to British outrages. Mr. Adams came at once to the front as a leading supporter of his political enemy, the President. Two motions for the division of the message and reference to committees were made by him. He was made chairman of one committee, reported a bill providing retaliatory measures, and then voted for it with Republican senators. In the following winter session he again and again voted against his party and with the friends of Mr. Jefferson whenever the subject of British aggression came up. The remnant of the Federalists declared him utterly unmanageable.

CHAPTER V.

Resigning a Seat in the Senate—Bitterly Denounced at Home—Minister to Russia—Another Exciting Sea Voyage—Studies of Russia and her People— American Sailors in Difficulties—Economy.

THE judgment of Mr. Adams did not approve of the embargo except as a temporary measure from which Great Britain might possibly take warning. With all his soul, however, he was opposed to a policy of submission, or to anything which looked like it. The leading interests and influences of Massachusetts, on the other hand, were commercial, and her people dreaded, with a too short-sighted selfishness, any law or policy which even temporarily interfered with the going and coming of their ships. Fear of open war with England was now the soul of New England Federalism, and kept it alive. The course of Mr. Adams was therefore looked upon as a betrayal of the very men who had sent him to Washington. Unstinted abuse was heaped upon him. Old friends turned away from him, and new and bitter enemies arose on every side. He was believed to have utterly ruined himself politically, and in his own mind had little doubt of it, neither he nor others at all understanding what strength would surely come to a man who already possessed the nerve and the courage to stand alone in so severe a storm.

His senatorial term was to expire on March 3d, 1809, and the men who condemned him determined to administer such a punishment as they deemed his perverse conduct required. On June 2d and 3d, 1808, nine months before the end of the term of Mr. Adams, the Massachusetts Legislature elected his successor. All the anti-British feeling rallied to his support, but it could give him only seventeen votes against twenty-one in the Senate, and two hundred and thirteen votes against two hundred and forty-eight in the House. James Lloyd was elected United States Senator, and anti-embargo resolutions were passed to add a point to the rebuke of Mr. Adams. They did but give him an opportunity for a practical application of one of his unswerving principles. Senators of the United States should represent not themselves, but the States sending them. The day following the election of Mr. Lloyd Mr. Adams addressed a letter to the Legislature. He rehearsed its action, pointed out that the anti-embargo resolutions, while plainly condemning the votes he had given as Senator, tacitly demanded of him a course of action in opposition to the policy of Mr. Jefferson's administration inconsistent with his own views and principles, and impossible for him to follow. He therefore tendered his resignation ; it was accepted, and Mr. Lloyd was at once chosen for the remainder of that term also.

Mr. Adams returned home to resume his law practice and to continue his labors as Professor of Rhetoric in Harvard College. With reference to both he pursued a severe course of study. He re-

turned also to be made to feel how deep and how
unsparing was the displeasure he had incurred. It
was even insinuated that he had been influenced by
promises of official place and pay. Old Federalists,
who had lost all hope of either when their party
went down, taunted and execrated him precisely as
if he had at some time been a party man, owing party
fealty. In their sense of the word he had never
been a Federalist at all. He had returned from a
long absence in Europe to take his place in a new
order of things, without much reference to the relics
of the old. His course of action had been uniform
and consistent, one step following another with inevitable precision, all the foot-marks made being ex-
actly alike. The country was going forward, and he
was going forward with it. One point which it
would surely reach was to be the War of 1812, the
supplement of the War of Independence. If John
Quincy Adams, in writings and speeches and senatorial votes, pointed out very clearly the causes
which must lead to a trial of strength with England,
the facts were to blame and not he.

The position he occupied prevented him from
taking any active part in the Presidential election,
in 1808, by which Mr. Madison was chosen to succeed Thomas Jefferson. In the winter following,
however, Mr. Adams had a law case before the Supreme Court, and was compelled to go to Washington. He was detained there while Mr. Madison was
making up his Cabinet and determining his diplomatic appointments before his inauguration. Mr.
Adams was not a Republican, and had no reason to

expect favors from the new administration, which was a continuance of the old. When, in 1805, something had been said to him about a foreign appointment to be given by President Jefferson, he had replied that there was no office in the President's gift for which he had any desire. During the political canvass of 1808 the Republican Party of his district had offered to send him to Congress, and he had refused the nomination. If not a party politician, however, he was well known as an able and experienced diplomatist, and Mr. Madison had need of him. Agents of the State Department, like Mr. Dana, had previously been sent to Russia, but no permanent mission had been established there, although the emperor had requested it. Mr. Madison was determined that a minister plenipotentiary should be sent, and was only two days in office before he offered the post to Mr. Adams, entirely because he was the right man for it. The offer was accepted, and the nomination was sent to the Senate. That body contained several Republicans who deemed the Russian mission needless, several more who did not like Mr. Adams, and also several Federalists. They were seventeen in all against fifteen who favored the appointment, and they immediately, March 7th, 1809, sent back to Mr. Madison a resolution declaring that " it is inexpedient at this time to appoint a minister from the United States to Russia."

It was as deep a stab as had been the action of the Massachusetts Legislature, for it was accompanied, on the tongues of many men, with the insinuation that now Mr. Adams had been paid his price for betraying Federalism. He replied through the press with a series of papers which forcibly expressed his reasons for not remaining in a political party so nearly dead years before that it could not go to the polls on a rainy day.

On June 26th, 1809, Mr. Madison again sent a message to the Senate, giving additional reasons for a Russian mission, and once more naming Mr. Adams. This time the Senate promptly confirmed the appointment, and on October 5th the new minister sailed for St. Petersburg, having closed up his law business and resigned his professorship.

Wars and the weather always interfered with the voyages and other undertakings of Mr. Adams. He continued his studies on board ship in spite of a rough passage until they reached the Baltic, but here vexations of a different sort began. They were of a sort well calculated to intensify any man's opposition to European views of the rights or no rights of American merchant vessels. Great Britain was at war with Denmark. The ship was first stopped by a British cruiser, and boarded. Her papers were examined, and she was permitted to proceed, only to be stopped again before night by a Danish cruiser. This time she was ordered to go to Christiansand, but a gale was blowing, and she went into Flecknoe Harbor instead. Mr. Adams afterward found thirty-eight American merchantmen at Christiansand, all seized during that summer. Eighteen had been already condemned as prizes and had appealed from the decision, and all the captains and crews were glad to have Mr. Adams undertake their relief, as he patriotically did. Sailing again, the ship was once more stopped by a British squadron, and the commanding admiral was with great difficulty induced to admit that he had no right to hinder the voyage of an American ambassador to Russia. One Yankee sailor from near Boston narrowly escaped impress-ment.

St. Petersburg was not reached until October 23d, owing to all these interruptions and delays, but the representative of the United States was well received by the Russian Government officials, and afterward by the Emperor Alexander in person.

At the first interview between the Czar and Mr. Adams the subject of conversation was the one up-permost in the mind of the latter, probably of both. It was the general insecurity of commerce and the necessity of a better international system for the protection of neutral rights in time of war. An official beginning was well made of the close friend-ship which has ever since existed between the two nations, the real beginning having a somewhat earlier date.

The empress and the empress-mother also re-ceived the American minister in full accordance with court etiquette, the Imperial family received Mrs. Adams, and the social position of the embassy was duly established. According to the commentary made by Mr. Adams :

" The formalities of these court presentations are so trifling and insignificant in themselves, and so important in the eyes of princes and courtiers, that they are much more embarrassing to an

American than business of greater importance.   It is not safe or
prudent to despise them, nor practicable for a person of rational
understanding to value them."

He did not forget or neglect his sailor friends at
Christiansand, but obtained the friendly interposition of the Russian Government, and the release of
the lawlessly detained vessels followed.   From that
time forward, during the long struggles which ended
in the downfall of Napoleon, the labors of Mr.
Adams on behalf of his harassed and plundered
countrymen were untiring.

There was much wealth among the Russian no-
bility resident at St. Petersburg, and their style of
living accorded with their ideas of magnificence.
So did that of the diplomatic representatives of other
European powers, while the United States had sent
a man without any considerable private income, and
upon a moderate salary.   It was not always easy to
keep his expenses down to the level of his resources,
but he rigidly insisted upon doing so, and for this he
received, on one occasion, the expressed approval
of the emperor.

Apart from diplomatic duties, the Russian capital
contained a superabundance of material to attract so
penetrating and persistent a student as Mr. Adams.
The system of government, the grades of rank, the
peculiarities of race and of customs, the habits of
all classes, the relations of Russia to other countries,
the language, history, coinage, weights, measures,
internal trade, external commerce—in fact, whatever
came within the scope of his very busy observation
was made a subject of thoughtful inquiry.

Besides the occupation given him by an attempt to analyze and understand the people to whom his own had sent him, Mr. Adams continued his earlier studies. These included astronomy, chronology, and the works of the ancient philosophers, to which he gave much time. He had made for himself an unvarying rule of reading daily five chapters of the Bible, and to this he added a selection of standard theologians. He might well remark, as he did : "Time is too short for me rather than too long. If the day were forty-eight hours instead of twenty-four, I could employ them all, if I had but eyes and hands to read and write." He was often extremely annoyed by the necessity he was under of wasting precious hours upon mere visits of ceremony and court formalities.

The course of the Emperor Napoleon with reference to American commerce was hardly less merciless than that of England. It was but another development of the great defect in international laws and usages against which Mr. Adams was contending. He could do but little, though doing all in his power to prevent or mitigate the distresses of American merchants and sailors in the North Sea and the Baltic, whether caused by French cruisers or British ; but a great change was very near at hand.

CHAPTER VI.

Life at St. Petersburg—The Moscow Campaign—The Treaty of Ghent—The Return of Napoleon from Elba—Mr. Adams Minister to England.

MR. ADAMS remained at St. Petersburg during the rapid series of events by land and sea through which Napoleon overstrained his ill-gotten power until it broke to pieces in his hands. The French invasion of Russia, the capture of Moscow, the great battles, the retreat and destruction of the invading army, sent exciting news to the capital of the empire. All the long tumult of European affairs, however, postponed the time when the principles and terms of a commercial treaty between Russia and the United States could be defined and adjusted to the claims and probable conduct of other nations. Meantime, the northern empire and the western republic gave each other continued proofs of mutual good-will, and the position of the United States Minister at St. Petersburg was made pleasant for him.

However much the law practice of Mr. Adams had been curtailed and interrupted by political and other demands upon his time, he had deeply impressed other members of the profession by the evidence he had given of natural legal ability and extended acquirements. A striking testimony to his standing at the bar was given in 1811. He was appointed an Associate Justice of the Supreme Court of the United States, and his commission was sent to him at St. Petersburg. High as was the honor and lifelong the dignity conferred, he declined to accept it.

In 1812 the long-standing difficulties between the United States and Great Britain drifted into open war. Shortly afterward, in September, 1812, the Russian emperor offered his friendly services as a mediator between the two nations with reference to peace, and the offer was promptly accepted by the United States. The American people had no liking for war, and in this war their disasters on land had been poorly compensated by a few brilliant successes at sea. England, having brought on the war by a course of action from which she had no purpose of departing, was differently disposed. She had no wish for peace, and rejected the offer of Russian mediation. Before the British refusal was known in America, President Madison appointed Mr. Bayard and Mr. Gallatin to act as peace commissioners jointly with Mr. Adams, sending word to the latter to continue his other functions as Minister to Russia. After Mr. Gallatin left home the Senate refused to confirm him as commissioner, on the ground that he was already Secretary of the Treasury, and could not hold two offices. So he and Mr. Bayard, on reaching St. Petersburg in July, 1813, found themselves in a peculiarly awkward position. As month after month went by, however, English commerce began to feel severely the harassing annoyances, and English taxpayers the needless burdens of the war. Reasons of home politics and public opinion induced the British Ministry to assent to the opening of peace negotiations, but with the United States directly, without Russian mediation. They also named three commissioners to meet those of the United States. Another man was made Secretary of the Treasury, and a new commission was issued to Mr. Adams, Mr. Gallatin, and Mr. Bayard, with the addition of Jonathan Russell and Henry Clay.

The meeting of the joint peace commission was to be at Gottenburg, and on April 28th, 1814, Mr. Adams left his family at St. Petersburg and set out to the performance of his new duties. On the way he heard that the allied armies were in Paris, and that Napoleon had abdicated. He was nearly a month in getting to Stockholm, and there learned that there had been a change, and that he must go on to Ghent. There the American commissioners met on June 30th in the apartments of Mr. Adams, but the British commissioners did not arrive until August 7th. When they came, both sides were so much disposed to stand upon their dignity that it was necessary to hold the first joint meeting at a hotel. Afterward the commissioners met alternately at the American or British apartments. The agents of the British Ministry had not been sent to negotiate a peace, but to relieve those who sent them of an accusation from their political opponents of rejecting the pacific overtures of the United States. They were representatives of the very spirit and policy which brought on the War of 1812. The first

propositions they offered in writing as the basis on
which peace might be declared were simply gro-
tesque and astounding. The manner in which the
intolerable demands of England were advocated,
after a few empty civilities at the beginning, is recorded thus by Mr. Adams :

" The tone of all the British notes is arrogant, overbearing, and
offensive. The tone of ours is neither so bold nor so spirited as I
think it should be. It is too much on the defensive, and too excessive in the caution to say nothing irritating. I have seldom
been able to prevail upon my colleagues to insert anything in the
style of retort upon the harsh and reproachful matter which we
receive."

There were many disagreements among the
American commissioners, who had been selected
very much as if Mr. Madison made an effort to get
together five men no two of whom were in the least
degree alike. Mr. Adams was as much alone among
them as he had been in the United States Senate,
but made himself pre-eminently useful from the beginning to the end of the very disagreeable conferences. The end did not come soon. The months
consumed at Ghent answered the political purposes
of the British Ministry. While their agents were
proposing impossible terms of peace, they themselves planned two memorable military expeditions
against the United States, each of which cost the life
of the general commanding it. The first, under
General Ross, brought lasting disgrace to its authors
by the burning of the public buildings at the city of
Washington. The other aimed at the seizure of the
mouth of the Mississippi River and the permanent

control of its navigation, treaty or no treaty, and ended in rout and failure at the battle of New Orleans.

A treaty of peace, with terms endurable but not satisfactory, was at last signed, December 24th, 1814. Polite expressions passed between Mr. Adams and Lord Gambier on the formal exchange of the signed and sealed copies, but there was almost a double meaning in the remark of Mr. Adams that he hoped this would be the *last* treaty of peace between Great Britain and the United States. Before it was ratified by the United States Senate its value and permanence had been greatly strengthened by General Jackson. Such as it was, its terms had been acceded to by the British Government only because of threatening complications in England's relations with other great European powers. The British newspapers opposed to the ministry insisted upon calling it a national diplomatic defeat, and they abused their adversaries in tirades which mingled the names of John Quincy Adams, Commodore Perry, and General Jackson.

The citizens of Ghent gave the joint commissioners a grand public entertainment in honor of the signing of the peace. After that Mr. Adams set out for Paris instead of St. Petersburg, for he was about to be named Minister Plenipotentiary to Great Britain as the reward of his unquestionably leading part in the peace negotiations. He was also about to be a witness of one of the most remarkable dramas in the world's history. He reached Paris on February 3d, 1815, met the other commissioners, and was presented with them by the American Minister to the Citizen King, Louis the Eighteenth, and to other members of the royal family. Several weeks passed very pleasantly, for Mr. Adams was at home in French society. Among the distinguished people with whom he now associated were Lafayette, Madame de Staël, Humboldt, and others who required no title. Suddenly, however, the restored Bourbon monarchy was startled by the news that Napoleon had escaped from Elba. Then came March 20th, 1815, when King Louis rode away from the Tuileries in the morning, and Napoleon took possession in the evening. There was no disturbance of the public peace. Mr. Adams was at the Théâtre Français not far away, and he did not know what had happened until the next morning's newspapers told him. He walked out to see Napoleon review the regiments forming the garrison of Paris, and there could be no doubt whose soldiers they were. There had been no time to remove the Bourbon insignia from belts or weapons, but the men who bore them saluted the emperor whose return to power they had refused to oppose. All things seemed to have been changed as if by magic, and when Mr. Adams called upon the Imperial Minister of Foreign Affairs, he was assured that the change had everywhere taken place peaceably, and would be permanent. That assurance left all the world but France out of the account. Mr. Adams expressed his hope for peaceable relations between France and the United States. He mentioned his approaching need of a passport to England, and was assured of prompt compliance with his wishes, or those of Mr. Crawford, the American Minister—the only minister of any power on earth then remaining in Paris.

Mrs. Adams arrived safely from St. Petersburg, and on May 16th, 1815, her husband left Paris with her for England, remarking : " War appears to be certain. The first thought of the inhabitants of Paris will be to save themselves. They have no attachment either to the Bourbons or Napoleon. They will submit quietly to the victorious party, and do nothing to support either."

CHAPTER VII.

Mr. Adams in England—Secretary of State—The War of the Succession—Society in Washington— Purchase of Florida—Candidates for the Presidency.

IT is difficult for the American or Englishman of to-day to comprehend the position of an American in England in the year 1815. No just view of men or events can be obtained, however, without an effort to perceive the facts. Wounded pride, with a consciousness of baffled, half-exerted power on the British side and a sore sense of injuries endured on the American side, kept the two nations apart, and affected the social conduct of individuals. It is a curious feature of that time that in America the so-called British party, opposed to the War of 1812, was aristocratic in its tendencies, while in England the most unrelenting dislike of America was to be found among the upper classes. Not many members of these understood the difference between conservative American democracy and destructive French radicalism.

John Quincy Adams, as United States Minister Plenipotentiary in London, found himself in a vastly different position from that which his father had held there years before. The son represented a national political experiment which was beginning to succeed, instead of one whose failure was confidently expected.   In the first work of his mission Mr. Gallatin and Mr. Clay had been commissioned with him, and they had already accomplished much of it before his arrival.   A commercial treaty was completed and they went home, leaving him to the performance of a vast mass of work, much of which may be described as the unfinished business left over from before the war, and by the occurrences of the war itself.

Personally Mr. Adams possessed many advantages over any other American who could at that time have been sent to England.   His father had been President of the United States, and the son carried with him the idea of good family, so important in a diplomatic circle which was also exclusively aristocratic.   His long official residence on the continent and his previous visits to England had brought to him a wide English acquaintanceship, and he had among all a high reputation as a diplomatist, scholar, and man of the world.   He could, therefore, be received without question by the best society, and when in it was peculiarly capable of maintaining his own dignity.   Society, in fact, made so many demands upon his time that a desire to escape was one of his reasons for removing his residence from London to Boston House, nine miles away.   Another important reason was the narrowness of his salary and the expense attending an attempt to live in good style. in London.   During the two years of his services as Minister to England, the honor he won was that no fault could be found with his administration of all the duties with which he was intrusted. If few opportunities occurred for doing anything brilliant, it was enough that the interests of his country had been thoroughly well cared for and substantially advanced.

The Secretary of State under President Madison, Mr. James Monroe, had a better opportunity than any other man for forming a correct estimate of the various capacities displayed by American diplomatists abroad. On March 4th, 1817, he became President of the United States, and immediately published his opinion of one of them in the most emphatic manner possible. He appointed John Quincy Adams Secretary of State. The commission did not reach London until April 16th, 1817, and Mr. Adams at once prepared to return to the United States.

With reference to the future political course of Mr. Adams, it must be noted that his appointment as Secretary of State had little to do with party or partisanship. It neither rewarded him for party services nor bound him by party obligations. It was purely and simply a fulfilment of George Washington's prediction, made in August, 1795 :

"I shall be much mistaken if, in as short a time as can well be expected, he is not found at the head of the diplomatic corps, let the Government be administered by whomsoever the people may choose."

He sailed from England on June 17th, 1817, and it was almost a matter of course that his voyage should be tedious. It lasted seven weeks, and he landed in New York August 7th, declaring that the

game of chess surpassed all other resources for kill-
ing time at sea.

His first visit was to his father and mother at
their home in Quincy, Massachusetts. It was eight
years since he had seen them, and they were growing old now. In September he reached the city of
Washington, and took up the duties of his office.

These were to be arduous, and he was to exert a
powerful influence upon the administration of Mr.
Monroe. All men at once took both facts for
granted. They knew Mr. Adams would make a
good Secretary of State, and that the foreign affairs
of the nation were safe in his hands. They therefore turned their attention away from them as from
business already settled, and devoted themselves to
a great political game of chess, in which Mr. Adams
had suddenly taken an advanced and very assailable
position. There was a sort of tradition, created by
the course of events, by reason of which the appointment of a strong man to be Secretary of State suggested him as a probable candidate for the Presidency. Of the first five presidents four had been
from Virginia, and that State therefore had no right
to present another name, nor had she another name
worth presenting. One President, John Adams,
had been from Massachusetts, and it was said that
her turn ought not to come again very soon. New
York had an ambition represented by De Witt Clinton. The far South asked for sectional recognition
in the person of Mr. Crawford, the Secretary of the
Treasury, and others. The West, speaking at first
only of Henry Clay, soon discovered that a new

party was forming of which he could not be the leader, and transferred much of its support to Andrew Jackson.

What was afterward called " the war of the succession" began at once, and aided greatly in maintaining the personal popularity of Mr. Monroe. Nearly all the fault found with his administration was concentrated upon Mr. Adams, and the President escaped.

The Secretary of State was not intriguing for the Presidency, and it was finally discovered that those who did so pitted themselves against each other even more than against him.

Some of his most severe trials and important services came to him very rapidly. The rebellion of the British colonies had been undertaken against a mother country in the full vigor of national life and power, and had succeeded. The Spanish colonies in South America were now breaking away from a mother country in the feebleness of long decline. Mr. Adams believed that they would succeed, but he also believed that it was the duty of the United States to observe a strict neutrality during the struggle. The administration faithfully strove to perform all its obligations to Spain, while not concealing its sympathy for the revolted colonies. There were barriers of international law and righteousness which it could not pass, and beyond them was the disagreeable certainty of a war with Spain. If American privateers, under South American republican flags, had been permitted to sail from the ports of the United States, then Spanish cruisers, and privateers of all sorts under the Spanish flag, would soon be working their will among the merchantmen of the United States. Regardless of such considerations, the mere effervescence of American public feeling was taken advantage of by politicians, notably by Henry Clay, to assail the policy of the administration — that is, its foreign policy, Mr. Adams.

An important heirloom of the State Department, ever since the purchase of Louisiana by Mr. Jefferson, had been a dispute with Spain as to the exact western boundary-line of Florida. A treaty for the settlement of this was under a slow process of negotiation from the beginning of Mr. Monroe's administration. It was complicated with negotiations for the purchase of Florida, and yet more by the apparent determination of the enemies of Mr. Adams to oppose any treaty he might make and any boundary-line he might agree upon with the very able and subtle Spanish Minister, Mr. Onis. There were minor complications too numerous to mention, and at last they were all made apparently worse, but were really settled by the extraordinary conduct of General Jackson. At the beginning of the year 1818 he was sent by Mr. Monroe to put a stop to the raids of the Seminole Indians into Florida, and in July news came that he had done so. He had also chased them across the Florida line, stormed Pensacola, and had otherwise given a vivid illustration of the fact that there was really no Spanish power at all in Florida. He had also approved of the hanging of two Englishmen, Ambrister and

Arbuthnot, accused of inciting the Seminoles to invade Georgia. On the latter account a small ghost of probable trouble with England arose, but Mr. Adams had no fear of extreme measures on her part, and the result justified him. With Spain it might easily have been a more serious matter at another time, but it was hardly worth while for her to take an additional war upon her hands on account of a mere border foray into some land she was selling. Too many people, however, saw how thin was her title, and how easily she might be made to part with so doubtful a property without obtaining much purchase money.

When the news came from Pensacola all the country was greatly excited, but the President and part of his cabinet did not understand the nature of the excitement. They feared that Congress and the nation would condemn both them and General Jackson for incurring peril of a foreign war. They were ready to declare that he had exceeded his instructions, and that all the blame belonged to him. They went just far enough to give him all the credit. Mr. Adams vigorously sustained the general from the outset, declaring that he had obeyed the spirit of his instructions, even if he had exceeded the letter. There were constitutional questions involved, as well as those of policy, which cannot be presented in a brief biography, but upon all of them the result vindicated the Secretary of State and the general. The treaty with Spain and the purchase of Florida suffered no hindrance, and Jackson at once passed ahead of Clay in the race for the Presidency. The treaty was agreed to by the Spanish Minister on February 22d, 1819, and was unanimously ratified by the Senate, in spite of the opposition of Mr. Clay. He and General Jackson became more determined enemies than before, and it was impossible for the enemies of Mr. Adams to deprive him of the honor justly due to him. He himself recorded the day of the signing of the Florida treaty as "perhaps the most important day of my life;" but he was greatly in haste, for more important days by far were yet to come.

During the two terms of Mr. Madison something had been done for the improvement of the town site known as the city of Washington, but the town itself was not yet there. The White House, burned by the British in 1814, had been reconstructed in time for its occupation by Mr. and Mrs. Monroe. Much had been done for the other public buildings. A number of private residences had been erected, but it was not possible for Mr. and Mrs. Adams to obtain a house which was a pleasant exchange for the domestic surroundings to which they had been accustomed abroad. The streets and the one avenue, Pennsylvania, of which much use was made, were unpaved, and were mere sloughs of mud during a large part of each year. There were no churches of any denomination. The social circle was narrow, and the political part of it contained many coarse and undesirable elements. Society gambling, although no more common than in Europe, was the order of the day, with high stakes and their sure accompaniments of varied evil. There was much hard drinking. The practice of duelling was strongly sustained by public opinion. On the whole, the political capital of the United States was a very unpleasant place of residence for a gentleman and lady of refined tastes and quiet manners. The Secretary of State and his wife made the best of it, and their house was a centre of good social influences, if not of the rude hospitality which would have been preferred by a large class of men who discovered that Mr. Adams did not in any respect resemble them, and who hated him accordingly.

CHAPTER VIII.

Colonization—The Missouri Compromise—Calhoun's Prophecy—The Third-Term Principle—The Presidential Succession—Weights and Measures—Second Election of Mr. Monroe.

THE great question of human slavery came into the foreground of American politics in the latter part of Mr. Monroe's first term. Its presence had been felt from the foundation of the republic, and it had several times stepped forward, but had receded or been pushed aside. It gathered strength now, and there was no human power to put it away without destroying it.

In 1819 the Colonization Society applied to the President for the purchase of a territory on the African coast, to which might be sent black men rescued from slave-traders and such others as might be sent out from the United States. The subject was referred to Mr. Adams. In reporting against the project, he set forth sufficient constitutional and legal objections, and added his opinion of the Society and its visionary scheme. "There are," he said, "men of all sorts and descriptions concerned in this Colonization Society ; some exceedingly humane, weak-minded men, who really have no other than the professed objects in view, and who honestly believe them both useful and attainable ; some speculators in official profits and honors, which a colonial establishment would of course produce ; some speculators in political popularity, who think to please the abolitionists by their zeal for emancipation, and the slaveholders by the flattering hope of ridding them from the free colored people at the public expense ; lastly, some cunning slaveholders who see that the plan may be carried far enough to produce the effect of raising the market price of their slaves."

None of the men he referred to felt any more kindly toward Mr. Adams after reading his pen portrait of them, and he successfully refuted such further arguments as were advanced in favor of making Liberia a national undertaking of the United States.

During the winter session of Congress of 1818–19 the bill for the admission of Missouri was defeated in the House of Representatives on account of the slavery-permission clause in the proposed State Constitution. Mr. Adams was at that time intensely occupied by the Florida treaty, and had no occasion for a public utterance of opinion. He had definite and strong opinions upon the slavery question, but as to practical measures relating to it, his mind was as yet, as he himself declared, "a chaos." He wrote concerning the Missouri matter in July following :

"The attempt to introduce that restriction produced a violent agitation among the members from the slave-holding States, and it has been communicated to the States themselves, and to the Territory of Missouri. The slave-drivers, as usual, whenever this topic is brought up, bluster and bully, talk of the white slaves of the Eastern States, and the dissolution of the Union, and of oceans of blood ; and the Northern men, as usual, pocket all this hectoring, sit down in quiet, and submit to the slave-scourging republicanism of the planters."

He was not what was then termed an abolitionist, for he fully respected the constitutionally reserved rights of the States, however clear may have been his Federalist perception of the right and power of self-preservation belonging to the national Government. He knew that the declared peril of violent Southern action was real, although he seems to have entertained an idea that a dissolution of the Union might take place without actual war. John C. Calhoun thought differently, and one day told Mr. Adams that, in case of a dissolution of the Union, the South would seek an alliance, offensive and defensive, with Great Britain. It was a very clear-headed political prophecy, and when the day of its fulfilment came the alliance Mr. Calhoun predicted was prevented only by the prompt vigor of President Lincoln and by the attitude of Russia.

While fettered by the Constitution and the laws in his conduct as a citizen and as a statesman, Mr. Adams thought much and felt deeply. At about this time he wrote :

"Never since human sentiments and human conduct were influenced by human speech was there a theme for eloquence like the free side of this question. Oh, if but one man could arise with a genius capable of comprehending and an utterance capable of communicating those eternal truths that belong to this question, to lay bare in all its nakedness that outrage upon the goodness of

God, human slavery ; now is the time, and this is the occasion, upon which such a man would perform the duties of an angel upon earth."

There were two other abstract questions, not before him in any shape requiring public utterance or political action, upon which his written expression of opinion should be noted. Concerning European views of the territorial extension of the United States, he declared that "until Europe finds it to be a settled geographical element that the United States and North America are identical, any effort on our part to reason the world out of the belief that we are an ambitious people will have no other effect than to convince them that we add to our ambition hypocrisy."

Vast regions have been added since then, but American ambition seems to have died out at the Rio Grande, on the south, and at the Great Lakes, on the north.

Concerning what is now called "the third-term principle," he wrote, having immediate reference to dissensions in the Cabinet caused by the war of the succession :

"I see them with pain, but they are sown in the practice which the Virginia Presidents have taken so much pains to engraft upon the Constitution of the Union, making it a principle that no President can be more than twice elected, and whoever is not thrown out after one term of service must decline being a candidate after the second. This is not a principle of the Constitution, and I am satisfied it ought not to be. Its inevitable consequence is to make every administration a scene of continuous and furious electioneering for the succession to the Presidency. It was so through the whole of Mr. Madison's administration, and it is so now."

The doctrine did not begin precisely in that manner, and is rather to be looked for in the fiery speeches of Patrick Henry before the Virginia Constitutional Convention; but the opinions of Mr. Adams have had many advocates at the present day.

The great Missouri Compromise debates in Congress began with the year 1820, and Mr. Adams could be no more than an interested spectator of the struggle, lamenting that in Senate and House the anti-slavery men had only one champion, Senator Rufus King, of New York, at all able to meet the Southern orators.

The apparent success of the treaty with Spain was marred for a while. The United States had ratified it, but Spain rejected it, sending over a new minister for the purpose of obtaining a better bargain. Mr. Adams also had discovered defects in the first treaty, and was not unwilling to have it revised. In the course of the two years following Spanish diplomacy wore itself out, and the treaty was ratified by both nations, with the improvements called for by Mr. Adams. Once more Mr. Clay tried hard to defeat a measure which added so much strength to a dangerous rival, but the national will was against him. He could influence only four adverse votes in the Senate, and these were caustically indicated by Mr. Adams as: " Brown, of Louisiana, who married a sister of Clay's wife ; Richard M. Johnson, of Kentucky, against his own better judgment, from mere political subserviency to Clay ; Williams, of Tennessee, from party impulses con-

nected with hatred of General Jackson ; and Trim-
ble, of Ohio, from some maggot of the brain.''

That was a bright day for Mr. Adams. Spain
had done him no harm by sending back his first
Florida success to be studied for two years by the
people of the United States, and then to be a
second time fully approved by them.

On the same day, February 22d, 1821, he sent to
Congress a report upon weights and measures, upon
which he had expended, during four years, a vast
amount of toil. He spoke of this report, with the
treaty, as being " two of the most memorable transactions of my life." Both were enduringly useful
to his country, and both had cost him the kind of
labor for which there is no pay. Even when Minister to Russia he had been preparing that report,
searching out the weights and measures of Europe
and of Asia, and striving to ascertain with the
minutest accuracy their comparative proportions. It
was pre-eminently a work of solid and practical
statesmanship, worth infinitely more than all the
electioneering performed by his rivals in the race for
the Presidency.

The great Missouri Compromise of March 1st,
1820, received most of its Northern assent by reason
of the hope it held out of restricting the agitation
of the slavery question, as well as slavery itself, to
the regions south of latitude 36° 30'. The hope
was delusive. Before the process of admission was
completed an article inserted into the Missouri State
Constitution declared it the duty of the State Legislature to pass laws prohibiting free negroes and

persons of color from coming into Missouri, although the Constitution of the United States provides that the citizens of each State, without distinction of race or color, shall be entitled to all privileges and immunities of citizens of the other States.

Mr. Adams was not in Congress, but he took strong ground, in public and private, against this act of pro-slavery aggression. The remedy he proposed was " for Congress to pass a resolution declaring the State of Missouri to be admitted from and after the time when the article repugnant to the Constitution of the United States should be expunged from its Constitution."

In conversation with Southern Senators he declared that if he were a member of any Northern State Legislature he would propose and advocate retaliatory measures. The growing intensity of his anti-slavery feelings and expressions can sufficiently be gathered from the following quotation from his written denunciation of the hated law :

" That article is itself a dissolution of the Union. If acquiesced in it will change the terms of the federal compact—change its terms by robbing thousands of citizens of their rights. And what citizens ? The poor, the unfortunate, the helpless, already cursed by the mere color of their skin ; already doomed by their complexion to drudge in the lowest offices of society ; excluded by their color from all the refined enjoyments of life accessible to others ; excluded from the benefits of a liberal education—from the bed, the table, and all the social comforts of domestic life. This barbarous article deprives them of the little remnant of right yet left them—their rights as citizens and as men. Weak and defenceless as they are, so much the more sacred the obligation of the Legislatures of the States to which they belong to defend their lawful rights. I would defend them, should the dissolution of the Union be the consequence ; for it would be not to the defence, but to the violation of their rights, to which all the consequences would be imputable ; and if the dissolution of the Union must come, let it come from no other cause but this. If slavery be the destined sword, in the hand of the destroying angel, which is to sever the ties of this Union, the same sword will cut asunder the bonds of slavery itself."

The Southern proposition for admitting Missouri unconditionally was defeated on December 4th, 1820. On January 24th a counter-proposition for her admission upon the condition outlined by Mr. Adams was also rejected. "It satisfies neither party," he wrote. "It is too strong for the slave party, and not strong enough for the free party."

The question lingered undecided until, on February 14th, 1821, it became the duty of the House of Representatives to count the votes by which James Monroe was a second time elected President. The votes of Missouri were reached, read, objected to on the ground that she was not yet a State, and then, after a stormy debate, were left upon the record with a vague declaration that they were of no consequence one way or the other.

The question of admission continued to be the leading subject of the debates in Congress and of public interest until February 28th, 1821, when it was settled by a compromise measure, arrived at by a joint committee of the two Houses. The slavery question was as far as ever from being settled, but a sort of political curtain was invented by means of which the great enemy of the republic was for a time hidden from the eyes of ordinary party politicians and mere voters.

CHAPTER IX.

The Monroe Doctrine—Territorial Expansion—United States Bank—The American System—The Right of Search and the Slave-Trade—Newspaper Controversies.

So many writers have asserted that the United States attained their present area "because slavery wanted more territory to make slave States of," that unthinking readers suppose the assertion to be accurate. It has some truth in it, but it is nevertheless untrue. The purchases of Louisiana and Florida were made by men distinctly and openly opposed to slavery. After that the belief in the further expansion of the republic was not confined to any section or party. John Quincy Adams held the opinion at one time that the United States and the continent of North America would become equivalent terms at an early day. He believed thoroughly in the extinction of European ownership or control of every part of either North or South America, and that such ownership or control, once extinguished, should not be renewed by or with the consent of the United States. A great majority of the people held the same opinion, but had no occasion to put it into shape for utterance. This general perception and opinion was the basis of what is known as "the Monroe doctrine." When the

second term of Mr. Monroe's administration began,
the war of the succession went forward with new
vigor, and the new parties in process of organization
searched the whole field of politics for great questions upon which the people might be asked to take
sides. Quite a number were discovered, and then
men voted for their favorite candidates with less
reference to problems of political economy than the
voters themselves imagined.

The territorial extension question was one of the
important subjects proposed for general debate,
although it was difficult to put it into available
shape for campaign uses. Much was accomplished
in this direction by overhauling the history of the
Florida negotiations, including Jackson's dash after
the Seminoles ; the history of the settlement of the
Louisiana south-western boundary ; and by dwelling
upon the exceeding value of the West Indies. So
far did the discussion go in the latter direction that,
in 1823, Mr. Adams wrote to the American Minister to Spain : " It is scarcely possible to resist the
conviction that the annexation of Cuba to our Federal Republic will be indispensable to the continuance
and integrity of the Union."

The Bank of the United States, as a vast and
dangerous financial monopoly ; the tariff, as an institution requiring unlimited discussion, invention,
and experiment ; internal improvements on a scale
which called out imitators of De Witt Clinton in
every State, if not in every county ; national
economy to the verge of national starvation—all
furnished materials for editors, pamphleteers, ora-

tors, and caricature artists, and "the era of good feeling," as Mr. Monroe's double term was called at the beginning, drifted into a very curious condition of things.   Behind all, under all, and through all the slavery question groped its steady way, and whatever the country contained of anti-slavery feeling or principle drew instinctively to the support of John Quincy Adams.

Neither the ability, nor the patriotism, nor the courage of President Monroe should be lost sight of in presenting the proof that he and his Secretary of State were in absolute accord with reference to European interference with American affairs, or the reverse.

On July 23d, 1823, Mr. Adams informed the Russian Minister that the United States "should assume distinctly the principle that the American continents are no longer subjects for any new European colonial establishments."   On December 2d, 1823, the language used in Mr. Monroe's message to Congress was : "The occasion has been judged proper for asserting, as a principle in which the rights and interests of the United States are involved, that the American continents, by the free and independent condition which they have assumed and maintain, are henceforth not to be considered as subjects for future colonization by any European powers."

This utterance was called forth by the apparent probability that the allied royalties of Europe, as part of a crusade against republicanism, were about to join hands with Spain in reconquering her lost possessions in South America. Nothing could be plainer than that such a crusade, if successful at all, must become so by crushing the head and front of all republicanism, the United States, and Mr. Adams went even further than Mr. Monroe in his declared conviction that the United States might as well begin to fight for its life at the beginning. The danger so promptly and courageously met soon vanished, and the United States added a long step to the great advance it had made by the War of 1812.

The Monroe doctrine had and has its counterpoise, formulated first in Washington's farewell advice against " entangling alliances with foreign powers." This other side of the subject Mr. Adams had also occasions for presenting. In the Greek struggle for freedom from Turkish tyranny he sympathized deeply, as did all his countrymen ; but he plainly declared that under no circumstances could Greece look to the United States for national aid or interference. Not even his strong feelings and convictions upon the question of human slavery prevented him from refusing to consider a proposition for uniting the United States with European powers in a league for the suppression of the slave trade. In the way of it, he said, was " the general extra-European policy of the United States — a policy which they had always pursued, as best suited to their own interests and best adapted to harmonize with those of Europe, which had never considered the United States as belonging to her system."

From that of which it did not and could not form

a part, the nation he represented must persistently separate its plans of action.

The far-seeing statesmanship of Mr. Adams looked forward to the day when North America would become the United States, not quite perceiving that such a result might be sufficiently attained without laboriously absorbing the local self-governments of either Canada or Mexico. In the year 1820, three years before the Monroe message, he had had an opportunity for presenting one phase of the Monroe doctrine and of its counterpart, and at the same time of defining still further the farewell advice of Washington. The Portuguese Minister suggested to him that the United States and Portugal, then controlling Brazil, were " the two great powers of the western hemisphere," and should concert together a comprehensive American system—that is, that by way of Portugal the United States should become mixed in European affairs, and by way of Brazil, help perpetuate European colonization in South America, forming a series of entangling alliances all the while. Mr. Adams was polite to the Portuguese Minister, but deemed the proposal grotesquely funny, as it undoubtedly was. He wrote, however : " As to an American system, we have it ; we constitute the whole of it ; there is no community of interests or of principles between North and South America." He did not add his opinion as to the political southern boundary of North America, which is by no means the same with its geographical boundary.

There was yet another old battle-field of the diplomatic career of Mr. Adams included in the proposition of Great Britain for joint action with the United States against the slave trade, and the Secretary of State was sure of the President's fiery support in any conflict which he might enter into with the British Minister, the moment it touched England's claim to the right of search. The right to search vessels under the American flag for possible black men, if agreed to, was dangerously related to her claimed right to search them for possible British sailors, and neither the one nor the other was to be admitted under any arrangement whatever. Mr. Adams declared : " All concession of principle tended to encourage encroachment, and if naval officers were once habituated to search the vessels of other nations in time of peace for one thing, they would be still more encouraged to practise it for another thing in time of war."

He suggested, however, with dry bitterness, that something might be done if Great Britain would consent " to bind herself by an article, as strong and explicit as language could make it, never again in time of war to take a man from an American vessel." Mr. Jefferson had pigeon-holed Mr. Monroe's hardly-won treaty with England because it did not contain precisely such an article, and Mr. Adams had toiled and argued vainly for the same thing at Ghent.

There were many stormy interviews between Mr. Adams and Mr. Stratford Canning, the British Minister, who was a perfect representative of the sharp law-practice maxim which was the soul of England's diplomacy, and led her representatives, in every case, to "begin by claiming everything and denying everything."

From time to time efforts were made to drag Mr. Adams into the continual newspaper skirmishing of the political war of the succession. As a rule, he maintained a dignified silence, but he defended himself with vigor and success from calumnies relating to his course at Ghent, and to other parts of his official career. All the while performing important public services and leaving behind him deep marks for good upon the history of his country, he toiled onward through the increasing excitement of the first severely contested Presidential canvass which the country had seen since the first election of Thomas Jefferson.

CHAPTER X.

The Canvass and the Candidates—Mr. Clay's Decision—Mr. Adams Elected President—An Unpartisan Administration—The Charge of Political Bargaining.

In March, 1818, Mr. Adams was asked by Mr. Everett if he was "determined to do nothing with a view to promote his future election to the Presidency as the successor of Mr. Monroe." "Absolutely nothing." replied Mr. Adams, and in adhering to that determination he did more than he could have done in any other way to make his nomination and election sure.

Mr. Crawford, of Georgia, who worked hardest and intrigued most successfully, obtained a nomination by a Congressional caucus such as had previously nominated three Presidents. It was a great success, with a great recoil, for it at once concentrated against Mr. Crawford all the intense popular jealousy of caucus tyranny throughout the land.

General Jackson was a much more dangerous rival, but Mr. Adams had generously been his champion, alone, in the Cabinet of Mr. Monroe and before the country, and therefore the personal popularity of the hero of New Orleans did not react against Mr. Adams as it did against Mr. Clay.

The old-time breach between Mr. Adams and

Mr. Clay did not widen in the Presidential canvass, but grew narrower instead, while Mr. Clay's relations with the other candidates became more and more personally and politically unpleasant.

The political canvass was everywhere pressed with a heat and vigor never before approached. No means existed whereby the acutest politician could estimate the causes or the probabilities of success. In one sense, Mr. Adams was not a politician at all, and he was now altogether in a fog. A member of Congress told him one day, while the result was yet in doubt, that there were sanguine hopes of his election, and in his reply he said :

"Whether I ought to wish for success is one of the greatest uncertainties of the election. . . . To me alone, of all the candidates before the nation, failure of success would be equivalent to a vote of censure by the nation upon my past services."

It could be nothing of the kind. When the votes᾽ were counted they declared a wide-spread conviction that he was a Northern man, opposed to slavery, and that a vast number of voters who had heard of him knew little or nothing about his services. The fathers of some of them had always hated old John Adams, and a son of his must have been born a Federalist. They passed a vote of censure upon him accordingly, without any reference to what he had done at Ghent or elsewhere, or to anything he had written about pound-weights and yard-sticks.

He said again : " You will be disappointed. To me both alternatives are distressing in prospect. The most formidable is that of success. All the danger is on the pinnacle. The humiliation of failure will be so much more than compensated by the safety in which it will leave me, that I ought to regard it as a consummation devoutly to be wished."

He declared that if elected he should turn no one out of office on account of his conduct or opinions during the election, but should do what he could to break up the remnant of all party distinctions. He was not and never had been a party man, and that was what now made him President.

When the several States reported the action of their electoral colleges, in December, 1824, it appeared that of the two hundred and sixty-one votes cast, Andrew Jackson had ninety-one, John Quincy Adams, eighty-four, William H. Crawford, forty-one, and Henry Clay, thirty-seven. The Vice-Presidency fell at once upon John C. Calhoun, who received one hundred and eighty votes, but the Presidential election went to the House of Representatives.

Delaware and Illinois each gave one vote to Mr. Adams, and Maryland gave him three. The only Southern votes which came to him were two from Louisiana, perhaps on account of his defence of General Jackson. His other seventy-seven votes were given him by New York and New England, and were as significant as was his failure to obtain any at all from the old, solid Southern interest.

In the House of Representatives Mr. Clay ceased at once to be a candidate. Mr. Crawford's failing health gave Mr. Clay an excellent public reason for not transferring to him the decisive vote which he now possessed. The sectional character of the Electoral College returns notified all clear-headed politicians that Mr. Adams could never again be a successful candidate. At the same time no other political fact could be plainer to Mr. Clay than that he and General Jackson were to be the leaders of the two great party divisions of the immediate future. He hated General Jackson too much to be selfishly wise, and gave the election to Mr. Adams, when, by taking the opposite course and putting General Jackson in, with little or nothing to stand on, the way would have been cleared for himself at the end of four years instead of being utterly blocked up.

When the vote was declared in the House of Representatives, February 9th, 1825, by two tellers, one from the South named John Randolph and one from the North named Daniel Webster, thirteen votes had been given to John Quincy Adams, seven to Andrew Jackson, and four to William H. Crawford.

It was not such an election as the just pride of Mr. Adams would have asked for. When notified of it, he responded to the committee in a manner which men who did not know him could not believe to be sincere. He spoke well of the character and public services of his defeated competitors, but added that he should refuse to accept if his refusal would bring the question once more before the people for their verdict. As it would not he accepted the trust, with confidence in the wisdom of the legislative branch of the Government and a trust in the direction of a superintending Providence.

Henry Clay had given abundant reasons for his

opposition to General Jackson year after year, and he gave them publicly now. There was not one shadow of a reason why any man should question the utter honesty of his preference for John Quincy Adams over a man whom he had denounced in public and private. Nevertheless General Jackson and his partisans did question it, vehemently charging upon Mr. Clay and Mr. Adams a corrupt bargain by which the one was to become President and the other Secretary of State, contrary to the will of the people.

That Mr. Clay accepted the office of Secretary of State from the man to whom he had awarded the Presidency gave point to the purely vindictive slander, kept it alive during the brief administration of Mr. Adams, and enabled General Jackson to then go before the people and demand the office of which, as he declared, he had been corruptly deprived. All of that was party politics, concerning which, apart from statesmanship and principles, Mr. Adams was never able to form any correct perception.

He made practically no removals from office, and in all new appointments he strove to disregard party lines, or rather any previous political affiliations. He did not found or foster any political organization, nor did the country contain any to which he could be said to be indebted for his elevation. On December 31st, 1825, he wrote in his diary :

"The year has been the most momentous of those that have passed over my head, inasmuch as it has witnessed my elevation, at the age of fifty-eight, to the Chief Magistracy of my country, to the summit of laudable or at least blameless worldly ambition ; not, however, in a manner satisfactory to pride or to just desire ; not by the unequivocal suffrages of a majority of the people ; with perhaps two thirds of the whole people adverse to the actual result."

By no means so large a proportion were really dissatisfied. The more intelligent classes throughout the land were disposed to expect good administration from a public servant so accomplished, so able, so thoroughly trained and experienced. All the outcry raised against him belonged to the preparatory malignities of the next Presidential canvass.

CHAPTER XI.

General Jackson's New Campaign—The Beginning of Nullification—A Powerless Administration—A Harvest of Calumny—White House Habits—Election of Andrew Jackson.

WHEN the administration of John Quincy Adams began it had a nominal working majority in both Houses of Congress, but this was made up of elements among which there was no real cohesion. It was ready to melt away, and rapidly did so. Even the officeholders throughout the country quickly understood that they had nothing to lose by abusing Mr. Adams.

In both Houses there were at the beginning a strong and cohesive opposition minority, with everything to gain and nothing to lose. The Legislature of Tennessee gave to them and to all the political driftwood in the country a centre and rallying-point by at once renominating General Jackson for the Presidency. From that time forward the long political campaign was fought right on, precisely upon the tactics which had directed his campaign in Florida. There he had put aside all considerations of treaties, international law, public policy, and had followed the Seminoles unflinchingly. So had his men followed him, and were ready to do it again. Now in and out of Congress, whatever might be plainly de-

clared as an administration measure was to be opposed, assailed, defeated, as a kind of political
Seminole.

Whatever else might be accomplished by such a
system of party warfare, vigorously and unscrupu-
lously carried on, the administration was crippled
and its usefulness was narrowed.

In his first message to Congress, in 1825, Mr.
Adams recommended :

" The maturing into a permanent and regular system the application of all the superfluous revenues of the Union to internal
improvement.

" The establishment of a uniform standard of weights and measures, which had been a duty expressly enjoined on Congress by the
Constitution of the United States.

" The establishment of a naval school of instruction for the formation of scientific and accomplished officers, the want of which
is felt with a daily and increasing aggravation.

" The establishment of a national university, which had been
more than once earnestly recommended to Congress by Washington, and for which he had made express provision in his will.

" Connected with a university, or separated from it, the erection
of an astronomical observatory, with provision for the support of
an astronomer."

Only one of these recommendations—the first—
offered any important political material, but the ut-
most possible use was made of that against Mr.
Adams in every place where it would serve any purpose to call him a " Federalist, proposing a magnifi-
cent national Government." As to that and all the
other recommendations, nothing was done with them
in the Congress nominally supporting the administration.

The storm which began with Mr. Clay's decision

against General Jackson, and which had pursued him into the Cabinet, blew harder and harder. No amount of proof was sufficient to kill that calumny, and there is reason to believe that the general refused to put it away long after other men grew ashamed of it.

The State of South Carolina had already taken an unconstitutional position with reference to the tariff question, which threatened to bring her into collision with the general Government.

The State of Georgia claimed the lands of the Creek Indians as within its boundaries, and popular feeling in that State was growing strongly opposed to an administration which found anything sacred in solemn covenants made with red men.

The struggles of local or State factions, in which the President refused to take a part, could but array against him in each case both contestants instead of only one. He declared that "neutrality toward parties is the only proper policy of a President in office." He pursued it conscientiously, and when the Twentieth Congress came together, in December, 1827, both Houses were controlled by the opposition for the first time in the political history of the country. The record of legislation during the term of Mr. Adams, for all these reasons, separated itself more and more from the life record which he was making, and requires no more extended analysis in his biography.

The Anti-Masonry party in New York accused him of being a Mason, but he refused to make a public denial, although not a Mason. The record of his official employments was made up, and all his salaries and expense accounts were added together to show how much public money he had received, and how he had been pampered and fed at the public cost. Every vote he had given in the Senate was searched out and criticised. Every step of his long diplomatic service was placed under a partisan microscope. Slanders came up everywhere, like Canada thistles. He refused to answer them then, and they are not worth mentioning now, so long have they been dead. There is a curious propriety in the fact that the rancor of mere party hate at one time went a step beyond calumny, and threatened him with assassination.

The old habits of study were for a time shattered. The exercise required for the preservation of bodily health was sometimes sought for in horseback-rides, and also by swimming daily in the Potomac River when the weather permitted. The middle hours of each day were given to public business, and only by establishing an early bedtime in summer, often between eight and nine o'clock, could any hours be rescued from the public service for such private life as was possible to a very hard-working President. Early to bed meant early to rise. Before the servants of the White House were awake, often in winter-time even as early as from four o'clock to five, Mr. Adams was up, kindling his own fire when fire was needed. The day invariably began with two or three chapters of the Bible, "with Scott's and Hewlett's commentaries." Then, if the weather allowed, came a walk for health, from which he sometimes returned before sunrise. Shortly after he and other men had eaten breakfast the daily stream of visitors set in, bringing with it duties of every shade and annoyances of every possible invention.

As time went on it became very plainly manifest that Andrew Jackson was to be the next President of the United States, but Mr. Adams received at last only one vote less than had been given him in 1824. He had eighty-four then in the Electoral College who believed he would make a good President, and eighty-three now declared that he had done so and deserved a second term. At that time one hundred and seventy-seven votes were divided among Jackson, Clay, and Crawford. One hundred and seventy-eight votes were now concentrated upon General Jackson, and the two parties of the future for the first time met face to face. Mr. Calhoun was re-elected Vice-President by one hundred and seventy-one votes, eleven less than in 1824, as if to show that the something or other which he represented reached over any party line then existing. It continued to do so through all the political history of that and the next generation.

Clearly as Mr. Adams had foreseen the result, and firmly as he had refused to lift a hand to prevent it, he permitted it to oppress him unduly. He was tired out, and he misunderstood the election. Too weary in body and mind and too sore in heart to understand that an honor had been conferred upon him by the sharp-eyed evils which had singled him out as their enemy, he wrote in his diary, on New Year's Day, 1829: " The year begins in gloom.

My wife had a sleepless and painful night. The dawn was overcast, and as I began to write my shaded lamp went out, self-extinguished. It was only for lack of oil, and the notice of so trivial an incident may serve but to mark the present temper of my mind.''

It was a temper from which both he and his sympathizing wife could easily recover. She had well maintained the social side of the White House during her husband's administration of the affairs of the nation. No previous occupants had ever left it with a more full and universal assurance that its simple dignity had been preserved, and that every influence and tone pervading it or going from it had been altogether pure and good. Mrs. Adams had taken her place well in the line of noble women which began with Martha Washington.

THE BIRTHPLACE OF JOHN QUINCY ADAMS.

CHAPTER XII.

The Quincy Homestead—Family Changes—Student and Gardener—Property—Anti-Slavery Position—Elected to Congress—An Utterly Independent Statesman—First Services.

ANDREW JACKSON took the oath of office as President of the United States on March 4th, 1829.

John Quincy Adams had already written in his diary :

"Three days more and I shall be restored to private life and left to an old age of retirement, though certainly not of repose. I go into it with a combination of parties and public men against my character and reputation such as I believe never before was exhibited against any man since this Union existed. Posterity will scarcely believe it, but so it is, that this combination against me has been formed, and is now exulting in triumph over me, for the devotion of my life and of all the faculties of my soul to the Union, and to the improvement, physical, moral, and intellectual, of my country."

He proposed to retire from all connection with public affairs, looking forward only to some " useful and profitable occupation, engaging so much of his thoughts and feelings that his mind might not be left to corrode itself."

During all the absorbing cares and toils of his official life after his return to America he had been in the habit of paying a yearly visit to the family homestead at Quincy, Massachusetts. Changes had

come which had made it altogether his own. His
brother Charles had passed away in 1800 ; his sister,
Mrs. Smith, in 1813 ; on October 26th, 1818, his
mother had been taken away. Of that event he
wrote :

"This is one of the severest afflictions to which human existence
is liable. The silver cord is broken, the tenderest of natural ties
is dissolved ; life is no longer to me what it was, my home is no
longer the abode of my mother. While she lived, whenever I returned to the paternal roof I felt as if the joys and charms of
childhood returned to make me happy ; all was kindness and affection. At once silent and active as the movements of one of the
orbs of heaven, one of the links which connected me with former
ages is no more. May a merciful Providence spare for many
future years my only remaining parent !"

The tie between father and son had always been
strong. They had been teacher and pupil, companions in fatigue and peril, and fellow-travellers in
foreign lands. Its earthly part broke at last, however, and on July 4th, 1826, the Quincy homestead
passed to its new owner. He was himself, at sixty-
two, almost an old man when he returned to it, in
1829, but the remarkable career which to him seemed
terminated when he crossed the threshold had had
nothing in it of greater value to his country than
filled the seventeen years of usefulness which then
began.

Mr. Adams came back to his home to find it
changed and to people it anew, but at first it seemed
as if there had been little or no change in the old-
time political animosities. The first important act
of what he deemed his retirement was to refuse,
with great dignity and forbearance, a public contro-

versy all but forced upon him by the most influential men of what had once been the Federal
Party.

Having been cut off, as he supposed, from the
politics of the present, he tried to sever himself from
annoyances belonging to the politics of the past.
He resumed his habits of study, with special attention to astronomy, Latin authors, and the Scrip-
tures. For the first time since he went on board
the Boston in Nantasket Roads, in 1778, he was able
to take up again some thoughts and things which
he had been fond of when a boy. The rocks, the
birds, the animals, the trees, the plants all around
him, were such as he had studied then, and he lov-
ingly renewed the long-interrupted acquaintance.
In the summer season the Quincy people were able,
two or three hours each day, to go and see how an
ex-President of the United States looked at work in
his garden. They all agreed very soon that Quincy
had as good a right to be proud as had Monticello,
or Montpellier, or Oak Hill.

It was at about this time that Mr. Adams began
preparations for a biography of his father, to which
he looked forward as an important part of his remaining work.

He was neither rich nor poor. Some property had
come to him by inheritance ; he had saved something from salaries and law fees ; he had invested
all so as to produce an income of six thousand dollars, a third of which was absorbed by the interest
of mortgages. Four thousand dollars per annum,
therefore, was left for the modest expenses of an al-

together retired statesman, and it was certainly none too much.

Now, as before, and as he remained to the end, Mr. Adams was an anti-slavery man without being an abolitionist. Slavery was an unmitigated evil to his mind, but one which the people of the Northern States had no right to attack so long as it kept within its own constitutionally guarded State lines. If it crossed them, if it assailed the Union, then by that act it destroyed for itself its constitutional wall, and could be smitten down. His position did not differ materially from that afterward held by William H. Seward and Abraham Lincoln. Shortly after his retirement he wrote :

"It [the abolition of slavery] is the only part of European democracy which will find no favor in the United States. It may aggravate the condition of slaves in the South, but the result of the Missouri question and the attitude of parties have silenced most of the declaimers on that subject. *This state of things is not to continue forever.* It is possible that the danger of the abolition doctrines, when brought home to Southern statesmen, may teach them the value of the Union, as the only thing which can maintain their system of slavery."

All through the rest of the year 1829 the people of the Quincy or Plymouth Congressional District talked more and more about the manner in which John Quincy Adams was conducting himself. Some of them had seen him at work in his garden. During the next season they saw him there again, and they began to say to one another : "We haven't anything really against him. Would he go to Congress ?"

One of them came and carefully made the inquiry of the gardening philosopher himself, and was answered : " No person would be degraded by serving the people as a Representative in Congress. Nor in my opinion would an ex-President of the United States be degraded by serving as a select-man of his town, if elected thereto by the people."

To another inquirer he said : " It must first be seen whether the people of the district will invite me to represent them.   I shall not ask their votes.   I wish them to act their pleasure."

They did so at the next election, in November, 1830, giving him eighteen hundred and seventeen votes out of twenty-five hundred and sixty-five.   It was sixteen years later before it was of any use for another man to run for Congress in that district.

The retirement dream had lasted long enough. Mr. Adams took his seat when the Twenty-second Congress met, December 22d, 1831, and one of the public questions to which he found his attention called was the course pursued by the State of Georgia toward the Indians, to which he had refused his co-operation while President.   All the other old political problems were there, some just as he had left them, some temporarily quiescent, some assuming new shapes full of peril to the nation.   All the sectional jealousies, all the personal enmities, all the slanderous political inventions which had embittered his four years at the White House, occupied seats in the legislative chamber when it was entered by Mr. Adams.

It was quickly understood that a new element had

been brought into the debates of Congress, a man
of vast experience and knowledge, deep and thorough scholarship, perfectly comprehending the men
and the time, without ambition and without fear,
owing no party allegiance, past or present, and
hampered by no subserviency whatever to the ambition of other men. This man had brought with
him a peculiar oratorical power, differing widely
from that of other men, yet of a grade which soon
obtained for him the title of "the old man eloquent." He had also brought with him a power of
withering analysis. To all this he added a capacity for invective and denunciation rarely if ever
surpassed. He had not studied Cicero and Burke
so faithfully for nothing, and he positively, keenly
enjoyed to the last the frequent exercise of every
faculty which he could bring to bear upon what he
regarded and declared the one great enemy of his
country.

Mr. Adams received his Congressional nomination
from what was first called the National Republican
and afterward the Whig Party, but he had been
elected by the people of the Quincy district, and to
them he at once announced that he should hold
himself bound to no party, sectional or political.
Now, as when first a member of the United States
Senate, it was necessary for him to stand alone.
No other man or set of men could be held responsi-
ble for his utterances or his votes. At the same
time, the untrammelled discharge of duty, guided
by principle only, was sure to render him of the ut-
most possible service to the nation as a whole.

The fact that Mr. Adams appreciated the social difficulties and respected the constitutional rights of the slave-holding South, that he was not an abolitionist, received a marked illustration at the outset. His first act as a member was to offer in the House fifteen petitions from the people of Pennsylvania, asking for the abolition of slavery in the District of Columbia. He moved their reference to the Committee on the affairs of the District, but accompanied the motion with the remark that he was not prepared to support such a measure, and should not do so.

CHAPTER XIII.

An Industrious Legislator—Appreciated by Political Enemies— The Censure of the House—Opposing Nullification—Enmity to Jackson.

SHORTLY after Mr. Adams made his appearance in the House of Representatives, he was asked by Henry Clay how he felt about turning boy again, his old associate adding that he would probably find it hard work. Mr. Adams replied only to the suggestion of toil : " I well know this ; but labor I shall not refuse so long as my hands, my eyes, and my brain do not desert me."

He kept his word year after year, no other member exceeding and few equalling his steady punctuality of attendance. He was each day one of the first to come and one of the last to go. He was a frequent speaker, closely watching the course of all business of any general interest or importance. It is this very industry which renders it both possible and impossible to trace with minute accuracy his opinions and his action. He gave to every question and subject as it came the best wisdom and knowledge that he had, and the record of his speeches and his votes is almost that of Congressional legislation during his long term of service.

Without any apparent desire or faculty for making friends, he was scornfully indifferent to the number or the bitterness of his enemies, and one result was that neither the character nor the value of his work was set before the country by any political following such as praised other statesmen in the hope of increasing their partisan usefulness. He was yet a distinct power upon the floor of the House, and hackneyed political partisans listened attentively to the very speeches in which he held them up for derision or scorched them with invective. What was more wonderful, he was able at times to sway the course of Congressional action remarkably.

The most laborious part of the duties of a Congressman is not always performed upon the floor or in debate. When Mr. Adams, in 1831, was appointed Chairman of the Committee on Manufactures, with part of President Jackson's message to consider and report upon, he reluctantly consented to serve, and only because assured that "the continuance of the Union might depend upon questions relative to the tariff."

He objected then because of unfamiliarity with manufactures, and, three months later, when named as one of a committee to investigate the affairs of the United States Bank, he added the second duty to the reasons he gave for again asking relief from the first. His request was opposed now by his political enemies. Members from New York, Virginia, and South Carolina vied with each other in tributes to his patriotism, his statesmanship, his standing before the nation, and especially to the ability and fidelity with which he had performed his duty as Chairman of the Committee on Manufactures.

Similar testimony accumulated rapidly in after years. Mr. Adams became known as one of the best practical legislators in one Congress after another during a period when such work as he was able to give was of the last importance to the longer endurance of the United States as one nation.

Highly as were his services appreciated by his committee, its majority compelled him, as chairman, May 23d, 1832, to present a report to only part of which he assented.

The features from which he dissented gave him an opportunity for a powerful speech assailing the idea then paramount at the South that the interests of that section were distinct from those of the North with reference to the tariff question. He unsparingly denounced a system based upon sectional selfishness, which " left our shores to take care of themselves, our navy to perish by dry rot upon the stocks, our manufactures to wither under the blast of foreign competition." Sectionalism in that day laid its hand upon all questions as it cannot do now, and Mr. Adams, in common with other leading men North and South, declared that the position taken by those who separated the interests of the manufacturer and the agriculturist was " striking directly at the heart of the Union, and leading inevitably to its dissolution." He advocated a protective tariff, national defensive preparation, internal improvements, and then went to the root of the matter by ascribing the perils which threatened the life of the nation as due " to that great, comprehensive, but peculiar Southern interest, which is now protected by the laws of the United States, but which, in case of severance of the Union, must produce consequences from which a statesman of either portion of it cannot but avert his eyes."

Upon every question yet before Congress, even including the question of slavery, not yet before it in tangible form, Mr. Adams had pretty numerous company, but in July, 1832, he managed to stand alone once more for a moment in defence of his rights as a member. A motion had been made censuring another member for words spoken in debate. The roll was called, and when the name of Mr. Adams was reached he, instead of voting, handed a paper to the clerk, and it was read—" I ask to be excused from voting on the resolution, believing it to be unconstitutional, inasmuch as it assumes inferences of fact from words spoken by the member, without giving the words themselves, and the fact not being warranted, in my judgment, by the words he used."

He had placed the House in a dilemma. It must condemn its own action or his, and it decidedly chose to condemn him. It refused to excuse him, and the roll was called again. Once more he claimed his right to decline from conscientious motives, without intending disrespect to the House, and asked permission to place on the journal his reasons for declining. He was told that the latter course would but be a record by the House of its own condemnation, and that he might easily have escaped the rule compelling him to vote, for he could have walked out before the vote was taken.

"I do not choose," said Mr. Adams, "to shrink
from my duty by any such expedient. It is not
my right alone, but the right of all the members
and of all the people of the United States which
are concerned in this question, and I cannot
evade it. I regret the state of things, but I must
abide by the consequences, whatever they may
be."

Seventy-four to fifty-four, the House again refused
to excuse him. The rule was read by the Speaker,
the votes were called again, and Mr. Adams was
again silent when his name was uttered. It was
necessary to pass the vote of censure upon the other
member without hearing aye or nay from him, but
two resolutions were offered, one declaring him
guilty of a breach of the rules, and another appointing a committee of inquiry to discover what should
be done with him, declaring the case "novel and
important." Before those resolutions were acted
upon the following day, members had had time to
consider whether the country as a whole was likely
to agree with them or with Mr. Adams. There was
a debate, not so stormy as the previous tumult
caused by his refusal, and his enemies were eager to
pass upon him so depressing a vote of censure as he
had seemed to call for; but Mr. Everett concluded
a few remarks of dignified remonstrance with them
by a motion to lay the whole matter on the table,
and the House agreed with him, eighty-nine to
sixty-three, that its wisest course was to pass that
motion. It had been a splendid test of the courage
and independence of Mr. Adams, and strengthened

notably his position as a man from whom utter devotion to principle was to be expected.

In December, 1832, the State of South Carolina began to take openly the dangerous ground in opposition to the tariff laws known in American political history as nullification, and the administration seemed to hesitate. Not until a year later, January 16th, 1833, did General Jackson send in a message to Congress declaring a vigorous policy. Mr. Adams then at once found himself side by side with his old enemy, ready to go as far or a little farther in crushing nullification than was the general himself. It was neither the first nor the last time that the administration received the support, accompanied by the terribly free and caustic criticisms, of its bitterest enemy ; of a man who described "the hero of New Orleans" as "a barbarian, who could not write a sentence of grammar, and hardly could spell his own name."

CHAPTER XIV.

The Texas Question—Old Issues Dying—The Flurry of War with France—Public Addresses—The Right of Petition—A Long War Begun.

ON March 4th, 1833, began the second term of President Jackson. The opposition could control only sixty-nine votes in the electoral colleges against the two hundred and nineteen which testified how well the general had read and how nearly he represented the general drift of popular feeling. As a grammarian, and in other respects plainly indicated from time to time by Mr. Adams and others, he was undoubtedly defective, but as a political leader not so much so. Had they been friends instead of enemies, if that could under any circumstances have been possible, the President might have been better understood by the member of the House from Quincy. As it was, neither of them was likely to perceive any good in the other, and both were uncommonly plain-speaking men.

One of the accusations brought against Mr. Adams during the latter part of his term as President was that, when Secretary of State under Monroe, he had failed in the negotiations with reference to the Southwestern boundary, and had lost an opportunity of obtaining the region which now constitutes the State of Texas. He was proved to have done his whole duty, but the party to which he was now opposed proceeded to do more. In various ways the Texas question was preparing during President Jackson's first term, especially by Southern planter-emigrants who went to Texas and took their slaves with them, contrary to Mexican law.

The United States Bank question reached its culmination, and was arbitrarily crushed, bank and all, by the President's iron hand, regardless of law, of the opposition of the Whig Party, and of the eloquent protests of Mr. Adams.

Other old questions died away, and so did men, and so did some personal animosities, for there were not lacking, South or North, those whose minds were broad enough to comprehend that Mr. Adams was now what is called an institution rather than an individual. He was a great mind, stored with and representing and uttering ideas, and was to be dealt with accordingly. The many enemies made by President Jackson in his own party by his arbitrary and oppressive dictatorship were apt to soften toward the general's old enemy when smarting under their grievances. On April 30th, 1834, in the course of a heated debate, a South Carolina member turned toward Mr. Adams with great earnestness, and said : " Well do I remember the enthusiastic zeal with which we reproached the administration of that gentleman, and the ardor and vehemence with which we labored to bring in another. For the share I had in those transactions—and it was not a small one—I hope God will forgive me, for I shall never forgive myself."

Uncompromising as was the enmity between Mr. Adams and the President, the latter was indebted to him, and to him alone, for the support he received at another critical juncture. It was when General Jackson turned toward France as unflinchingly as once against the Seminoles, ordered Mr. Livingston, Minister to France, to get his passports, leave Paris, and go to London, and then sent to Congress a message advising war measures unless the French Government should at once comply with the terms of the treaty of 1831, including its cash indemnity payments. Timid men were alarmed, party ties were not strong enough to hold them, and the President's support in the House was breaking to pieces under the sudden shock, when Mr. Adams came to the rescue. The speech he made, eloquent, patriotic, convincing, turned the tide, and solidified the House in support of the administration. It was a speech which at the same time risked the reputation and influence of the speaker. His fear that it might destroy his political future, however, was unjust to the people of his district. That sort of remarkable and unexpected thing was precisely what most of them expected him to do. Even those who were angry with him for it were quite ready to vote for him again, while the anti-slavery men and women were somewhat indifferent to his course upon other matters, so long as they received accounts every now and then of fiercely dramatic scenes on the floor of Congress, when their representative fearlessly expressed for them all the wrath they had in them.

General Jackson saw no occasion for melting, and

there really was not any. Mr. Adams said of him, in November, 1837 : " Though I had served him more than any other living man ever did, and though I supported his administration at the hazard of my own political destruction, and effected for him, at a moment when his own friends were deserting him, what no other member of Congress ever accomplished for him — an unanimous vote of the House of Representatives to support him in his quarrel with France—though I supported him in other critical periods of his administration, my return from him was insult, indignity, and slander."

It was so. General Jackson unerringly read the deep-seated personal antipathy which, more than a year later, impelled Mr. Adams to oppose the action of Harvard College in conferring upon the President the degree of doctor of laws, and, when unable to prevent it, still to refuse his presence at the Commencement exercises when the honor was conferred.

Again and again the "old man eloquent" found himself called upon to deliver public addresses, and notable civic occasions were considered to have received a cap-sheaf when it was possible to announce that John Quincy Adams was to be the orator of the day. Even his mere presence was worth especial effort to obtain. In Congress also his eulogies of public men were asked for and listened to with profound respect as, one after the other, the old worthies passed away. No more notable instance of this need be sought for than the unanimous vote of both Houses, in December, 1834, naming him as the proper person to address them upon the life,

character, and services of Lafayette. Of that address the House of Representatives ordered fifty
thousand printed copies and the Senate ten thousand, while Henry Clay in the Senate declared that
" if he were to be guided by his opinion of the great
talents of the orator and the extraordinary merit of
the oration, he should be unable to specify any
number."

Mr. Adams was a bodily representative of the
natural right of all men to freedom of speech,
although he had deprecated the agitation of the
slavery question as imperilling the public peace and
the stability of the Union.   He now saw, more and
more clearly, that the really perilous agitation came
from slavery itself, and that, having secured the
Missouri Compromise, it was taking new form in
the movement for the annexation of Texas.   He
had been all his life an annexationist, and had so
declared himself ; but he was now forced into a
different position by his antipathy to slavery, first,
and then to the methods employed or projected for
the further increase of the national domain.   The
movement for the annexation of Texas was distinctly a movement to restore the tottering balance
of power in Congress, particularly in the Senate, by
the creation of one or more slave States.   Southern
leaders, far-sighted men, regarded it as an act of
self-preservation.   They were not wise, however, in
adding to their other political difficulties a war upon
the constitutional right of petition, making Mr.
Adams its champion.   In January, 1835, it became
his duty to present a petition from one hundred and

seven women of his district, praying for the abolition of slavery in the District of Columbia. He
moved its reference to a committee, with instructions to report. This was a long step forward, and
was so understood. It was a warning of trouble
to come. Not but what other petitions, many of
them, had been presented, but all had been merely
handed in as so much waste paper, to be put aside
at once, while now, in very impressive language, a
report was asked for. In so doing Mr. Adams
keenly denounced the absurdity of declaring the
slave trade at sea piracy, and of punishing as pirates
the felons who carried it on, while the same pursuit
was declared respectable when followed within sight
of the windows of the Capitol.

This time the petition was received, but its com-
mitment was refused, and it was laid on the table.
Others followed from time to time, until, a year
later, January 4th, 1836, when Mr. Adams presented
an abolition petition, Mr. Glascock, of Georgia,
moved at once that it should not be received at all.
Stormy debates followed day after day, and these
grew more bitter as other petitions came in. On
February 8th the whole subject, including several
parliamentary devices for defeating the right of
petition, was referred to a committee. In ten days
they reported a set of resolutions which set forth :
First, that Congress had no power to interfere with
slavery in any State. Second, that Congress ought
not to interfere with it in the District of Columbia.
Third, that because of the offensive and dangerous
nature of the subject, " all petitions, memorials,

resolutions, or papers relating in any way or to any extent whatsoever to the subject of slavery or the abolition of slavery shall, without being either printed or referred, be laid upon the table, and that no further action whatever shall be taken thereon."

In spite of every effort of Mr. Adams, he was refused an opportunity to speak. The first resolution was passed with only nine votes against it. He was excused from voting upon the second. The roll was called upon the third, and when his name was reached he sprang to his feet, exclaiming : " I hold the resolution to be a direct violation of the Constitution of the United States, the rules of this House, and the rights of my constituents."

He spoke amid a storm of angry calls to order, and the resolution passed by a vote of one hundred and seventeen to sixty-eight. Its advocates had made a blunder, and loaded themselves with the odious " gag rule," and Mr. Adams became, to the day of his death, the acknowledged champion of the right of petition. The people of his district would have continued him in Congress for that if for no other reason. Petitions poured in to him to be presented and laid upon the table under the " gag," each presentation being accompanied by some arrowy sentence which did its work. On one day, February 14th, 1838, he handed in at once three hundred and fifty, and on one or two later occasions he even exceeded that number. It was one long battle, or, rather, a long succession of skirmishes, in which no man who came into wordy collision with Mr. Adams came off with profit or glory, and his wiser antagonists prudently let him alone. New members, young hot-heads especially, were very apt to come forward in haste for lessons which they were not apt to forget.

On March 4th, 1837, Martin Van Buren became President of the United States, his administration being a political continuation of that of Andrew Jackson. Among its heirlooms was the sure and tireless enmity of John Quincy Adams.

CHAPTER XV.

The Whig Party—An Important Clerk—The Third Party—Mr. Adams Organising the House of Representatives—All Rise to do him Honor—The Last of Earth.

THE diary of Mr. Adams offers an invaluable study of a human life. His state papers, his speeches, addresses, correspondence, his reported conversations, are all worth reading. While continuing to be, year after year, the central figure of the anti-slavery contest in Congress, his services went on as a legislator to whom other subjects of public importance were committed as by common consent whenever, at least, a wise and non-partisan result was wished for. The struggle against the annexation of Texas, with its almost sure corollary of a war with Mexico, went vainly on during the term of Mr. Van Buren. The opposition or Whig Party was gaining power steadily, and at the opening of the Twenty-sixth Congress, in 1839, expected to contest with the supporters of the administration the Speakership and control of the House of Representatives. It could not hope to do so if the clerk, in calling the roll for purposes of organization, should omit the names of five members from New Jersey whose election was nominally contested. Upon the action of the clerk, therefore, and upon its expected determination of the contest for the Speakership, might depend the subsequent course of legislation, and with it party success or ruin, national peace or war, or life or death. Under such circumstances the two parties met in the House chamber, December 2d, 1839, in great need of a third party, to act as umpire, with the unlimited confidence of the other two. The required third party was there. He was growing old now. His once resonant voice cracked a little when highly pitched or unduly exerted. His hairs were white and few, and his eyes were dimmed, except for an inner fire which could yet burn very brightly on occasion. His right hand was partly paralyzed and required a special support in writing, while it had become something of an effort for him to rise in his place to address the House.

The clerk called the roll in the usual way, the members-elect answering to their names, until the State of New Jersey was reached. Here he paused, and stated that he should pass over the five contested names, not taking the responsibility of deciding whether they were elected or not. The act of omitting them was a decision against them so far as their right to take part in the organization of the House was concerned, and a scene of Bedlamite confusion followed. Resolutions were offered which the clerk refused to put. The mob of puzzled members of a House of Representatives which somehow did not yet exist or could not put itself together swayed and raved helplessly hither and thither during three whole days. The third party sat at his desk, writing busily, watching the course of the helpless confusion around him, and waiting for the proper time for interference. On the morning of the fourth day the clerk, Mr. Garland, began once more the calling of the roll, prepared to repeat his previous refusal to call the New Jersey names. They had just been reached, the words " New Jersey" were on the lips of Mr. Garland, but before he could add another the voice of Mr. Adams rang through the chamber :

" I desire to interrupt the clerk—"

" Silence ! Silence ! Hear ! Hear him ! Hear what he has to say ! Hear John Quincy Adams !" shouted many members.

He paused for a moment, while all the tumult subsided into utter silence, and then addressed the listening members :

" It was not my intention to take any part in these extraordinary proceedings. I had hoped this House would succeed in organizing itself ; that a Speaker and clerk would be elected, and that the ordinary business of legislation would be progressed in. This is not the time nor place to discuss the merits of conflicting claimants from New Jersey. That subject belongs to the House of Representatives, which, by the Constitution, is made the ultimate arbiter of the qualifications of its members. But what a spectacle we here present ! We degrade and disgrace our constituents and the country. We do not and cannot organize, and why ? Because the clerk of this House—the mere clerk, whom we create, whom we employ, and whose existence depends upon our will—usurps the throne, and sets us, the representatives, the vicegerents of the whole American people, at defiance, and holds us in contempt! And what is this clerk of yours? Is he to suspend, by his mere negative, the functions of Government, and put an end to Congress? He refuses to call the roll! It is in your power to compel him to call it, if he will not do it voluntarily." At this point Mr. Adams was interrupted by a member, who assured him that the clerk would resign rather than call the State of New Jersey. "Well, sir," said Mr. Adams, "let him resign, and we may possibly discover some way by which we can get along without the aid of his all-powerful talent and genius.

"If we cannot organize in any other way, if this clerk of yours will not consent to our discharging the trust confided to us by our constituents, then let us imitate the example of the Virginia House of Burgesses, which, when the colonial Governor Dinwiddie ordered it to disperse, refused to obey the imperious and insulting mandate, and, like men—"

That was enough. They all knew the story of the old Raleigh Tavern and of what was done in the Apollo ball-room. Mr. Adams was interrupted by deafening cheers. The right chord had been touched, for he had made the faces around him crimson with shame. He let the applause die out, and then stated that he would now offer a resolution "ordering the clerk to call the members from New Jersey possessing the credentials from the Governor of that State."

He was at once asked by several voices : " How shall the question be put ?" " Who will put the question ?"—for that had been a main difficulty during the entire chaos. Instantly came his answer : " I intend to put the question myself !"

There was not another man in that assembly who possessed, in his own personal character and standing, before the nation and the world, the unquestionable authority to make that answer and have the high assumption promptly submitted to. It was the voice of a Tribune of the People.

Mr. Richard Barnwell Rhett, of South Carolina, from the top of a desk, shouted : " I move that the Honorable John Quincy Adams take the chair of Speaker of the House and officiate as presiding officer till the House be organized by the election of its constitutional officers."

He put his own motion, and it was unanimously, enthusiastically carried. On motion and order he and Mr. Williams, of North Carolina, conducted Mr. Adams to the chair, while Mr. Wise, of Virginia, remarked to the latter :

" Sir, I regard it as the proudest hour of your life ; and if, when you shall be gathered to your fathers, I were asked to select the words which, in my judgment, are best calculated to give at once the character of the man, I would inscribe upon your tomb this sentence—'*I will put the question myself.*' "

Mr. Adams had now a difficult and delicate duty upon his hands, for the temporary admission of the New Jersey members left parties about evenly divided, and the struggle for the Speakership went on until December 16th. Eleven days of turmoil, electioneering, balloting for the members, and of severe trials of temper and of judgment for Mr. Adams, ended in the defeat of the administration. Mr. R. M. T. Hunter, of Virginia, was elected Speaker, and a severe break was made in the long, uninterrupted control of the dominant party.

Two years later the same personal eminence which had enabled Mr. Adams to break the deadlock and organize the House enabled him to take a stand with reference to duelling and its Congressional accompaniments of threat and insolence which its advocates would not have tolerated from another man. He held the barbarism up to scorn and derision, and lashed it with bitter invective.

The administration of Van Buren died out, and the Whig Party elected William H. Harrison to take his place, giving him two hundred and thirty-four votes out of two hundred and ninety-four. One month later, by the death of General Harrison, Vice-President John Tyler, of Virginia, became President.

The times were changing, and Mr. Adams lamented the political degeneracy of the present as compared with that very past whose evils he had so vividly portrayed in their day. He was not changing. He had abandoned no principle, he ceased no warfare, he took not his hand away from the plough. He was wearing out nevertheless. His wife had grown old with him, and was to survive him only four short years. The old couple seemed altogether to belong in the public place and work to which the reverent people of the Plymouth district persisted in sending them.

There was one undying reason why they did so. Their representative stood in their minds for several great human rights. One of these was the right of petition, and he was fighting its battle. It was won for them at last. The majorities which sustained the gag law melted away year by year, until, on December 3d, 1844, by a vote of one hundred and eight against eighty, the barrier was removed. Mr. Adams had fought long, had gained the last great triumph of his life, and wrote in his diary : '' Blessed, forever blessed, be the name of God.''

The annexation of Texas, the war with Mexico, another Presidential election, an endless procession of subjects affecting the welfare of the nation, received their wonted attention from a mind which had not lost its power, but there came increasingly warning symptoms that the work of the body was nearly done. The earlier career of Mr. Adams as a member of the House had been marked by a number of intensely dramatic scenes, and several more had occurred even in these latter years, but only two can be recorded within the narrow limits assigned to this biography.

On November 19th, 1846, while walking in the street in Boston, he was attacked by paralysis. He lost the power of speech, and his right side was affected. Three months later he was sufficiently recovered to proceed to Washington, and on February 16th he made his appearance in the House of Representatives. As one man the members arose in their places to honor his return. All business was suspended until he had been formally conducted to his accustomed seat, but he excused himself, on account of feebleness, from responding to the congratulations tendered him.

Only once after that, although as punctual as ever in his attendance, did he take any part in the debates, and then but briefly. On February 21st, 1848, his answer to the roll-call seemed as clear and prompt as usual, but he had responded for the last time. Shortly after the opening of the session he arose, with a paper in his hand, and addressed the Speaker. That officer himself had arisen to put a question, but was interrupted by a cry of "Stop! Stop! Mr. Adams!"

The Nestor of the House had tottered and fallen, caught in the arms of his next neighbor. He had been again stricken by paralysis. The House at once adjourned, he was carried into a cloak-room, and Mrs. Adams and his family were sent for. They were with him, some hours later, when he seemed to be striving to say: ' Thanks to the officers of the House."

Then followed a silence, and when it was broken the uttered words were : " This is the last of earth. I am content."

Entire unconsciousness followed, and he passed away in the evening of February 23d. He had fought a good fight, and had been given the last, high honor of falling at his post of duty.

THE END.

THE LIVES OF THE PRESIDENTS
— OF THE —
UNITED STATES.

A new series of importance, which will be completed in about ten volumes.

By WILLIAM O. STODDARD,

*Author of " The Life of Abraham Lincoln," " Dab Kinzer,"
" Esau Hardery," etc., etc.*

Written so as to interest all readers, especially young people, and designed to be strictly accurate and valuable, and to give the results of the latest research.

The intention is to make it the STANDARD series of its class.

Each volume, 12mo, from new type on good paper, with illustrations. Bound uniformly in red cloth, with attractive design in black and gold on covers, showing portraits of Washington, Lincoln, Grant, and Garfield. Each volume, $1.25.

1. **George Washington.**

2. **John Adams and Thomas Jefferson.**

3. **James Madison, James Monroe, and John Quincy Adams.**

4. **Andrew Jackson and Martin Van Buren.**

*5. **Ulysses S. Grant.**

*Other volumes in preparation. The *Life of Grant* is published out of its chronological order because of the present great interest in the subject.

Any of these books can be had of your bookseller, or will be sent, postpaid, on receipt of advertised price, by the publisher,

FREDERICK A. STOKES,
Successor to WHITE, STOKES, & ALLEN,
182 FIFTH AVENUE, NEW YORK.

CPSIA information can be obtained at www.ICGtesting.com
Printed in the USA
BVOW04s1017160414

350836BV00017B/414/P